Linux!

I Didn't Know You Could Do That...™

Nicholas D. Wells

SYBEX®

San Francisco • Paris • Düsseldorf • Soest • London

Associate Publisher: Gary Masters

Contracts and Licensing Manager: Kristine O'Callaghan

Acquisitions & Developmental Editor: Ellen Dendy

Editor: Sally Engelfried

Project Editor: Malka Geffen

Technical Editors: Eric Ray, Don Hergert

Book Designers: Franz Baumhackl, Kate Kaminski

Electronic Publishing Specialists: Kate Kaminski, Adrian Woolhouse

Project Team Leader: Leslie Higbee

Proofreader: Rich Ganis

Indexer: Ted Laux

Companion CD: Ginger Warner

Cover Designer: Daniel Ziegler

Cover Illustrator/Photographer: PhotoDisc

Library of Congress Card Number: 99-65755

ISBN: 0-7821-2612-X

Manufactured in the United States of America

10 9 8 7 6 5 4 3 2

To all those talented people who created something new or better and then shared it with the rest of us. Many thanks.

Acknowledgements

Thanks to the staff at Sybex—Ellen Dendy, Gary Masters, Malka Geffen, and Sally Engelfried—for shepherding this book through the creation process, an inherently challenging process when designing a new series as it's being written. Thanks to Eric Ray for his patience in working to improve the book technically and to Don Hergert for some speedy work to get everything ready. Thanks to Neil Salkind and everyone at StudioB for their continuing support. And thanks most of all to my wife Anne and baby Annie, my two girls, for making it all worthwhile.

Table of Contents

Introduction

With all the noise about Linux being perfect for tasks such as running a Web server or acting as a router, you may be wondering what else you can do with this newly popular operating system. This book is about some of the other really handy things Linux can do that you probably didn't know about—things like graphically setting up a firewall or Apache server, using all sorts of sound and video tools, increasing your system security, playing with programs to balance your checkbox, managing your business contacts, cataloging your videotapes, and checking the weather. This book covers dozens of gee-whiz Linux programs and features that will make you go, "Wow! That's just what I need!"

Is This Book for Me?

The pages that follow don't assume that you know much about Linux. If you've installed Linux and can open a command line window and follow directions, you can use nearly everything in this book. A few of the advanced topics will apply more to system administrators. If you know a little about compiling Linux programs, that's helpful, but I've tried to walk you through the steps. Again, some packages may require a programmer to get them to run if you're not using a Red Hat Linux system.

The packages on the CD have been tested on Red Hat 6. If you're not using a Red Hat Linux system, many of the prebuilt binaries on the CD will still work for you; others will need to be compiled from source code. Each package includes a README file to guide you through that process, but you may have better luck if you're a little more experienced with Linux.

N O T E The section titled "The CD" below and the README file on the CD itself both provide helpful guidelines.

What Will I Get out of This Book and How Is It Organized?

Two types of information are included in this book. Some sections provide instructions on using parts of Linux that you might not know about yet, like using a RAID system or working with the vi editor and tar backup command to help you optimize your system. Most of the book is about additional free software packages that you can install on your Linux system for added functionality. These packages are included on the book's CD.

NOTE   See the section titled "The CD" for more information.

This book is divided into 12 parts that highlight different aspects of what you can do with Linux:

1. **Do it Faster, Easier, and Better:** How to make a few basic Linux tasks like entering commands go more smoothly and require less effort on your part. Also, an introduction to the venerable vi editor and instructions on tracking system and network usage.

2. **Manage Your Files Like a Pro:** Tools for checking your hard disk status, recovering files, and generally doing advanced stuff with your Linux files.

3. **Automate Your Entire System:** How to use standard Linux features to run programs any time, from making a message pop up in 30 minutes to running a script every morning at 2 A.M.

4. **Spice Up Your Desktop:** A variety of add-ons for Gnome and KDE desktops, including system administration utilities and personal productivity tools just for fun.

5. **Make Your Linux System a Desktop OS:** Run numerous word processors, spreadsheets, and full office suites on Linux, or run existing Windows programs on Linux.

6. **Turn Linux into the Ultimate Gamer:** Run all sorts of great games on Linux, from chess and NetHack to fast-paced games like flight simulators and arcade favorites. You can even play Minesweeper and solitaire.

7. Make Your System Entertaining: Play video clips, audio CDs, and even watch TV on your Linux desktop. Learn about audio mixing studios and digital synthesizers for Linux.

8. Turn Your System into a Web Server: Use the Apache Web server to its fullest, with configuration hints for high performance, information about dozens of add-on modules, and a graphical configuration tool.

9. Turn Your System into a Super-Server: Use Linux features to connect multiple systems through one Internet connection, use multiple addresses on one server, and manage server security with browser-based tools. Add a firewall with graphical configuration tools.

10. Clone Windows NT: Use Linux add-ons to share data with Windows NT and NetWare servers on your network. Or replace an NT server with the Linux Samba tools. Learn about the NetWare for Linux server product.

11. Use Linux as a Business Server: Check your files for viruses (including files on a Linux e-mail server), send and receive faxes, and learn about Linux conferencing software.

12. Disaster-Proof Your System: Learn about Linux backup utilities and add-on programs, plus how to use a Linux-controlled UPS (uninterruptible power supply), a battery-based power supply.

The CD

The CD includes dozens of applications and files including helpful utilities, entertaining games, and even a full office suite. Most of the programs on the CD include complete source code as well as a binary executable file.

A note of warning: some of the add-on packages are easier to use than others. I've included a lot of tools that you can run right off the CD; others require that you work with the source code a little, especially if you're not running a standard Red Hat Linux distribution, which is what all the packages were tested on. If you're not a programmer, don't worry. I'm confident that you'll still find all sorts of useful tips and tools in this book. If some that you want to try are harder to use, consider that as incentive to learn more about the inner workings of Linux.

For detailed information about a package, browse the documentation that comes with that package. A long README file on the CD includes a list of all packages on the CD with a short description. A few technical notes may help you along the way:

◆ The packages on the CD were tested with a standard Red Hat 6 installation. The rpm_list.txt file on the CD shows you what was installed on my test system.

◆ Depending on how you have your CD mounted, you may need to copy a binary file to your hard disk before you can run it. Check the options in your /etc/fstab for information. Once you've copied the file to your hard disk, be sure it has the execute bit set (use the command chmod a+x *filename* if needed).

◆ The binary files (executables) may not work on other Linux systems like Caldera OpenLinux, Slackware, or Suse, because each system is configured slightly differently. To use the CD programs on other Linux systems, you'll probably need to compile the source code. Instructions are included in the main README file on the CD, with specifics included in each program archive, but basically it amounts to using these three commands:

```
./configure
make
make install
```

◆ If you do need to work with source code, you'll need some additional packages installed on your Linux system from your original Linux CD. These packages provide programming tools. They include the word *devel*. For example, you probably have the qt package installed already. If you want to compile source code, you need the qt-devel package as well.

◆ I can't help you get all these packages working on your particular system. Too many variables exist, and it would be impossible for me to know the source code for the many programs included to be able to diagnose problems. If you're having trouble, the best course of action is to contact the author of the individual software program. An e-mail address and Web page are generally provided in the README file for each individual package.

Enjoy Your Tinkering!

I wish you a lot of fun exploring all the great programs for Linux that so many talented people have created. If you want to look for more of them (or check for updates on the ones I've described) check out the Internet resources at the back of the book. Let me know what you think! I'm at nwells@xmission.com.

Conventions Used

The following typographical conventions are used in this book:

Program names, commands, and directories within a paragraph are shown in a program font like this.

Commands that you enter are shown on separate lines like these.

```
$ make install
# rpm -Uvh qt-devel-1.44-1.i386.rpm
```

The first character is the Linux command line prompt, which you should not enter. I've used the "$" as a standard prompt, or the "#" when I think you may need to be logged in as root to complete the commands (sometimes a note in the text explains that as well).

For some sections, the output of commands is shown in the same style, but without the prompt before it, like this:

```
Supported ethernet device found. (eth0)
Sniffit.0.3.5 is up and running.... (192.168.100.3)
Packet ID (from_IP.port-to_IP.port): 192.168.100.3.80-
192.168.100.2.2793
```

Throughout the books are scattered Notes, which are generally asides about the subject at hand, and Warnings, which caution you when you need to be extra careful about performing an action.

Do it Faster, Easier, and Better

Your basic Linux system is designed to be all things to all people. It includes a nice graphical desktop, it functions as an Internet server, and it includes software development tools. Unfortunately, all things to all people can mean mediocre results for everyone.

This section is full of shortcuts and tricks to help you do a myriad of tasks faster and easier and to fine-tune your Linux system so it better suits your personal style. You'll also learn how to configure and check system information that's not always easy to see.

1 Use Your DOS Know-How to Save Time

If you're new to Linux, you may have more experience with DOS and Windows. By using aliases in Linux, you can put all that DOS experience to work without having to relearn everything in Linux.

Using DOS Commands in Linux

An alias is a text substitution: When you type one command, your command shell replaces it with another command, according to the alias that you defined.

For example, if you're accustomed to typing

```
DIR
```

to see a directory listing in DOS, you can make Linux use it the same way. Just enter this command at your Linux shell prompt (use quotation marks around the right side because it includes spaces):

```
$ alias dir="ls -la --color"
```

Now enter dir at the Linux prompt and you'll see a directory listing, just as you would in DOS.

You can use as many aliases as you like. To see the aliases that are currently in effect, enter alias with nothing after it:

```
$ alias
```

Every user can have a separate set of aliases. Table 1.1 shows a list of some common DOS commands and their Linux equivalents. Remember to watch for each space, hyphen, and period. (And don't try entering all of these until you learn the trick in the next section!)

WARNING   Linux commands are always case-sensitive and are almost always lowercase. You'll probably want to make all your DOS aliases lowercase as well; leave the Caps Lock key turned off.

TABLE 1.1   DOS Commands and Their Linux Equivalents

DOS Command	Linux Equivalent
DIR	ls –la
DIR /P	ls –la | less
CD..	cd ..
COPY	cp –i
REN	mv
DEL	rm –i
TYPE	cat

Aliases substitute text even in the middle of a command. If you use this alias:

```
$ alias copy="cp -i"
```

and then enter this command:

```
$ copy file1 file2
```

The shell will substitute the alias text so that the command executed is really:

```
$ cp -i file1 file2
```

NOTE Some of the Linux equivalent commands in Table 1.1 include safety features that will help you avoid overwriting or deleting files in Linux. For example, removing a file with rm -i (for "interactive") is always safer than just removing a file with rm.

Make Your New Commands Permanent

If you play with the alias command, you'll find that the next time you log in all your aliases have disappeared (enter alias without any parameters to see what aliases are in effect).

Because every user and every login session can have a different set of aliases defined (a different *environment*), you need to set up your aliases to be executed each time you log in.

If you're the system administrator, you can set these up in the system-wide startup script, /etc/bashrc, which applies to all users. You can also place the alias commands in the startup script in a user's home directory: .bashrc. This will make the commands effective only for that user. Follow these steps to set up permanent aliases for yourself:

1. From your home directory, open the .bashrc file in a text editor.

You can use vi, as described later in this section, or any of the easy-to-use graphical text editors that are included with Linux (kedit, xemacs, crisp, etc.).

NOTE Notice that .bashrc has a period at the beginning of the filename. This makes it a hidden file.

2. Go to the end of the .bashrc file

3. Add lines for each of the aliases that you want to have in effect each time you log in. For example, the last few lines of your file might look like this:

```
alias dir="ls -la"
alias cd..="cd .."
alias copy="cp -i"
alias del="rm -i"
```

4. Save and exit the text editor.

Now, every time you log in, the commands in .bashrc are executed, including the alias commands that you added.

One final point. As useful as aliases can be as you transition to Linux, they can also be a crutch. Using an alias hides the true Linux command from you and may prevent you from learning the full command suite of Linux and using the many additional options that Linux commands provide. Don't be afraid to move away from aliases as you learn more Linux commands (except perhaps for the safety-related aliases that save you from overwriting and deleting files).

2 How to Type Less and Do More

The more you work at a command line, the better your typing becomes. At least, that's how it's supposed to work. For the rest of us, Linux provides some easy ways to avoid typing lengthy filenames and commands. Read on for some tips on how to do this.

Reuse Commands without Retyping

When you type a lengthy utility name or complex expression on the command line, wouldn't it be nice to use the same command again without retyping it? DOS had a feature like this—you could press F3 to bring up the last command. Or, if you used the DOSKEY program in DOS, you could use the up arrow to view the last few commands.

The standard command line interface in Linux (the Bash shell) goes a lot further in making it easy to use previous commands that you've entered. By using the history feature of the default shell, you can quickly access the full range of previously entered commands, editing them slightly if needed.

Over 100 commands are stored by the shell for each user. To see them listed, use this command:

```
$ history | less
```

Or, to see a shorter list, include the number of commands you want to see. The most recently used command is listed last:

```
$ history 10
125 cd shells
126 ls bashrc
127 more bashrc
128 cd /etc
129 ls b*
130 more profile
131 history | less
132 df
133 cat /etc/passwd
134 history 10
```

To execute any of the commands in the history list, type an exclamation point, then the number of the command. For example, if I wanted to execute the df command, I'd enter:

```
$ !132
```

In this example, the df command is shorter to type. But when you've entered a very long command, using the history number is much easier than retyping the entire command. For example, if I had entered this command:

```
$ ps aux | grep httpd > /mnt/sundance/pidlogs/httpd/current
```

it would be much easier to use the history than to retype the command.

An even easier way to access recent commands is with the up arrow. When you press the up arrow in Linux, the command line changes to show each of your recent commands—and you can continue to press the up arrow to list over 100 commands in all.

Once you see the command that you want to use, you can use the left and right arrow keys to move the cursor over it and edit the command as needed to fit your current situation. Press Enter when you're ready to execute the command.

N O T E   The cursor doesn't need to be at the end of the line before you press Enter.

You can control the number of history entries that are saved for your user account by setting the HISTSIZE environment variable. This variable will normally be set to something like 100, so 100 commands will be saved. If you'd like to save more commands, enter something like this:

```
$ export HISTSIZE=500
```

If you want to set a larger history size permanently, you should include this line in the .bashrc startup script in your home directory.

Of course, when you have 100 previous commands saved, it may be hard to find the one you want. Here's a workaround to that problem.

Suppose you entered the long command example given above (ps aux…). To locate that command again in a list of hundreds of history commands, use a search command, choosing a few characters that you know are part of the command you need to locate (httpd in this case). So, for example:

```
$ history | grep httpd
43 ps aux | grep httpd > mnt/sundance/pidlogs/httpd/current
135 history | grep httpd
```

With this information, you can immediately execute the previous command you need with this statement:

```
$ !43
```

If you already know the number of the previous command you want to use, you can enter it at any time using this syntax. But be careful, since the numbers are updated each time you enter a new command.

Access Files and Directories More Quickly

Although the history feature of the Bash shell is great when you've already typed in a command once, some commands are difficult to enter the first time. This is often because of long directory names or filenames that include punctuation and numbers.

To help ease the task of entering these commands, the default Linux command line (the Bash shell) includes a feature called tab-completion that you can use with any Linux command. It works like this:

1. Type the first letter or first few letters of the filename you need to enter.

2. Press the Tab key.

3. If only one file or directory in your current directory matches the first letter or letters that you type, the entire filename or directory name is filled in for you.

4. If more than one file or directory starts with the letter or letters you type, your computer beeps. At this point, you have two options:

   ◆ Type another character or two and press Tab again to see if the file or directory name can be filled in.

   ◆ Press Tab again to see a list of options that match the first letters you typed.

To see how this can save you time as you work, I'll show how you can use tab-completion to change to one of the directories on the CD for this book.

1. Change to the directory where the CD is mounted.

```
$ cd /mnt/cdrom
```

2. Type the **cd** command, followed by a space and a **B**, but don't press Enter.

$ cd B

3. Press the Tab key.

The word `Binaries` appears in your command.

4. Type **D** and press the Tab key.

The directory `Disk Tools` is added to your `cd` command. The entire path is automatically enclosed in quotation marks because the `Disk Tools` directory contains a space.

5. Type **d** and press the Tab key.

The computer beeps but adds nothing to your command because several items in the `Disk Tools` subdirectory start with d.

6. Press the Tab key again.

A list of options starting with d is shown (defrag and diskerase).

7. Type i (so you have di) and press the Tab key again.

The diskerase directory name is added to your command.

8. Press Enter to change to the directory that you entered using Tab completion. Your command will look like this:

```
$ cd "Binaries/Disk Tools/diskerase"
$
```

Using tab-completion in this example may seem like tending to a lot of little details just to save a few keystrokes. However, after you become accustomed to using the Tab key for long filenames, you'll find it's easy to use and will be grateful not to have to type all those extra characters.

3 Become a Linux Guru: Master vi

If you really want to show off your Linux skills, you need to know how to edit text files using the vi (pronounced "vee-eye") editor. Nearly everyone laments how hard vi is to learn, but those who have learned the basics can wear it as a badge of honor.

The vi editor is very powerful, if you can memorize arcane command strings. But there's another, more practical reason that you need to know some vi basics: vi is the lowest common denominator. Every Linux system and every UNIX system will have vi installed. If you know something about vi, you can always edit a text file in Linux. And since Linux is configured using text files, this is a key skill to have.

NOTE Another Linux editor that has a following of die-hard fans is called emacs. Emacs is arguably more powerful than vi, but it's also a huge program, so you won't find it on all Linux systems.

Of course, if you're running Gnome or KDE and have a slick graphical editor at your fingertips, you normally won't resort to vi (unless you've become a fan).

Get Started with Your First vi Session

The vi editor is a character-based program. You can start it from any console or terminal emulator window using this command:

```
$ vi
```

After you start vi, you see a blank screen with a few tilde characters (~). Don't panic; you'll soon learn how to deal with all this empty space. The tilde characters aren't part of your file. They just indicate lines on screen that are empty.

If you have a text file that you want to edit, start vi with the filename. For example, if you want to edit the file report.txt, you enter this command:

```
$ vi report.txt
```

The file appears on-screen, ready to edit.

Secrets of Adding and Deleting Text

You can move around in your text file using your arrow keys (up, down, left, right, Page Up, Page Down).

The first secret of editing in vi is learning about Insert mode and Command mode.

◆ If you see the word --INSERT-- or --REPLACE-- at the bottom of the screen, then you are in Insert mode and text that you type appears as part of your document.

◆ If you don't see anything on the bottom of the screen, you're in Command mode. Characters that you type are interpreted as commands.

◆ Another mode, Visual, is also available by pressing V in Command mode. But learning too much vi at one time isn't healthy, so I'll leave that one for you to explore on your own.

You can start typing text in Insert mode using a few methods:

◆ Press i to start regular Insert mode.

◆ Press a to start inserting text after the current cursor position.

◆ Press o to insert the text you type on a new line.

◆ Press Shift+R to start inserting text that will replace (overwrite) the current text.

To change from Insert mode back to Command mode, press Esc. If you press it again, your system beeps, but this doesn't do any damage.

Table 3.1 describes how to use Command mode to complete some basic functions in vi. As you look at this table remember that:

◆ vi provides several ways to accomplish the same thing. This table shows just one good way for basic tasks.

◆ Memorizing commands is how you become skilled with vi.

◆ The commands follow patterns that make it easy to build on your existing knowledge so that you can do new things with vi.

◆ Many things that can be done in vi with a couple of keystrokes are almost impossible to do in a regular word processor (but I won't ask you to memorize everything that vi is capable of).

N O T E When keystrokes are listed in this table separated by commas, they should be pressed one after another, *not* at the same time.

TABLE 3.1   Command Modes for Basic vi Functions

Action	Keystrokes
Delete a character	**X** (or d, ← or d, →)
Delete a word	**d, w**
Delete a line	**d, d**
Search for a string	**/ (then enter the search string and press Enter)**
Undo a change	**u**

TABLE 3.1 Command Modes for Basic vi Functions(Continued)

Action	Keystrokes
Redo a change	Ctrl+Shift+r
Go to end of the file	Ctrl+g
Go to the top of the file	1, Shift+G
Get more help on vi	:, h, Enter (colon, h, Enter)
Save your file	:, w, Enter (colon, w, Enter)
Exit vi	:, q, Enter (colon, q, Enter)
Quickly exit vi, saving all changes	Shift+z, z (hold down Shift and press z twice)

Remember, if it seems like you're stuck in Insert mode and the commands in this table don't work, press Esc a couple of times to get back to Command mode (it also doesn't hurt to check to make sure that the Caps Lock key isn't active).

4 Monitor Your System the Easy Way

For system administrators, keeping track of system resources is a constant need. The tools in this section let you graphically track the usage of CPU time, system memory, swap space, and so forth in real time.

Use Bar Graphs to Monitor CPU and Memory

The xsysinfo utility provides a graphical display of

◆ The average system load

◆ The immediate CPU load

- ◆ The physical memory usage
- ◆ The swap space (virtual memory) usage

All of these values are displayed as bar graphs that are updated instanta-neously as your system is used. Although not as precise as some other tools, xsysinfo provides a nice display of basic information.

The xsysinfo utility is located at /Binaries/System Tools/xsysinfo on the CD. You can run it from any graphical command line. The basic display looks like the dialog box shown below.

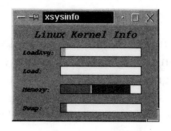

When you start xsysinfo from a command line, you can use several options to determine which labels and bar graphs are included. The README file in the /Binaries/System Tools/xsysinfo directory on the CD explains these options.

Track System and Network Usage with xperfmon++

Another excellent tool for monitoring system activity, including network packets sent and received, is xperfmon++. The activities monitored include

- ◆ Load average
- ◆ User CPU %
- ◆ System CPU %
- ◆ Idle CPU %
- ◆ Free memory KB
- ◆ Free swap MB
- ◆ Pages swapped in
- ◆ Pages swapped out
- ◆ KB paged in

- ◆ KB paged out
- ◆ Disk transfers
- ◆ Interrupts
- ◆ Processes
- ◆ Context switches
- ◆ Input packets
- ◆ Output packets
- ◆ Collision packets

xperfmon++ features a color-coded set of graphs that track system activity. When activity reaches certain levels in any category, the box containing that graph changes from green to yellow to red. You can set threshold values to meet the needs of your own system by modifying the xperf-mon++.ad file or using command line options.

The xperfmon++ utility is located on the CD in /Binaries/System Tools/ xperfmon. It includes a detailed man page with instructions for using command line parameters to set bar graph behavior, color choices, and many other options.

The main window of xperfmon++ is shown in Figure 4.1.

While xperfmon++ is running (and the main window has focus), you can press various keys to change how the graphs are updated:

- ◆ s to slightly decrease the update interval (make the graph a little slower)
- ◆ S to make the graph run a lot slower
- ◆ f to slightly increase the update interval (make the graph run a little faster)
- ◆ F to make the graph run a lot faster

By using command line options when you start xperfmon++, you can include or exclude any of the monitor graphs from the main window display.

Similarly, the threshold values for yellow and red level warnings in each category can be set using command line options when the program is started. See the man page at /Binaries/System Tools/xperfmon on the CD for details.

FIGURE 4.1 The `xperfmon++` utility shows color-coded graphs of various CPU, memory, and network activities.

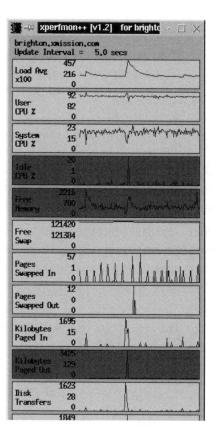

5 Secure Your System Against Intruders

With more and more sites being cracked by malicious or curious intruders, you need to be certain that all the users on your system use passwords that can't be easily cracked to allow access from unauthorized users.

Sniff Out At-Risk Passwords Using hardcrack

NOTE Many password-cracking programs are available on the Internet. The hardcrack program described here is just one example of the tools available to those seeking to break into your system.

A single valid login account to your system can provide a gateway for a cracker (a malicious hacker) to exploit other security holes and gain additional access. As a system administrator, you can use hardcrack to see if users on your system are using short or easily guessed passwords, then warn them to update their passwords.

Many sources recommend using special characters in passwords, such as numbers and punctuation marks. These make it harder to guess the password right off, but they don't make it much more difficult for a password-cracking program like hardcrack. Length is the real key to password security.

The author of hardcrack recommends using at least seven letters in a password. The README file shows that it takes the following amount of time to crack a password of various lengths on a slow (100MHz) Pentium system.

3 letters	1 minute
4 letters	1 hour
5 letters	3 days
6 letters	190 days
7 letters	30 years
8 letters	Hundreds of years

Of course, much faster machines are standard fare these days, so the time needed to discover each of the above password lengths is usually less.

The hardcrack program is located on the CD in Binaries/System Tools/hardcrack. It works by default on the /etc/passwd file of your system. If you want to check the password of a given user account, use that account name like this:

```
# hardcrack -1 username
```

If you have the encrypted password text (a string that looks like garbage letters and numbers), you can enter it character by character on the command line to have hardcrack work with that password.

```
# hardcrack -1 23 -2 15 -3 55 -4 33
```

Each digit of the encrypted password is given as a number between 0 and 64 (the code of the characters used for encrypted passwords).

After hardcrack has worked on the password for a time, it prints a simple message stating what the password is. It's up to you to take corrective action.

Hide Password Files with Shadow Passwords

The hardcrack program and others like it assume that a potential intruder can get a copy of your password file (/etc/passwd) or at least one encrypted password from it.

The shadow password method is used on most Linux systems today, including Red Hat 6 (if you left the installation defaults as they were set). This method uses modified password utilities to access a file that can only be read by the root user. In contrast, the standard /etc/passwd file can be read by any user, giving everyone access to the encrypted passwords.

By using shadow passwords, you can also enforce security features like minimum password lengths and maximum time between password updates.

Shadow password information is stored in /etc/shadow on your Linux system. To learn more about shadow passwords, see the man pages for the shadow file, the passwd utility, and the usermod utility, which are included with all recent Linux distributions. These man pages should also be installed on your Linux system. For further reference, point your browser to this document on the CD: /Doc/Shadow-Password-HOWTO.html.

Use Nonpassword Authentication

If all this talk about passwords is making you nervous about the security of your system (as it should), consider using Pluggable Authentication Modules (PAM) to avoid standard passwords altogether.

By using PAM, you can specify one of several methods of authenticating users to your system, rather than comparing against a text-based password file (or even a more secure one, like shadow passwords). Various modules for the PAM system are available, including MD5 and database authentication systems. (Red Hat 6 uses MD5 by default.)

For more information about PAM, see `http://www.kernel.org/pub/linux/libs/pam/index.html`. Additional information about password security can be found in the Security HOWTO document, which is available at `http://www.kernelnotes.org/HOWTO/Security-HOWTO.html`.

6 Keep an Eye on All Your Network Traffic

A busy network generates a lot of traffic. This section describes utilities that enable you to monitor traffic to make certain that your network isn't overloaded or being misused.

NOTE Some of the tools in this section are like those used by intruders to attack your system. By knowing how they work, you can locate potential security problems before someone else does.

Monitor the Load on Your Network

The `netload` utility is a very simple utility that shows the number of packets being received and transmitted over a given network interface and computes a relative load on the interface.

By using `netload`, you can determine if your network is near its capacity. An overloaded network will slow down all traffic, especially for collision/multiple-access networks like Ethernet.

The `netload` utility is located at /Binaries/System Tools/netload on the CD. You can start it from any command line (it is a text-based program) by including the network interface that you want to watch:

```
# netload eth0
```

Some common network interface names are shown in the following table.

Interface name	Description
eth0	First Ethernet card
lo	Localhost (local loopback for testing)
ppp	PPP interface (usually over a modem)
eth1	Second Ethernet card
tr	Token ring card

When you start `netload`, you see a list of statistics and a bar graph showing the relative load on your network. Although the relative load is not as precise as some utilities, it lets you watch in real time as the traffic load builds and declines. The computed Maximum device load is shown in the top line of the box (see Figure 6.1).

FIGURE 6.1 The `netload` utility monitors the real-time network load.

```
┌────────────────────────────────────────────────────────┐
│ 🖳 ─⋈ Terminal <3>                              · □ ✕   │
│  ┃ File    Options                               Help   │
│  ┃                                                      │
│  ┃        PACKETS ERRORS  DROP   FIFO   FRAME     ▲     │
│  ┃   REC    82900    ○      ○      ○      ○              │
│  ┃   TRANS  97955    ○      ○      ○      1              │
│  ┃                                                      │
│  ┃   ┌──────────────────────────────────────────┐      │
│  ┃   │ Maximum device load 76 (Fri May 28 15:21:09 1999) │
│  ┃   │          Relative Load                    │      │
│  ┃   │      Received           17                │      │
│  ┃   │      Transmitted        19                │      │
│  ┃   │      Total load         36                │      │
│  ┃   │                                           │      │
│  ┃   │   ┌───────────────────────────────────┐   │      │
│  ┃   │   └───────────────────────────────────┘   │      │
│  ┃   │            device eth0                    │      │
│  ┃   └──────────────────────────────────────────┘      │
│  ┃        By Luis Falcon (lfalcon@csun.edu)      ▼     │
└────────────────────────────────────────────────────────┘
```

Of course, netload doesn't keep track of the network load over time, as some utilities do (such as xperfmon++, described previously in this section). But netload is much simpler to use if you just want to review how heavily your network is being used.

Press Ctrl+C to end the netload program.

Track Detailed Networking Statistics with IP-Traf

The utilities described so far in this section (such as netload and xperfmon++) don't show you much detail about the network activity; they only display how much activity there is.

The IP-Traf utility is a powerful tool for tracking what is actually happening on your network. You can track requests and responses by hostname, IP address, and port; watch requests in real time as they are serviced; and see general statistics for your network interfaces.

All of the IP-Traf functionality is easy to use from the menu-based (character-mode) interface. The binary is located on the CD at /Binaries/System Tools/iptraf; the complete documentation for this program is also included in the Binary subdirectory. Start the program from any Linux command line (you must be logged in as root to run iptraf):

```
# iptraf
```

After a couple of initial messages (press any key to continue after reading these), you see the main menu of IP-Traf, shown in Figure 6.2.

The General interface statistics option provides a summary of traffic flow on each of the active interfaces of your system. The information provided includes the throughput (KB per second, for example).

For more detailed information on a single interface, choose the Detailed interface statistics option and select an interface from the list presented. The window that appears shows you real-time activity on the selected interface, with traffic broken down by packet size and type.

The throughput and any IP errors are also tabulated in this detailed view of the network interface (see Figure 6.3).

Press Esc to return to the main menu from any of the screens described here.

FIGURE 6.2 The main menu of IP-Traf **provides access to statistics, filters, and configuration options.**

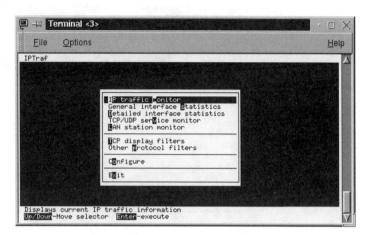

FIGURE 6.3 **A detailed view of a network interface shows traffic broken down by type and size.**

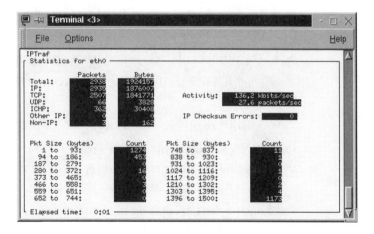

Most of the traffic that crosses your IP network will be using the TCP/UDP protocols. The TCP/UDP service monitor menu option is used to break down traffic on a single interface based on the TCP port that the network packet arrives on. This is shown in Figure 6.4.

Other non-TCP requests, such as ICMP (used for the ping command) are viewed using the first menu option, IP traffic monitor. This screen, shown

FIGURE 6.4 The activity on specific TCP/UDP ports can be monitored with IP-Traf.

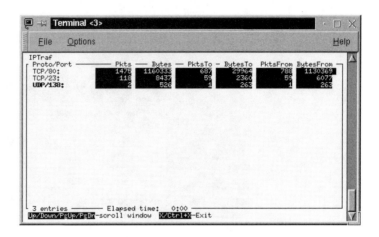

in Figure 6.5, is a good one to leave open on the system administrator's desktop to watch the network. It displays the following information:

◆ Source and destination IP addresses, with port numbers, for each connection

◆ The number of packets and bytes exchanged for each connection

◆ Flags to indicate the state of each connection from moment to moment

◆ A listing of other requests for UDP, ICMP traffic, etc.

On a LAN, one client often causes trouble for the entire network by inadvertently flooding the network with packets or making invalid requests that other systems attempt to process.

By choosing the LAN station monitor option on the IP-Traf main menu, you can see the activity on your network divided into individual workstations, as noted by their hardware Ethernet card addresses (see Figure 6.6).

If one of the workstations shown in the LAN station monitor screen is flooding the network with traffic (as shown by the PktsIn and BytesIn fields), you can check that machine to see what software the user has that is causing the problem.

With so much information available in IP-Traf, you may want to configure it more specifically to your needs. The Configure option on the main menu

FIGURE 6.5 IP traffic monitor shows detailed information about all packets and protocols passing through your system.

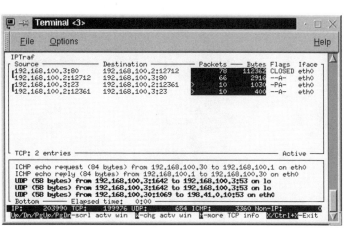

FIGURE 6.6 The network traffic can be shown divided by which workstation on the network the packets relate to.

opens a window where you can select from over a dozen configuration options. (See Figure 6.7.)

Configuration options include:

◆ Reverse DNS lookups to display connection information as host-names instead of as IP addresses (this is set to Off by default because of the extra processing required for reverse lookups)

FIGURE 6.7 The comprehensive configuration screen in IP-Traf lets you define how the utility operates.

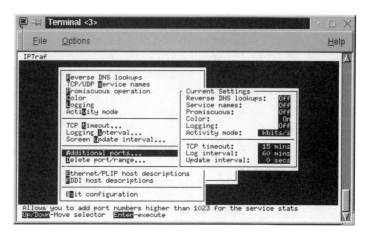

◆ TCP/UDP service names to use the standard names of services instead of port numbers (for example, display Telnet instead of 23)

◆ Color options to display the screens in color

◆ Logging options to define whether activity is logged to a file and how often the log is updated

◆ Activity mode to select "bits per second" or "bytes per second" for displays

◆ Screen update interval selection to refresh the screen more or less frequently

A final feature of IP-Traf that deserves mention is the filtering option for TCP and other protocols. Here I focus on describing a TCP filter, but you can choose Other protocol filters on the main menu to define non-TCP filters.

By setting up the TCP display filters option, you can watch for specific traffic within IP-Traf. This limits the amount of information that you have to wade through to find what you're looking for.

To define a new filter, choose TCP display filters on the main menu, then choose Define new filter and enter a filter name for the TCP filter you will create. The filter definition screen shown in Figure 6.8 appears.

Within this filter definition screen, you enter the hostname or IP address of the machine that you want to filter and the TCP port to filter on. You can then either include or exclude packets that match these filter criteria.

FIGURE 6.8 Filters for TCP traffic (or other protocols) can be defined within `IP-Traf`.

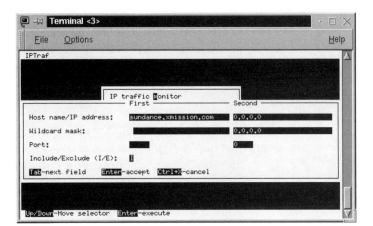

 WARNING The filters in `IP-Traf` define what to look for. They don't have any effect on what is allowed on the network. `IP-Traf` is not a firewall.

By defining a series of filters, you can check for certain activities on your network without being bothered by extraneous data.

 Additional details about using `IP-Traf` are provided in the documentation files that are included in the directory `/Binaries/System Tools/iptraf/Documentation` on the CD.

Capture Data Directly from the Network

When people talk about the dangers of using the Internet for electronic commerce, they often mention how someone can "sniff" information directly from the Internet. Information that isn't encrypted can then be easily read.

The `sniffit` utility shows you how easy it is to do this. It also provides a useful tool for network administrators trying to debug very challenging problems on their network.

TIP   By using the `sniffit` utility, you will see how important it is to use secure communication over the Internet and your internal networks. You will also become more aware of how easy it is for malicious users to gather information using these basic tools.

Tools like `IP-Traf`, described in the previous section, are used to manage network load based on traffic levels of different protocols. The `sniffit` program is different. Rather than providing statistical information based on protocols, it stores individual packets as they are sent over your network.

NOTE   Many issues affect which network packets are received at your computer's network card. Unless you are working at a server, much of the network traffic is never seen by your system.

You can use `sniffit` is several ways, including setting up configuration files to determine how network packets are tracked and stored. The `sniffit` program can also use plug-ins to support various functions and has an Interactive mode where you can control how network traffic is analyzed as the program works.

The `sniffit` program is located on the CD at `/Binaries/System Tools/ sniffit`. A few simple command line examples follow. Remember that `sniffit` can only track network packets that pass through your network card. If you're on a local network, most of the traffic won't be seen on your network card. (If you don't have networking set up on your computer, don't run `sniffit`.)

Each packet on your network has fields that define the IP address that the packet originates from (the source) and the IP address that the packet is headed for (the target).

If you want to see packets that are coming from IP address 192.168.100.3, regardless of protocol or target (destination), use this command (you must be logged in as root to use `sniffit`):

```
# sniffit -d -s 192.168.100.3
```

When you press Enter, all the packet data (the actual data sent in the packet) is dumped to the screen, as requested by the -d option. The information dumped to the screen looks something like this:

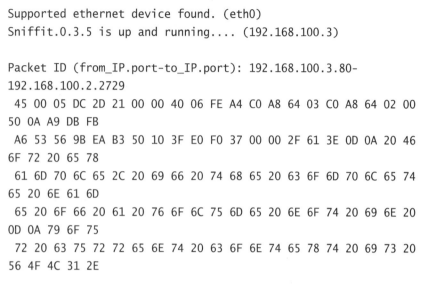

```
Supported ethernet device found. (eth0)
Sniffit.0.3.5 is up and running.... (192.168.100.3)

Packet ID (from_IP.port-to_IP.port): 192.168.100.3.80-
192.168.100.2.2729
 45 00 05 DC 2D 21 00 00 40 06 FE A4 C0 A8 64 03 C0 A8 64 02 00
50 0A A9 DB FB
 A6 53 56 9B EA B3 50 10 3F E0 F0 37 00 00 2F 61 3E 0D 0A 20 46
6F 72 20 65 78
 61 6D 70 6C 65 2C 20 69 66 20 74 68 65 20 63 6F 6D 70 6C 65 74
65 20 6E 61 6D
 65 20 6F 66 20 61 20 76 6F 6C 75 6D 65 20 6E 6F 74 20 69 6E 20
0D 0A 79 6F 75
 72 20 63 75 72 72 65 6E 74 20 63 6F 6E 74 65 78 74 20 69 73 20
56 4F 4C 31 2E
```

Capturing network traffic generates a lot of data. If you want to store that data to a file, called savedata in this example, use a redirection symbol:

```
# sniffit -d -s 192.168.100.3  > savedata
```

To see packets coming from this IP address but only those that specify a certain TCP port (normally associated with a protocol, such as 80 for the Web), use this command:

```
# sniffit -d -p 80 -s 192.168.100.3  > savedata
```

Changing from -d to -a changes the numeric (hex) dump to ASCII, so you can actually see the data flowing across the network:

```
# sniffit -a -p 80 -s 192.168.100.3  > savedata
```

In this case, the data looks more like this:

```
Supported ethernet device found. (eth0)
Sniffit.0.3.5 is up and running.... (192.168.100.3)

Packet ID (from_IP.port-to_IP.port): 192.168.100.3.80-
192.168.100.2.2793
```

```
    E . . . 7 . . . @ . .     . . d . . . d . . P . . . e . . . . . .
P . ? . . .
    . . / a > . .  Select    this    option    if
you    want
    the    old    name    saved    as    a    . . value
in    the    "Other    Names"    field    of
the    "Details"
```

To see all traffic that is headed for a certain IP address, use the -t option for target, instead of -s for source:

```
# sniffit -a -p 80 -t 192.168.100.3  > savedata
```

This command might be used with the IP address of a Web server, to see packets destined for port 80 on the Web server.

To see all traffic related to a certain IP address, either coming from it or going to it, add the -b option with either -t or -s to specify the IP address.

```
# sniffit -ab -p 80 -t 192.168.100.3  > savedata
```

The Interactive mode can also be used with the -i option if you have compiled in the correct parts of the source code.

Many other similar tools are available on the Internet, but sniffit provides an easy to use utility for checking network packets that pass by your computer.

Manage Your Files Like a Pro

You've used all the standard Linux utilities for copying and deleting files (cp, rm), managing your directory structure (cd, pwd, mkdir), and so forth. This part describes a few of the tools you *wish* you had all along. Now you can use them to manage your files like a pro.

WARNING Some of the tools showcased in this section require quite a bit of knowledge about how your hard disk is set up. Read the documentation carefully if you need to learn about the more technical details before using these special utilities.

7 Optimize Your Linux Hard Disk

With some operating systems, you need to optimize, or defragment, your hard disk regularly to prevent serious performance problems. This is because the pieces of a single file are scattered (fragmented) over the entire area of your hard disk.

Linux doesn't suffer from this problem to any serious degree because the design of the Linux native file system (called ext2, for extended file system, version 2) allocates space for files in a way that allows files to grow in size without becoming fragmented.

Still, on a Linux system with a lot of disk activity (or one where the hard disks are quite full) you can increase your disk performance by 5 to 25 percent by defragmenting your Linux file system.

The defrag package enables you to quickly defragment your Linux file system to improve performance. The binary package is located on the CD in the /binaries/Disk Tools/defrag directory; the source code is at /Source/Disk Tools/defrag-0_70_tar.gz. (The source code is for a slightly older version of the program.)

To install the binary package, use this command while logged in as root with the CD mounted:

```
rpm -Uvh "/mnt/cdrom/Binaries/Disk Tools/defrag/defrag-0_73
   5_i386.rpm
```

A separate binary file is also included on the CD in the same directory as the rpm package, but install the rpm if possible.

Once the defrag package is installed, you can use this example to defragment the third partition of my IDE hard disk. The device name for this partition is /dev/hda3. You can change this device name to match your own partition. To run the e2defrag utility (for the Linux ext2 filesystem) in the defrag package, follow these steps while logged in as root:

1. Back up any important data on your hard disk.

WARNING This step is crucial. If the e2defrag utility has any serious difficulty with your hard disk, all of your data may become unusable.

2. Enter this command and review the output to make certain that the partition you want to defragment is not mounted (e2defrag should never be used on a mounted partition).

```
# mount
```

WARNING If you need to defragment your root partition, you must reboot your system from a boot diskette and run the e2defrag utility from diskette. The root partition cannot be unmounted while using your system.

3. Run the fsck utility on the partition that you want to defragment to test for errors:

```
# fsck /dev/hda3
```

4. Run the e2defrag utility in read-only mode.

This will not update your hard disk, but it will check that the defrag utility can operate correctly on your hard disk.

```
# /sbin/e2defrag -r /dev/hda3
```

5. Run e2defrag to optimize your hard disk.

```
# /sbin/e2defrag /dev/hda3
```

Running the e2defrag utility can take from 5 to 30 minutes, depending on the size of your hard disk and the speed of your computer. As e2defrag works, you see a graphical screen like the one in Figure 7.1.

FIGURE 7.1 The e2defrag **utility displays progress as disk areas are optimized.**

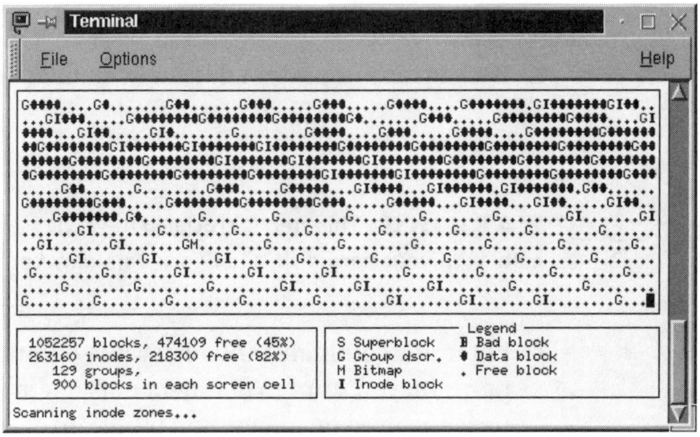

6. If you used e2defrag on your root partition, run the lilo command to update the hard disk map file that tells lilo how to boot Linux.

```
# lilo
```

NOTE You don't need to change the /etc/lilo.conf file.

If you're really interested in high performance, you can take other steps to optimize specific files on your disk. Each file on your Linux file system is assigned a number called an inode. This number is used to locate the file on your hard disk each time it's accessed.

To see the inode numbers associated with your files, use the ls command with the -i option:

```
# ls -i
  92458 CHANGES
  92459 ChangeLog
  92460 INSTALL
  92462 Makefile
  92461 NEWS
  92463 README
  92465 buffers.c
  16657 defrag-0_70_tar.gz
  92464 defrag.8
  92467 defrag.c
  92468 defrag.h
  92484 xdump.c
  92485 xia.c
  92486 xia.h
```

You can use e2defrag with a list of inodes that should be given priority during the disk defrag operation. The files that these inodes refer to may include commonly accessed database files, the main pages of your Web server, and so forth.

When you use an inode list to optimize your hard disk, the e2defrag program takes special care to make the files referred to by those inodes the most efficient to access.

To learn how to create an inode list file for e2defrag, see the manual page in /Binaries/Disk Tools/defrag on the CD.

8 Recover Lost Files with a Linux Undelete

When you learned about the Linux command to delete files (rm), you probably also learned that Linux *really* deletes files. It's not easy to recover them by simply marking disk areas as "used" again. Linux also doesn't have a special area for deleted files like the Macintosh Trash Can or Windows Recycle Bin.

The good news is that several tools will help you save yourself from disaster when you've deleted a file that you want to use again.

Plan for the Future with safedelete

If you'd like to play it safe when you delete files on Linux, install the safedelete package and get in the habit of using it.

When you use the safedelete command, safedelete automatically compresses the files you delete and moves them to a special hidden directory, out of your way.

If you discover that you've deleted a file that you need to retrieve, you can use the undelete command (part of the safedelete package) to retrieve the deleted file.

The safedelete program keeps a log of files that you delete so that the undelete command can correctly locate them. The files are completely reconstructed because they were never actually deleted, just compressed and moved out of your way.

Because using safedelete regularly would fill your hard disk with discarded, compressed files, safedelete automatically permanently deletes some files after a certain number of days. You can set up a configuration file in your home directory (the file is named .safedelrc) to specify how long files of different types should be saved before permanently deleting them.

The safedelete package is located in Binaries/Disk Tools/safedelete on the CD. This package is different than many of the binary packages in the Disk Tools subdirectory. No source code is included for safedelete, but when you unpack the archive file, a complete set of binary programs (based on the latest Linux library functions: glibc) are installed on your Linux system, along with documentation and man pages. The binaries included are:

- ◆ safedelete, the main program to safely delete files

- ◆ undelete, which you can use to retrieve deleted files

- ◆ savedelchk, which you can use to check the log and status of all the compressed, safely deleted files

◆ `safecnvt`, a tool to convert `safedelete` logs from an older version of this package

You must install the `safedelete` package in the root directory of your Linux system so that the files in the package are copied to the correct locations. Use these commands while logged in as root:

```
cd /
tar xvfz "/mnt/cdrom/Binaries/Disk Tools/safedelete/safedelete
   1_3-5.tgz
```

To use the `safedelete` package, you must start with the `safedelete` command instead of the `rm` command. These steps illustrate how this works:

1. Create a test file:

```
cp /etc/termcap /home/nwells/jnk
```

2. Delete the test file.

```
safedelete /home/nwells/jnk
```

3. Check that the file is deleted.

```
ls /home/nwells/jnk
```

4. Undelete the file.

```
undelete /home/nwells/jnk
```

You must use the complete pathname in the `undelete` command. To see the files being archived by `safedelete` (and to see which files are available to be undeleted), view the `.safedeletelog` file in your home directory.

The best way to use `safedelete` is to use an alias in your `.bashrc` script so that every time you use the `rm` command, `safedelete` is used instead. By doing this, you can use the commands you're already accustomed to in Linux and still have the benefits of the `safedelete` program. To add this alias, put a line like the following at the end of the your `.bashrc` file (or other shell startup file, if you're not using the `bash` command shell) in your home directory:

```
alias rm=safedelete
```

Make certain that you test the functionality of `safedelete` on your system before using this alias command.

Retrieve Files When You Didn't Plan Ahead

Even if you didn't use a tool like `safedelete` to store deleted files, the `e2recover` utility can attempt to recover your files and sometimes do a good job of it, depending on how much your hard disk has been used since you deleted the files.

Linux allocates space for files via a series of pointers on the hard disk. Once the pointers have been deleted, the original location and contents of a file may be very hard to put back together.

The `e2recover` utility operates using information provided by the `debugfs` utility, which is a part of most Linux distributions.

To use `e2recover`, you don't specify the filename you want to undelete. Instead, you specify a directory where all the recovered files will be placed. The binary for `e2recover` is located on the CD at `/Binaries/Disk Tools/ e2recover`.

Part of the `e2recover` package is the `fsgrab` utility. This program grabs raw blocks of data from a device like your hard disk. E2recover uses `fsgrab` to gather blocks of data from deleted files and assemble them into regular files.

To use the `fsgrab` utility, you specify a device, the number of blocks to skip before reading, the number of blocks to read, and the regular file to write the blocks into. Additional options are possible, but these will usually do the job.

For example, you might have an `fsgrab` command like this to read five blocks from the device /dev/hda3, starting at block 147, and write those blocks to the file `restored.file`:

```
# fsgrab -d /dev/hda3 -s 147 -c 5 -o restored.file
```

To learn more about `fsgrab`, use the following command or read the man page in the `Binaries` directory on the CD:

```
# fsgrab -help
```

NOTE The `fsgrab` command can be useful in its own right, but you don't need to use it explicitly to recover deleted files. The `e2recover` command will do it for you.

9 Completely Destroy Sensitive Files

Although it's nice to have an undelete command with e2recover, sometimes the *last* thing you want is for someone to be able to recover a file that you deleted. Financial data and other personal or business files sometimes need to be obliterated from your system for security reasons.

The shred utility is just the right tool to erase a file so that it cannot be reconstructed or undeleted. When you use shred, the contents of a file are actually overwritten six different times, ending with random data. The file is then deleted normally so the filename no longer appears on your system.

The shred utility is located in /Binaries/Disk Tools/shred on the CD. To use this utility, simply include the filename that you want to permanently erase from your system:

```
$ shred   filename
```

WARNING Remember that when you use shred to delete a file, the file cannot be recovered. Be especially careful when using shred with any wildcard characters. Avoid running shred when you are logged in as root.

10 Completely Destroy an Entire Hard Disk

Using the shred utility is a great way to protect sensitive data files from prying eyes that might try to undelete them. Occasionally, you may need to destroy the data on an entire hard disk or disk partition as well.

This might be useful when you rent or borrow a computer and need to erase your data before returning it, for example, or if you are changing to a new department at work and must leave your old PC behind.

The `diskerase` utility can be used to erase all of your data in situations like these. The program can be used in two ways:

◆ To erase all partitions on a hard disk

◆ To erase all information on a single partition of a hard disk

This utility is located at `/Binaries/Disk Tools/diskerase` on the CD. Several optional parameters are available when you use `diskerase`. The most useful fills your hard disk with a string of characters that you choose.

To use `diskerase` to erase an entire hard disk (all of the partitions and partitioning information on the hard disk), use a command like this.

```
# diskerase /dev/hdb
```

In this example, `/dev/hdb` is the second IDE hard disk. You can use any Linux hard disk designation as the device name. To fill the hard disk with a repeated string, such as "Sybex," use a command like this:

```
# diskerase /dev/hdb -s "Sybex"
```

If you don't specify an `-s` option, the disk is filled with zeros.

To use `diskerase` to erase a single partition on your hard disk, use a command like this:

```
# diskerase /dev/hda3
```

This example wipes out the contents of the third partition on the first IDE hard disk. The other partitions on the hard disk and the partitioning information itself is not touched by this command. The `-s` option can also be used to fill a partition with a repeating string.

WARNING   Don't forget the partition number on the device name, or your entire hard disk will be erased. Be certain that you know which partition number needs to be erased!

11 Keep Your Disk Resources in Constant View

When you have a large or busy Linux system, disk space can disappear rapidly. A common way to display your available disk space is to use the df utility. The results of df would look something like this:

```
$ df
Filesystem        1024-blocks   Used  Available Capacity Mounted on
/dev/hda4             956173   804104     102670     89%  /
/dev/hda3            1018329   644689     321028     67%  /mnt/redhat5.9
/dev/hda1            2039996  1121588     918408     55%  /mnt/win
//sundance/d         3070336   735168    2335168     24%  /mnt/sundance_d
```

This section describes two other utilities that provide the same information in different ways.

Graphically View Your Disk Space

The xdiskinfo command provides a graphical method of viewing your available disk space. xdiskinfo is a tcl/Tk script that uses the wish interpreter.

Xdiskinfo is located in /Binaries/Disk Tools/xdiskinfo on the CD. To run xdiskinfo, use a command like this within a graphical command line window:

```
$ xdiskinfo &
```

A dialog box appears like the one in Figure 11.1. This dialog box shows you graphically how much space is used and how much is free on your root disk partition. The text lines above the pie chart show you the exact numbers represented by the chart.

If you have more than one partition mounted on your Linux system, as I do, a button appears at the top of the dialog box for each of the different file systems. Click a button to see a chart of free space for that file system.

When you have finished looking at the chart, click the OK button to end xdiskinfo.

FIGURE 11.1 Xdiskinfo displays the free space on each of your partitions.

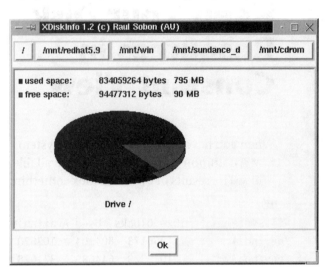

12 Fine-Tune Your Hard Disk Format

The standard Linux hard disk format provides very good performance for most users. The Linux file system can be fine-tuned, however, to add a few improvements for those who know specifically what they need from their hard disks.

Fine-Tune the Optimum File Size for Your System

The default block size for a Linux file system is 1,024 bytes. This works great for most users. But if your Linux system is chock full of files that are less than 512 bytes (such as icon graphics files), then you could improve your disk performance by changing your block size to 512. (The disadvantage of using a smaller block size is that larger files will have slightly reduced performance.)

Similarly, if your system is mostly larger files (for example, huge database tables), you could change your block size to 2,048 or 4,096 bytes. Because Linux reads from disk drives one block at a time, you could see performance improvements by doing this.

Of course, if you make the block size larger, you have to contend with two downsides:

◆ Potentially reduced performance when reading numerous files that are very small

◆ Wasted space for all the files that are far below the block size (because the block size is the minimum allocation of space on the hard disk)

The problem with using a nonstandard block size is that you must select the block size when you format your hard disk. You can't change it later without reformatting the disk. But if reformatting doesn't bother you (perhaps because you're starting with a new system), use the mke2fs command (a default part of every Linux system) with the -b option to specify the block size.

A sample hard disk formatting command would look like this:

```
# mke2fs -b 4096 /dev/hdb2
```

Be very careful about using this command. If you use a device name incorrectly, you might wipe out a partition that you didn't intend to format. Also, remember that only unmounted partitions should be formatted. Formatting a mounted partition will give unpredictable results.

N O T E Many other options can be included with the mke2fs command, but because they can be set using the tune2fs command after formatting, they are discussed in the next section.

Tune-Up Your File System Without Reformatting

The mke2fs command lets you define many options for your Linux file systems at the time you create (format) them. By using the tune2fs command, you can change many of those options without reformatting your hard disk.

The `tune2fs` command is a default part of standard Linux distributions.

WARNING Never use `tune2fs` on a file system that is mounted. If you need to update your root file system, start your computer from a floppy diskette so your regular root partition isn't being used.

The following table lists items that can be updated using the `tune2fs` command:

OPTION	DESCRIPTION	EXAMPLE
-c	Maximum number of times the file system can be mounted between automatic integrity checks (using the `fsck` program).	tune2fs –c 5
-i	Maximum amount of time the file system can go between automatic integrity checks (using the `fsck` program). Days (d), weeks (w), or months (m) can be specified. (Days is the default if no letter is included.)	tune2fs –i 1w
-m	Reserves a certain percentage of the file system for files owned by the superuser (root) or other specific users. This allows the superuser to still use the system when all the "normal" space is used up. This could be set to zero on something like a /home partition. A certain number of blocks can be specified rather than a percentage (use the -r option).	tune2fs –m 5
-u, -g	Defines a user or group (by name or ID number) who can use the reserved blocks.	tune2fs –g wheel
-L	Defines a label for the file system.	tune2fs –L usenet

13 Access Linux Files from DOS or Windows

Most of us use several operating systems regularly—or at least we have friends who do and we often need to share information with them. The tools described in this section show you how to share information between DOS or Windows and your Linux system.

Access DOS Floppies without Mounting

Most Linux systems (including Red Hat 6) install the mtools package by default. This package provides easy access to DOS-format diskettes using DOS-style commands with drive letters. For example, if you have mtools installed on your Linux system, you can copy a file from a DOS diskette with this command:

```
$ mcopy A:report /home/nwells
```

The mtools package is included in /Source/Disk Tools on the CD. Binaries aren't prebuilt on the CD because most distributions include this package already installed or available. Mtools includes a full set of "DOS-like" utilities. The most used utilities are listed in the following table:

MTOOLS COMMAND	EXAMPLE	DESCRIPTION
mdir	mdir A:	Shows the contents of the floppy drive named
mcopy	mcopy A:report /home/ nwells	Copies a file to or from a floppy drive
	mcopy report.ps A:	
mread	mread A:report /home/ nwells	Copies a file from a floppy drive to the Linux hard disk

MTOOLS COMMAND	EXAMPLE	DESCRIPTION
mwrite	mcopy report.ps A:	Copies a file from the Linux hard disk to a floppy drive
mformat	mformat A:	Formats a floppy (DOS-format)

Remember that when you use an mtools utility, you don't have to mount the floppy disk drive first. These utilities are about the only time you'll see the old DOS drive letters used in Linux.

NOTE If you have mounted a floppy drive using the mount command or an automounter program (including something like the Desktop icons in KDE or Gnome), the mtools utilities may have trouble accessing your floppy drive.

Access Windows Partitions within Linux

If your Linux system dual boots between Linux and Windows, you probably need to access the data on your Windows partition from time to time while you're running Linux.

Instead of rebooting and copying data to a floppy disk, you can use the standard mount command in Linux to access other partition types (such as DOS or Windows 98) as if they were part of your Linux file system. You can view, copy, and create files on the Windows partition. Any new files you create will also appear within Windows. Long filenames are supported as well for FAT32 file systems.

To access your Windows partition within Linux, you need to know the hard disk and partition number that Windows is using. For example, if you have three partitions on your first hard disk, Windows might be stored on /dev/hda3, the third partition of the first hard disk. You can use fdisk to carefully look at your partition information.

◆ Create a directory to use as a mount point for accessing Windows.

```
# mkdir /mnt/win
```

◆ To mount a DOS or older Windows partition, use this command:

```
# mount -t msdos /dev/hda3 /mnt/win
```

◆ To mount a newer Windows partition (with FAT32), use this command:

```
# mount -t vfat /dev/hda3 /mnt/win
```

◆ If your kernel doesn't support FAT32 (vfat) by default, you may need to add a kernel module using this command: `insmod vfat`.

Access Linux Partitions within Windows

Windows doesn't permit you to "mount" or otherwise access different file systems unless you use the networking features of Windows. The ext2tool package, however, gives you a few standard utilities to access a Linux partition while you're running Windows.

Use the ext2tool utilities when you have a dual boot system and have started up Windows but need to access files on your Linux partition. Unfortunately, the ext2tool programs don't let you write files to the Linux partition.

The ext2tool programs are DOS programs, not Linux programs. Don't try to run these EXE programs in Linux. The source code is included in the /Source/Disk Tools directory on the CD, however.

The programs included with ext2tool are shown in the following table:

EXT2TOOL PROGRAM	DESCRIPTION
GO32.EXE	Needed by all other programs in ext2tool; don't execute it directly.
E2PART.EXE	Lists the partitions on your hard disk (requires a parameter of 128 for your first hard disk or 129 for the second).
E2LS.EXE	Lists the files in the current working directory of your Linux partition (like ls in Linux).
E2PWD.EXE	Prints your current working directory in the Linux partition (like pwd in Linux).
E2CD.BAT	Changes the current working directory that you're looking at on the Linux partition.

EXT2TOOL PROGRAM	DESCRIPTION
E2CAT.EXE	Dumps the contents of a file on the Linux partition (like TYPE in DOS or cat in Linux).
E2CP.EXE	Copies a file from the Linux partition to your DOS/Windows partition. (You cannot copy from DOS/Windows to the Linux partition.)

All of these programs are located in /Binaries/Disk Tools/ext2tool on the CD. The procedure for using them is shown here:

1. Start your DOS or Windows system and change to the directory containing the ext2tool programs (/Binaries/Disk Tools/ext2tool).

2. Run the E2PART utility to see the partition number of your Linux system. Use a parameter of 128 for the first hard disk, or 129 for the second:

```
C:>e2part 128
PARTITION      LENGTH        FILESYSTEM TYPE
1              2047 MB       MS-DOS (FAT)
2              71 MB         Linux swap space
3              1028 MB       Linux ext2
```

3. Define the variable E2CWD to point to the correct hard disk and partition. Again, use 128 for the first hard disk or 129 if Linux is stored on your second hard disk. The second number (3 in this case) is the partition number.

```
C:> set E2CWD=128:3
```

The current directory is set to the root of the Linux file system. You can change that default setting by adding a number to the E2CWD variable. The README file provides details.

4. Use the E2CD command to set your working directory.

```
C:> E2CD /home/nwells
```

NOTE Remember to use forward slashes, as in Linux, not backward slashes, as in DOS.

Once you've followed the above steps, you can do any of the following:

◆ Use the E2LS command to view the contents of any directory.

```
C:> E2LS /home/nwells
```

◆ Use the E2CAT command to view the contents of text files.

```
C:> E2CAT /home/nwells/gimp.kdelnk
```

◆ Use the E2CP command to copy a file from Linux to Windows.

```
C:> E2CP /home/nwells/gimp.kdelnk gimp.kde
```

14 Hack Your Hard Disk

If all of the tools described so far for managing your hard disk don't give you the access you really crave, try this: with the Linux Disk Editor (lde) you can view and edit any byte on your hard disk. This is a low-level tool to see what codes are actually written to the hard disk—how a file is constructed— and maybe help you update or reconstruct it.

WARNING The lde tool is not for novices. You can use it in read-only mode to explore and learn about your hard disk. But a single bad edit could make your hard disk unusable without expert help.

Why use such a low-level tool? Many tools in Linux (such as fsck) provide an automated way to correct problems. If those automated tools don't work, however, the lde helps you correct things manually, much like some of the old DOS utilities such as the Norton Disk Doctor did.

To use the `lde`, you should have a partition that is not mounted as a read/write partition (if you need to edit your root partition, boot your system from a floppy disk—see Number 47, "Boot Linux in Emergencies," for more information). The `lde` is located at /Binaries/Disk Tools/lde on the CD.

> **NOTE** Another low-level disk editor similar to `lde` is called `ext2ed`. The source code for this package is located at /Source/Disk Tools/ on the CD if you want to explore this tool.

Many command-line options are available when you start `lde` (see the man page in the doc directory). If you use command-line options, you can use `lde` to dump information from specific disk blocks or perform similar operations. If you don't use those options, `lde` provides a menu-based interface to explore your hard disk. The only required option is the device name you want to explore. In this example, I'm working with the third partition of the first IDE hard disk on my system.

```
# lde /dev/hda3
```

After entering this command, the screen goes blank for a moment. Press Enter to see the first screen of `lde` (see Figure 14.1) which displays the superblock information for your selected device.

FIGURE 14.1   The initial screen of `lde`, the Linux Disk Editor, shows the superblock information for the device you are viewing.

```
 □ ⋈ Terminal <2>                                               ·  □ ✕
   File   Options                                                   Help
                    lde v2.3.4 : ext2fs : /dev/hda3
  Inode:       2 (0x00000002)  Block:        0 (0x00000000)  0123456789!@$%^



                    Inodes:        263160 (0x000403F8)
                    Blocks:       1052257 (0x00100E61)
                    Firstdatazone:      1 (N=1)
                    Zonesize:        1024 (0x0400)
                    Maximum size: 16843020 (0x0101010C)

                    ✳ Directory entries are 255 characters.
                    ✳ Inode map occupies 33 blocks.
                    ✳ Zone map occupies 129 blocks.
                    ✳ Inode table occupies 32895 blocks.




                    F)lags, I)node, B)locks, R)ecover File▮
```

The lde has three modes and several flags that you can set. You can enter one of these modes by pressing one of the keys shown at the bottom of the screen or by viewing the menu and choosing an item there.

To view the menu, press F2 or Ctrl+O (see Figure 14.2).

FIGURE 14.2   **The menu of** lde **shows mode options (inode, blocks, and recover) as well as configuration options.**

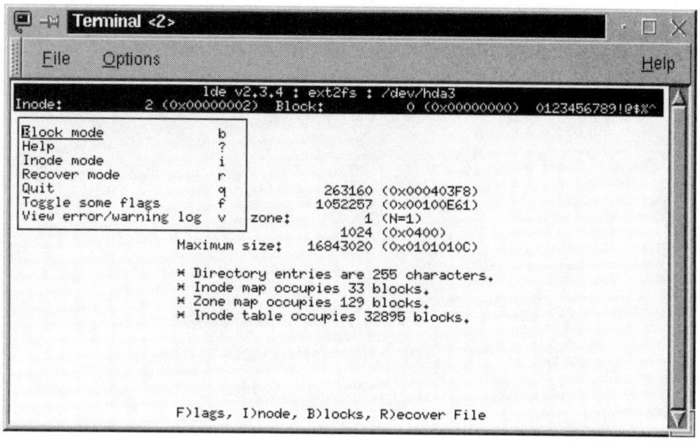

```
┌─────────────────────────────────────────────────────────────┐
│ 🖳 ⊣⊠  Terminal <2>                                    · □ ☓ │
├─────────────────────────────────────────────────────────────┤
│    File    Options                                    Help   │
│                 lde v2.3.4 : ext2fs : /dev/hda3              │
│  Inode:        2 (0x00000002)  Block:        0 (0x00000000)  0123456789!@#%^ │
│ ┌─────────────────────────┐                                 │
│ │Block mode          b    │                                 │
│ │Help                ?    │                                 │
│ │Inode mode          i    │                                 │
│ │Recover mode        r    │                                 │
│ │Quit                q    │        263160 (0x000403F8)      │
│ │Toggle some flags   f    │       1052257 (0x00100E61)      │
│ │View error/warning log  v│ zone:       1 (N=1)             │
│ └─────────────────────────┘          1024 (0x0400)          │
│                       Maximum size:  16843020 (0x0101010C)   │
│                                                             │
│                       ⋇ Directory entries are 255 characters. │
│                       ⋇ Inode map occupies 33 blocks.       │
│                       ⋇ Zone map occupies 129 blocks.       │
│                       ⋇ Inode table occupies 32895 blocks.  │
│                                                             │
│               F)lags, I)node, B)locks, R)ecover File        │
└─────────────────────────────────────────────────────────────┘
```

Before you can make any changes to your hard disk, you must change the "Write" flag to YES. It is always off by default as a safety precaution. Leave it at NO unless you feel comfortable editing your hard disk at this level. Press F to view the flags and then set OK to write to filesystem to Yes.

Inodes are the file descriptors for everything on your Linux file system. They point to the actual location of data for a file; they also contain owner and permission information and the dates and times related to a file or directory.

When you use inode mode in lde, you see all of the information about an inode in a summary fashion. You can then change this information for any inode.

To enter inode mode, press i or choose inode mode from the menu. The first inode is shown, as in Figure 14.3.

You can press F1 or H to see a full screen of help about using the inode mode. You can also press F2 or Ctrl+O to view the inode menu (which is different than the main menu, though it appears in the same location on screen).

FIGURE 14.3 Inode mode lets you view information about a file or directory, as stored in the inode for that item.

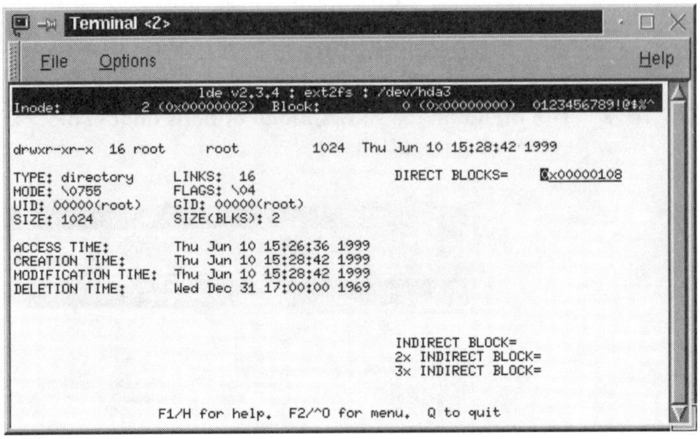

When you are feeling adventurous, press B to see Block mode, shown in Figure 14.4. In this mode, you are viewing the raw information on the hard disk. The numbers you see are accessed in a structured way by all the other tools you use in Linux. This utility presents them at the lowest level, allowing you to alter and repair things as necessary.

FIGURE 14.4 Block mode lets you view and edit every number stored on your hard disk.

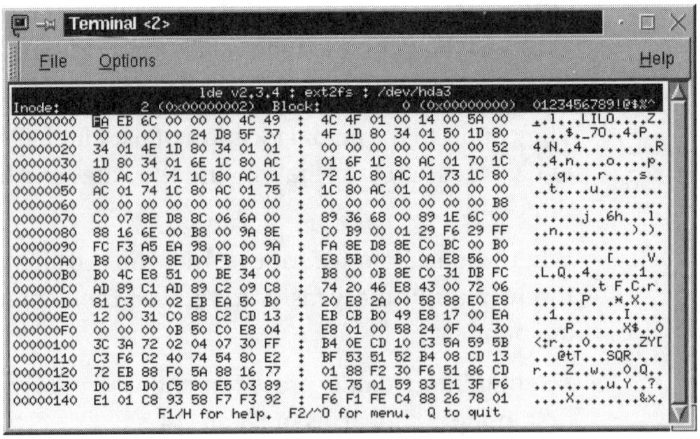

Once again, pressing F1 or H displays a set of help for Block mode; pressing F2 or Ctrl+O displays the Block mode menu, where you can select different operations to perform on the current block.

A few basic commands for viewing your hard disk blocks are shown in the following table:

ACTION	KEY TO PRESS IN BLOCK MODE
Highlight different characters in the block.	Arrow keys
View the next or previous block (sequentially).	Page Down or Page Up
View the next or previous block for the inode that applies to the current block.	N, M
Write this block to a recovery file.	R

One final mode is available in lde: The recovery mode. This mode shows you the disk blocks that are associated with an inode. These are the blocks that are used by normal file access methods and which may be damaged and need repair because a file was corrupted or deleted.

By setting the blocks used by an inode in recovery mode, you can reconstruct a file from the disk blocks of data that you discover by exploring your disk with lde.

The recovery mode screen is shown in Figure 14.5. You should read the documentation for lde to understand how inode indirection is handled before trying to reconstruct a file using recovery mode.

FIGURE 14.5 **In recovery mode, you define the disk blocks associated with an inode.**

```
 ┌──────────────────────────────────────────────────────────────────┐
 │ ◱ ⊶ Terminal <2>                                      · □ ✕       │
 ├──────────────────────────────────────────────────────────────────┤
 │  File   Options                                          Help      │
 ├──────────────────────────────────────────────────────────────────┤
 │              lde v2.3.4 ; ext2fs ; /dev/hda3                       │
 │ Inode:        2 (0x00000002)  Block:      0 (0x00000000)  0123456789!@#%^ │
 │                                                                    │
 │                           DIRECT BLOCKS:    0 : 0x00000000         │
 │                                             1 : 0x00000000         │
 │                                             2 : 0x00000000         │
 │                                             3 : 0x00000000         │
 │                                             4 : 0x00000000         │
 │                                             5 : 0x00000000         │
 │                                             6 : 0x00000000         │
 │                                             7 : 0x00000000         │
 │                                             8 : 0x00000000         │
 │                                             9 : 0x00000000         │
 │                                             ! : 0x00000000         │
 │                                             @ : 0x00000000         │
 │                        INDIRECT BLOCK:      # : 0x00000000         │
 │                     2x INDIRECT BLOCK:      % : 0x00000000         │
 │                     3x INDIRECT BLOCK:      ^ : 0x00000000█        │
 │                                                                    │
 │   Change blocks with adjacent characters.  Q to quit.  R to dump to file │
 └──────────────────────────────────────────────────────────────────┘
```

NOTE When you have finished using lde and you return to a command line, you may find that your screen behaves strangely. Don't be concerned—it has nothing to do with your hard disk. The menu features of lde sometimes confuse the screen management controls. To fix it, type this command and press Enter (even if you can't see it as you type it): stty sane.

Automate Your Entire System

Remember the old days of using DOS AUTOEXEC.BAT files and Windows Start folders? This section describes how to do the same sort of thing with Linux. You can automatically start in graphics mode, run programs, set system variables, or do anything else you choose.

Some additional functionality for automatically running programs is dependent on your graphical environment (such as KDE or Gnome). Those features aren't discussed in this section.

15 Start Automatically in Graphics Mode

The latest Linux products make it so easy to configure the graphical X Window System that you might never see a character console again (unless you choose to).

For older systems where you have to log in and then start the graphical system, Linux provides a simple way to jump right to a graphical log in screen, so you never have to log in via character mode. Avoiding character mode can be a benefit for several reasons, such as:

◆ If you always log in and start the X Windows System, going to X automatically saves you some time when you boot your system.

◆ If you install or manage Linux systems for users who are nervous about entering character-mode commands, you can configure Linux so they never see character mode again.

Linux has several modes of operation, called run levels. The standard character mode that Linux starts with is run level 3. By switching Linux to run level 5, you always stay in graphics mode. Typical run levels in Linux are shown in the following table (some Linux distributions may use variations of this numbering, but the arrangement shown here is fairly standard and applies to Red Hat 6).

RUN LEVEL	DESCRIPTION
0	System is halted.
1	Single-user mode, used by the system administrator for maintenance.
2	Multiuser mode without networking. Not often used.
3	Standard multiuser mode with networking active.
4	Not defined.
5	Like run level 3 but uses the graphical X Window System interface.
6	Reboots the system (shuts down all system services).

Before you can use run level 5, you must have the X Window System working already. If you can use KDE, Gnome, fvwm, or other graphical window managers or desktops, you're ready to use run level 5.

Switching to run level 5 is easy. Just execute this command while logged in as root:

```
# init 5
```

After a few seconds, the xdm graphical login prompt appears, and you can enter your username and password to start using your system. When you log out of your X Window graphical session, you return to the graphical login screen; you never return to the character-mode screen unless you execute this command within a graphical terminal window:

```
# init 3
```

Having tested run level 5 with the init command, you can now make it the default on your system so that every time you start Linux, it begins with a graphical login prompt. To make run level 5 the default, you must edit the text file /etc/inittab while logged in as root.

In the /etc/inittab file, you should locate a line that looks like this one (usually one of the first noncomment lines in the file):

```
id:3:initdefault:
```

Using your text editor, change the 3 to a 5, so the line looks like this:

```
id:5:initdefault:
```

If you're curious, look at the last line in the /etc/inittab file. It looks something like this:

```
x:5:respawn:/usr/bin/X11/xdm —nodaemon
```

Or, in Red Hat 6, it looks like this (they use a symbolic link here to the gdm Gnome Display Manager):

```
x:5:respawn:/etc/X11/prefdm —nodaemon
```

This is the command that is run to start run level 5, the xdm graphical login program. You can read about xdm options in the xdm man page. These options allow you to update the background image, the text messages, and so forth in the graphical login screen.

Save your updated /etc/inittab file and exit your text editor. That's all there is to it. Next time you restart Linux, you will go directly to run level 5 and the graphical login.

A simpler way to configure the graphical login screen if you're running Red Hat 6 is to use the LinuxConf utility (under System on the Gnome main menu). Within LinuxConf, choose the Configuration ➤ boot mode ➤ Mode section to view a dialog where you can select a graphical mode or text mode.

If you're using KDE as your desktop, you can also use the KDE version of xdm, called kdm. This program is configured graphically within a section of the KDE Control Center (under the Applications tab).

By setting the Linux run level to graphical mode as described in this section, all users on the system start automatically in graphical mode. If you just want to have the graphical mode launched automatically after you log in at a text-mode prompt, you can add the startx command to one of your initialization scripts (such as .profile in your home directory), as described in the next section.

16 Run a Program Automatically Each Time You Start Linux

Linux follows a standard process each time you start the system and each time you log in using your username and password. Part of the standard process on both occasions is running any startup commands that are found in certain files (I'll call these startup scripts).

You can add lines to these startup scripts to start programs that you need each time you begin using Linux or to set configuration information.

A script is simply a text file containing lines with commands as they would be executed from any command line. Linux scripts are similar to DOS batch files, but Linux provides much more programming functionality, such as control structures and complex conditional tests. You can learn more about that from the `bash` man page.

Each time you start Linux, the following script is executed.

```
/etc/rc.d/rc.local
```

Actually, many other system configuration scripts are executed as well, but `rc.local` is a good place to add commands that you want to have executed once for the entire system each time you turn on your Linux computer.

Each time you log in, other script files are executed (if they exist):

- ◆ `/etc/profile` (for every user on the system)
- ◆ `.profile` (in your home directory, executed only when you log in)

Each time you start a new Bash command shell (such as by logging in or opening an xterm window), your working environment is set up by Linux. To do this, the following scripts are executed:

- ◆ `/etc/bashrc` (if it exists)
- ◆ `.bashrc` in your home directory

On Red Hat 6 Linux, another script named `.bash_profile` is part of your home directory and is executed as well as those listed here. The Bash shell is the default for all Linux systems. If you've selected another shell as your working environment, such as the C or Korn shell, a corresponding script is executed each time you open a new shell, for example, the `.csh` or `.ksh` scripts in your home directory.

Another set of scripts is run each time you start the X Window System. These scripts are more complex than the others just mentioned; don't alter the existing lines in these files unless you know what you're doing. The scripts that are run for X may also depend on which version of Linux you are running and which graphical tools you use (such as KDE, Gnome, fvwm, or CDE). The basic scripts to be run probably include:

- `.xinitrc` in your home directory
- `.Xclients` in your home directory
- `.Xsession` in your home directory
- `/etc/X11/xinit/xinitrc`
- `/etc/X11/xinit/Xclients`

Because these files are used to determine which graphical window manager and desktop to start for you, they are executed in the order shown above. For example, if you have a file named `.xinitrc` in your home directory, it can specify which desktop to start for you when you enter the `startx` command.

Programs that you want to start when you start X are normally listed at the end of the `.Xclients` file in your home directory. The system-wide `Xclients` file in `/etc/X11/xinit` might contain the names of programs that will be started for all users when they run `startx`, for example, a desktop pager or clock program.

Defining Programs and Environment Information

To make a program start each time you boot your Linux system, just add that command to the end of your `/etc/profile` script.

For example, suppose that you want to send an e-mail to a system administrator account on another system each time Linux is started. You can do this by adding a line like this one at the end of the `/etc/rc.d/rc.local` script:

```
mail -s "Starting Linux system Brighton" robert@whistler.
xmission.com < /dev/null
```

This command appears in the script exactly as it would appear if you were typing it from any command line.

In addition to starting programs, you may need to set up information about your environment, such as environment variables and alias commands, each time you start a shell or use the su command to access your user account. Any commands used to set up your environment can be added to the end of your .bashrc script in your home directory.

TIP The filename .bashrc begins with a period, making it a hidden file. Use the ls -a command to view hidden files.

For example, suppose you need to define an environment variable each time you log in so that the programs you run have that information available to them. The environment variable is specific to your user account, so you place it in your .bashrc file. It might look like this:

```
export HISTSIZE=250
```

It's also common to include environment variable definitions in the .xinitrc or .Xclient files in your home directory, so that any graphical programs you need will have that information available. This type of information can apply to all users on your Linux system if you place it in the /etc/profile or /etc/X11/xinit file.

WARNING If you are using run level 5 (the graphical login screen), be careful about changing any scripts that are run at system startup. If you add a command that doesn't work correctly, the system may not be usable because the script cannot exit normally. Test commands as a regular user first.

17 Run Any Program Any Time

Running programs automatically when you log in is a great feature, but even DOS can do that. Linux also lets you set up specific times and dates to run any program you choose. As long as your computer is on, the program will run unattended and e-mail you the results.

Running programs automatically is great for all sorts of administrative tasks and little electronic "errands" such as:

◆ Sending yourself reminder messages about meetings or other things you need to take care of

◆ Backing up your system in the middle of the night

◆ Automatically checking system logs with log analysis programs

◆ Downloading large files while you sleep

◆ Querying a stock price every 10 minutes and compiling a graph

All of these can be done easily in Linux using the `crontab` and `at` commands. The root user on your system can set up files to allow or deny rights to run automatic programs using `crontab` and `at`. This is done by setting up a text file named `/etc/cron.allow` or `/etc/cron.deny` and including usernames in one of these files. If neither of these files is present (which is the default on most Linux systems), all users can run automatic programs using `crontab` and `at`.

Setting Up a One-Time Task

The two commands `crontab` and `at` are used a little differently: `crontab` is for recurring tasks; `at` is for single tasks that are scheduled for a later time but are not necessarily recurring. However, using either program is often referred to as setting up a "cron job."

To use `at` to schedule a one-time task for automatic execution later, follow these steps:

1. Run the `at` command with the date or time when you want your commands executed. A prompt for entering the `at` command appears.

```
$ at 19:30
at>
```

The methods of specifying dates and time for at can be very complex if you need them to be. The following table shows some examples of how to format the date and time. The man page for at describes more specifics about how to specify execution times.

at 19:30	7:30 P.M. tonight (or tomorrow if it's past that time already)
at now+10 minutes	10 minutes from when you press Enter
at Jun 3 6:00	6:00 A.M. on June 3
at 11/10/99	Right after midnight on November 10, 1999

2. At the at> prompt, enter the commands that you want to execute as if you were entering them on a regular command line.

```
at>ps
```

3. After entering all of the commands you need to execute, press Ctrl+D.

The at command responds with the job number and date and time that the job will be executed. For example:

```
Job 5 at 1999-11-01 19:02
```

NOTE The programs that process at and crontab commands check for something to do each minute, so you can't be more precise than using these commands.

◆ If you need to see when you have tasks (jobs) scheduled using at, run the atq command:

```
$ atq
6    1999-11-01    19:14a
8    1999-11-02    00:05 a
```

◆ If you want to cancel the execution of a job that you scheduled with at, use the atrm command with the job number (if you don't know the job number, you can find it using atq).

```
$ atrm 6
```

4. The job numbers are specific to your user account. Each user has a separate queue of tasks that have been submitted using at.

What happens to the output generated by commands that you enter using at? It is automatically e-mailed to your user account. This allows you to review the output whenever you choose to (a helpful feature when running programs at 2:00 A.M.).

Setting Up Recurring Automatic Programs

The at program is great for single tasks, but if you want to run a program at regular intervals, such as once per week or once per hour, the crontab program can set up a regularly scheduled task for you.

Using crontab is a little more complicated than using at because the time formats are more complex, and you must create a text file containing the information about your task.

To use crontab, create a small text file containing the commands you want to execute. An example is shown here, taken from the crontab man page:

```
# use /bin/sh to run commands, no matter what /etc/passwd says
SHELL=/bin/sh
# mail any output to `paul', no matter whose crontab this is
MAILTO=paul
#
# run five minutes after midnight, every day
5 0 * * *          $HOME/bin/daily.job >> $HOME/tmp/out 2>&1
# run at 2:15pm on the first of every month -- output mailed to
  paul
15 14 1 * *        $HOME/bin/monthly
# run at 10 pm on weekdays, annoy Joe
0 22 * * 1-5mail -s "It's 10pm" joe%Joe,%%Where are your kids?%
23 0-23/2 * * * echo "run 23 minutes after midn, 2am, 4am ...,
  everyday"
5 4 * * sun        echo "run at 5 after 4 every sunday"
```

Each line of the text file contains a description of when to run that command and the command itself. Lines can also contain environment variables such as MAILTO=paul, which defines a user who should receive the e-mailed output from these commands.

N O T E As with the at command, output from any commands you run using crontab is mailed to you. If you don't include a MAILTO setting as in this example file, the e-mail will come to whomever submitted the command file using crontab.

Figuring out the definition of when to execute the command is the challenge with crontab files. Each of the five fields are described in the following table, from left to right as they appear on each command line of the sample file above.

1	Minute	0–59
2	Hour of the day	0–23
3	Day of the month	0–31
4	Month	0–12 (or names, using the first three letters, upper- or lowercase)
5	Day of the week	0–7 (0 or 7 is Sunday; names can also be used, as with months)

If a field contains an asterisk, all possible values are used for that field. For example, if an asterisk is in the Month field, the command is executed every month; if an asterisk is in the Hour field, the command is executed every hour.

Looking more closely at the example file, the following line will run the command portion (starting with $HOME/bin/daily.job) every date of the year at five minutes after midnight (hour 0):

```
# run five minutes after midnight, every day
5 0 * * *        $HOME/bin/daily.job >> $HOME/tmp/out 2>&1
```

The output from the daily.job script will be added to the end of the out file (the /tmp/out path within your home directory) because of the >> operator. Any errors that occur are also sent to the file as regular output (the 2>&1 does this).

To change this to run only on Mondays, the first five fields would change like this:

```
5 0 * * 1        $HOME/bin/daily.job >> $HOME/tmp/out 2>&1
```

To run on the 1st, 10th, and 20th of every month, they would be:

```
5 0 1,10,20 * *        $HOME/bin/daily.job >> $HOME/tmp/out 2>&1
```

When you use a list or range of times like this (1,10,20), don't use a space between the commas. A space is only used to separate the five fields.

Once you have a file set up with your commands and their times and days of execution, you simply submit that file to the system using the crontab command:

```
$ crontab my_cron_file
```

That's the only step. All the commands in the file are stored internally. The cron process checks once each minute as long as your system is turned on. Any commands that are scheduled for execution are run and the output is e-mailed to you.

Spice Up Your Desktop

With the growing sophistication of the KDE and Gnome desktops, new users of Linux are becoming accustomed to the power of a full-featured GUI. Still, the desktop you download or install by default on Linux doesn't include all the tools and toys that you want.

This part describes some slick add-ons for KDE and Gnome that you can integrate with your desktop, such as attractive graphical toys and practical utilities. The focus in this part isn't just on system administration, however—it's on adding features to your desktop that you didn't know were possible to add.

If you don't yet have a copy of KDE or Gnome installed on your Linux system, look on the CD under /Binaries/KDE1.1.1 or /Binaries/Gnome and get the software you need. Packages are provided in several formats and for several Linux distributions. If you're running Red Hat 6, you can choose to install KDE as part of the Gnome desktop used by Red Hat. When you do this, a menu item labeled KDE Menus includes most of the standard KDE options.

To switch to the KDE desktop completely within Red Hat 6 so that you aren't using Gnome at all, run the program switchdesk-kde. If you decide to build some of the programs described in this part from source code (though that's rarely necessary), you should also install the qt-devel package from your Red Hat 6 CD.

18 Personal Productivity Tools and Toys

This section describes specialized programs to help you get the job done. Serious productivity programs like financial managers, special databases, and Internet searching tools have been slow in coming to Linux, but there are some really impressive ones here.

Also included in this section are productivity applications that enable you to appear busy while you're actually doing something that isn't in your job description, such as checking the weather or cataloging your video collection.

Manage Your Finances and Track Your Stock Portfolio

Several tools are available for Linux to help you manage all those Internet stocks you bought last year. Stock tracking and management, personal finance (checkbook tracker), and other financial tools are all available.

The Gnome portfolio manager uses the Yahoo! stock quote service to help you track a selected portfolio of stocks. You use the Update button to update all the stock prices, then use the Chart button to see a graphical display of how your portfolio is performing. Features include multiple portfolio support and symbol lookup. The program was designed to replace the Java-based portfolio manager provided by Yahoo! Finance.

The Gnome portfolio manager (`gnome-pm`) is located at `/Binaries/Desktop/gnome-pm` on the CD. You must have Gnome installed to use it.

If you use Quicken to maintain your checkbook, you should look at Gnofin, a Gnome-based personal finance tool (see Figure 18.1).

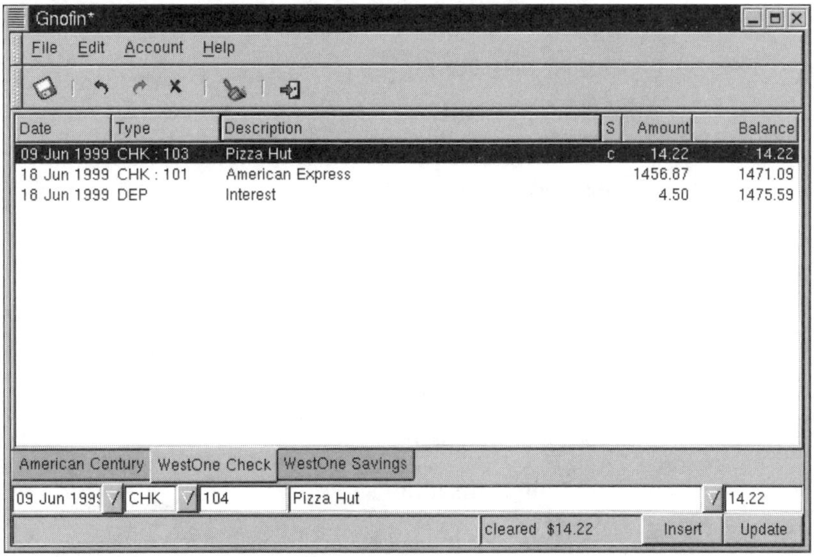

FIGURE 18.1   Gnofin lets you enter checks and track account activity.

Date	Type	Description	S	Amount	Balance
09 Jun 1999	CHK : 103	Pizza Hut	c	14.22	14.22
18 Jun 1999	CHK : 101	American Express		1456.67	1471.09
18 Jun 1999	DEP	Interest		4.50	1475.59

American Century | WestOne Check | WestOne Savings

09 Jun 1999 / CHK / 104 | Pizza Hut / 14.22

cleared $14.22 | Insert | Update

Gnofin lets you define multiple accounts and enter checks and other trans-actions (EFT or ATM, for example). A running balance is maintained for all your transactions.

Gnofin is located at /Binaries/Desktop/Gnofin on the CD.

When you're ready for more advanced financial management, try CBB. CBB is a scripted program (written in Tcl/Tk and Perl) that manages your personal finances like Quicken. CBB is not a Gnome or KDE program, but it's much more complete than Gnofin. It even imports Quicken data files.

CBB is located at /Source/Desktop/ on the CD. Because CBB is a scripted program, a single command to place the files into correct system directo-ries is the only step needed before running the program. Use these com-mands to copy and untar the package.

```
$ cp /mnt/cdrom/Source/Desktop/cbb-0_78_tar.gz /home/nwells
  part4
$ tar xvfz cbb-0_78_tar.gz
```

The following commands install the package. You need to be logged in as root to install the package in the default location. Answer the questions that the script asks about your system during the installation (you can just press Enter for the default if you're using Red Hat 6 or most other Linux systems).

```
$ cd cbb-0.78
$ make install
```

After using these commands to install the program, you can start it with this command:

```
$ /usr/local/bin/cbb
```

CBB includes features like:

- Memorized transactions
- Balloon field help
- Default category lists
- Split transactions
- A full set of reports and graphs

The CBB interface is shown in Figure 18.2.

FIGURE 18.2   The CBB financial package lets you track your personal accounts with powerful Quicken-like features.

Track Your Business Contacts

For businesspeople or home users who want to track contacts or friends on their KDE desktops, PeopleSpace provides an easy-to-use specialized database. PeopleSpace keeps track of names, addresses, and up to eight contact methods (fax, mobile, pager, e-mail, etc.) in a simple on-screen form.

The PeopleSpace program is located at /Binaries/Desktop/Peoplespace on the CD. When you start the program, a Wizard walks you through the initial configuration of the database (see Figure 18.3).

As you enter new data for people whom you want to record information about, you scroll between all the records with the left and right arrow buttons on the toolbar. Several types of additional notes and comments can be stored for each person. You can then search the database for people matching various criteria, such as name, company, city, or last meeting (see Figure 18.4).

FIGURE 18.3 PeopleSpace begins with a configuration Wizard to help you set up your contacts database.

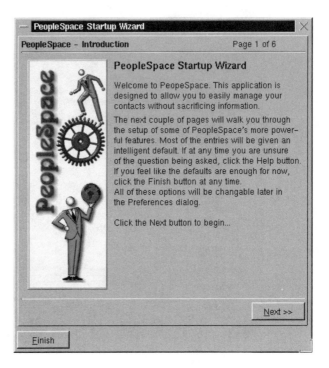

FIGURE 18.4 PeopleSpace includes fields for name, address, notes, and contact information.

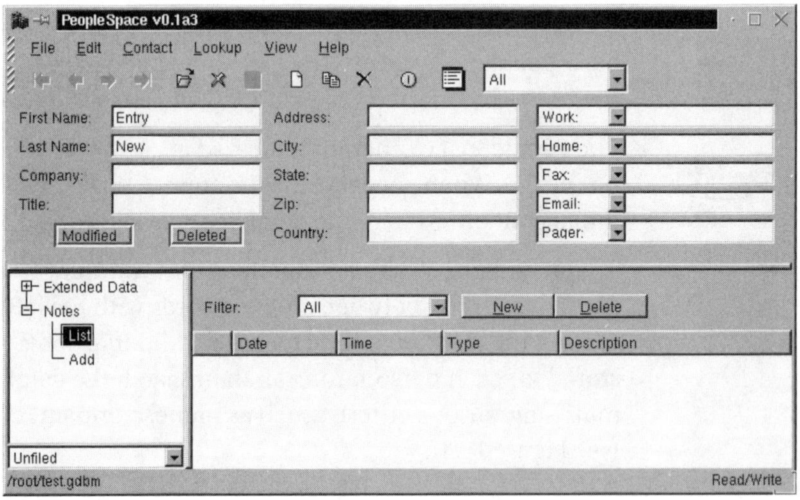

Separate lists of personal and business contacts can be created, or multiple complete databases can be used. The configuration established by the Startup Wizard can be updated at any time by choosing Edit ➤ Preferences.

Manage Multiple File Downloads

When you're busy working on your computer, managing large or multiple downloads can really interrupt your workflow. Transfer Manager can take care of that for you. By using Transfer Manager, you can download multiple files without opening a separate browser window for each one and without returning to a browser window repeatedly to click on the next file in a series that you want to download.

To use the Gnome Transfer Manager, you specify the URL that you want to download (Web, FTP, etc.) and the directory where the file to download should be placed.

The Transfer Manager then starts the download. The window is refreshed once per second (you can set the refresh rate). As the download progresses, the fields shown for each file include:

- ◆ The status of the download (active, stalled, etc.)

- ◆ The number of bytes retrieved and the total size of the download

- ◆ The amount of time used so far and the estimated time to complete the download

- ◆ The session speed

 The interface to Transfer Manager is shown in Figure 18.5. The program is located at /Binaries/Desktop/transfermanager on the CD. It can be started with this command:

```
$ ./gtm
```

Transfer Manager includes a Preferences dialog box where you can select which network interface to use for downloads (such as the modem, cua0, or the Ethernet card, eth0). You can also specify a default directory for all downloads (though each download can have a different directory specified) and use a proxy server for both HTTP and FTP downloads.

FIGURE 18.5 The Gnome Transfer Manager tracks multiple downloads while you work on other things.

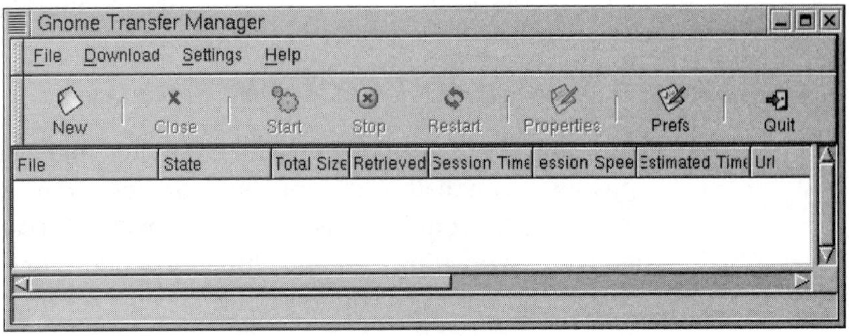

Create Custom Web Searches

Another task that sometimes interrupts your workflow is searching for something on the Web. You may have to repeatedly click on links and try new sites and wait for new pages to download.

The AQSS utility automates a simple Web search so you can do other work until the search results have been gathered. This utility is located at /Binaries/Desktop/AQSS on the CD. The interface is shown in Figure 18.6.

Four tabs in the middle of the window display remaining sites to search, completed searches, successfully located items, and any errors that occurred. You add new URLs to search in the *Direccion* field and the text to search for in the Search Rule field. As you can see, a little Spanish is scattered throughout the interface because the author (in Spain) hasn't quite finished things (the Preferences dialog box is also not yet functional).

Catalog Your Videos

Videobase is a handy specialized database for recording information about your videocassette collection. Fields such as these are tracked by this program:

◆ Video name

◆ Director

◆ Cast members

◆ Release date

FIGURE 18.6 The AQSS utility searches Web sites for you.

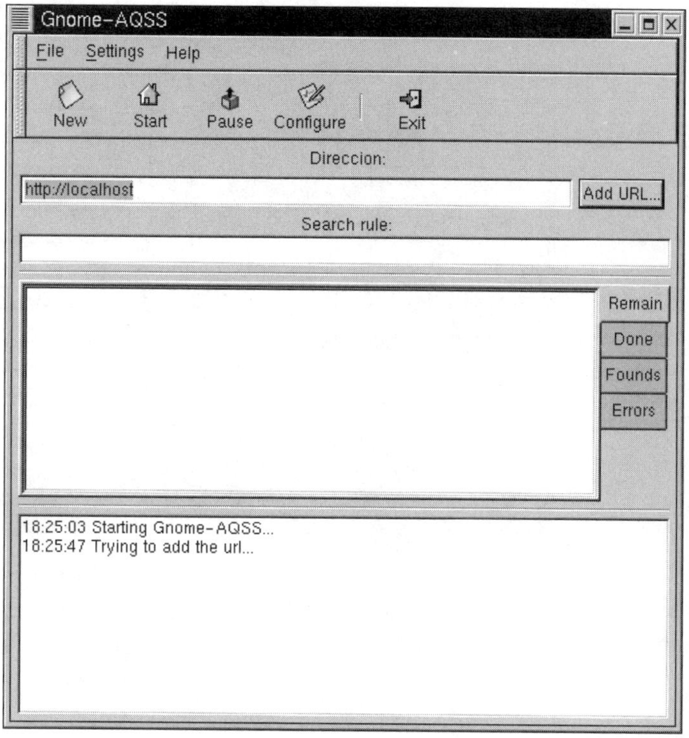

◆ Length

◆ Last date seen

◆ Category

◆ Remarks

Videobase runs on Gnome. It's located on the CD at /Binaries/Desktop/
Videobase. Start the program with this command:

```
$ videobase
```

Figure 18.7 shows the main window of Videobase along with the Details
screen that you use to enter information about a new video. You can fill in
all of these fields and return and edit them later if needed.

Once you have a complete list of videos recorded in Videobase, you can use
the Filtering feature to search for information in the database. The filter lets

FIGURE 18.7 Videobase stores information about your video collection.

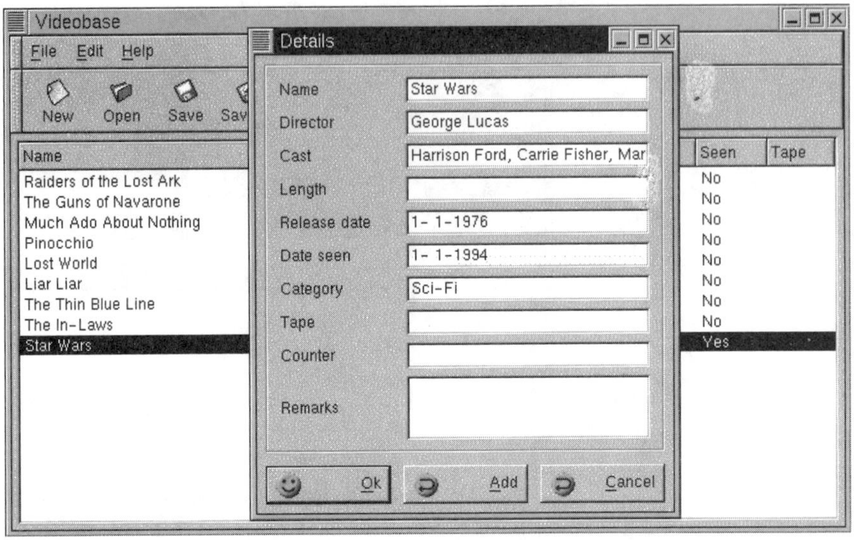

you choose a field and enter a condition for that field. Two fields can be combined for more complex filtering. When you apply the filter (see Figure 18.8) only the videos matching your criteria are included on screen.

FIGURE 18.8 The Filter feature of Videobase lets you view only the videos that match certain criteria.

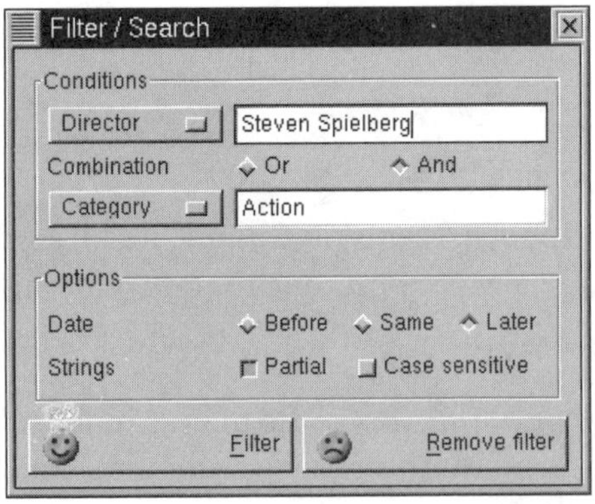

For example, suppose you wanted to see which videos you have with Harrison Ford in them that Steven Spielberg directed. Choose the Director and

Actor fields, and the display is updated to show only matching entries. Partial string matches and date options are also supported in the Filter dialog box.

Check the Weather

If you need to keep track of the weather as you work, install SkyApp on your Gnome system. This little tool appears as a scrolling window with in your Gnome panel. It retrieves information from the Web site http:// www.weather.com and displays lines of updated information as you work, as shown here.

The program for SkyApp is located at /Binaries/Desktop/skyapp on the CD. This package doesn't include a standard make file, so if you decide to build your own binary, review the README file carefully.

19   System Admin Tools

Both Gnome and KDE include a full suite of system administration tools. However, there are a few tools that are new, specialized, or still relatively unknown. This section tells you how to take advantage of some very useful tools that aren't included in the default desktop distributions.

Manage File Systems Graphically

If you need to access multiple file systems either locally (on hard drives attached to your PC) or remotely (using the NFS remote mounting protocol), you're probably familiar with the mount command and the /etc/ fstab file. The kfstab utility gives you a graphical interface through which you can review and add mounted file systems.

Kfstab is located at /Binaries/Desktop/kfstab on the CD. When you start the program, you see the window shown in Figure 19.1. From this window, you can add to or remove any of the available or mounted file systems.

FIGURE 19.1 Kfstab helps you set up your file system table with all the appropriate options.

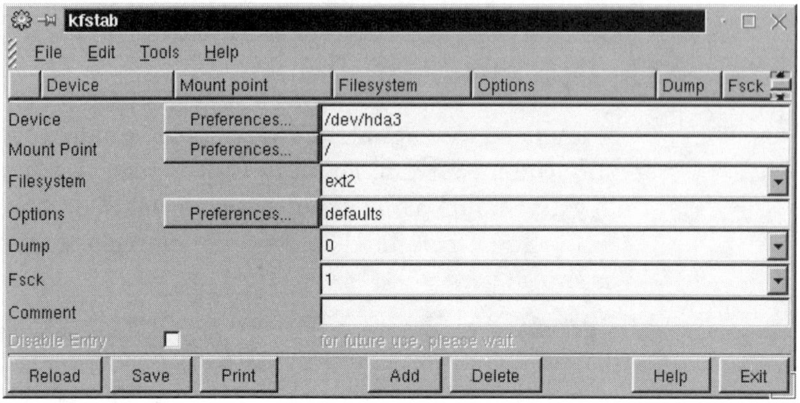

You can alter the configuration for how your file system will be mounted on your system by changing any of the fields in the main kfstab window. When you want to define a new file system, change all of the fields, starting with the device name and mount point, then click the Add button.

Although the kfstab utility is simply acting as an editor for the /etc/fstab file, it makes it much easier to see all the available options (click Preferences next to the Options field) and so forth. When you have made any needed changes, click the Save button to update your /etc/fstab configuration file. Remember that the file systems are not accessed directly via the kfstab program; this utility just helps you define the file system table that other programs use to automount devices such as floppies, CDs, and even remote NFS servers.

If you have the kdu or kdf utilities installed on your KDE system, they are made available via the Tools menu. These utilities can be used to see the free space and disk devices mounted on your system, as well as the space used by a directory.

Monitor Program Activity

As you work with your Linux system, starting multiple programs and working in multiple windows, it's helpful to have access to a list that shows which programs were started from within a particular environment. For example, if you start a graphical program from within a command-line window and then close the command-line window, the graphical program will end as well. The kpstree utility helps you avoid shutting the wrong application down. This tool shows the relationships between processes as a graphical tree within KDE (see Figure 19.2).

FIGURE 19.2   Kpstree displays all system processes, showing the relationship between them.

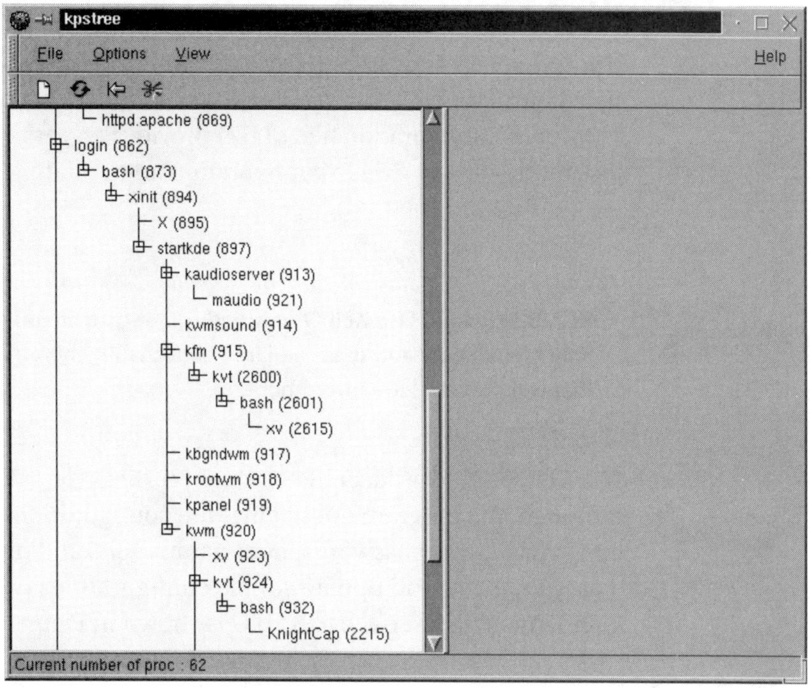

```
 kpstree                                                  □ ×
 File   Options   View                                              Help

 ⟍ httpd.apache (869)
 ⊞ login (862)
    ⊞ bash (873)
       ⊞ xinit (894)
          ├ X (895)
          ⊞ startkde (897)
             ⊞ kaudioserver (913)
                ⟍ maudio (921)
             ├ kwmsound (914)
             ⊞ kfm (915)
                ⊞ kvt (2600)
                   ⊞ bash (2601)
                      ⟍ xv (2615)
             ├ kbgndwm (917)
             ├ krootwm (918)
             ├ kpanel (919)
             ⊞ kwm (920)
                ├ xv (923)
                ⊞ kvt (924)
                   ⊞ bash (932)
                      ⟍ KnightCap (2215)
 Current number of proc : 62
```

The utility is located at /Binaries/Desktop/kpstree. Although you can't do much else with the kpstree utility besides look at the process tree, this alone can be informative, especially for those new to Linux. You can see how the login program starts a shell, which then starts another program, and so forth.

Kpstree does let you sort the process tree by name or by process ID number (PID). You can also remove (kill) a process that you click (be careful which ones you kill!), and you can set the refresh rate for how often the information is updated on screen.

Kpstree is similar to using the ps and top utilities on a command line. In conjunction with kpstree, you may find the ktop KDE utility useful. It doesn't display the processes in a tree diagram, but it does allow more interaction with the processes, such as changing process priorities.

Ktop is included with the latest release of KDE (and is included in the KDE Utilities package (kdeutils) on the CD at /Binaries/KDE). You can also find the ktop package in the /Source/System Tools directory on the CD.

Configure How Your Hard Disk Boots

If you've set up your system to handle multiple operating systems or multiple Linux kernels, you've probably used the lilo command and the /etc/lilo.conf configuration file. KLILO provides an easy-to-use graphical interface for modifying the lilo configuration and updating on your hard disk.

WARNING Use KLILO only with great care. If you're not familiar with how Linux boots and uses the LILO boot manager, you could make changes that will prevent Linux from booting.

The KLILO utility is located at /Binaries/Desktop/klilo on the CD. Although this program doesn't include configuration of all possible LILO features (such as passwords, boot parameters, and message text), it makes it easy to review and update simple configurations without using the command line. The interface to KLILO is shown in Figure 19.3.

FIGURE 19.3 Configuring basic boot options for LILO is easy with KLILO.

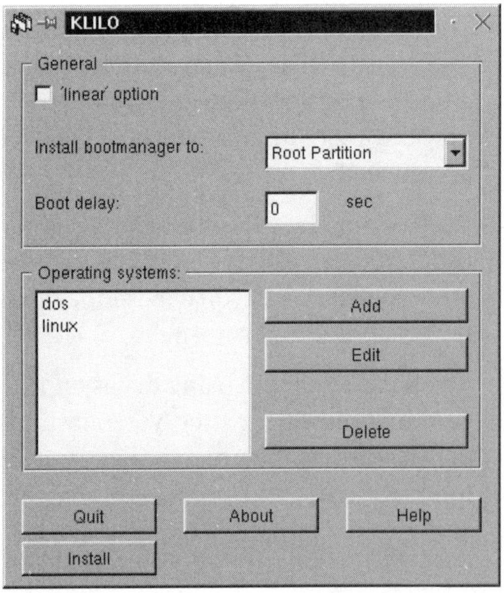

Using KLILO, you can add a configuration for additional operating systems or Linux kernels on your computer by clicking the Add button. Once a system is added, you can use the Edit button to set up the hard disk device, select which kernel to run, and so forth. The overall configuration options at the top of the dialog box let you set up where to install LILO and determine the delay before starting up the default operating system (the first one listed in the Operating Systems list).

After configuring your `lilo.conf` file using KLILO, press the Install button to run the `lilo` command and copy this configuration to the boot sector, Master Boot Record, or a floppy diskette (you must be logged in as root to install LILO).

Manage All Your Passwords

The more you use the Internet, the more accounts you have set up around the world. Where before you had just an ISP account, now you're likely to have a separate username and password to access your online bank, your ClickRewards account, Amazon.com, Consumerreports.org, a mutual funds company, and a few others as well. Using the same username on all these accounts is usually not possible; using the same password on all of them is downright foolish.

The Gpasman utility provides a simple solution. It stores all your usernames and passwords for various accounts that you maintain. The passwords are shown in cleartext (readable) on screen so that you can refresh your memory when you need to access an account. The data, however, is stored on disk in an encrypted form, so that others who may have access to the hard disk cannot see the passwords in your Gpasman file.

To use the Gpasman utility (located at `/Binaries/Desktop/gpasman` on the CD), use this command:

```
$ gpasman
```

The interface is shown in Figure 19.4.

Of course, you could also use Gpasman to record the passwords or ID numbers for your ATM card, your car entry code, and so forth, but it's dangerous enough to have all your Internet passwords stored in one place!

FIGURE 19.4 The Gpasman utility records usernames and passwords for the multiple accounts you maintain on various Internet sites.

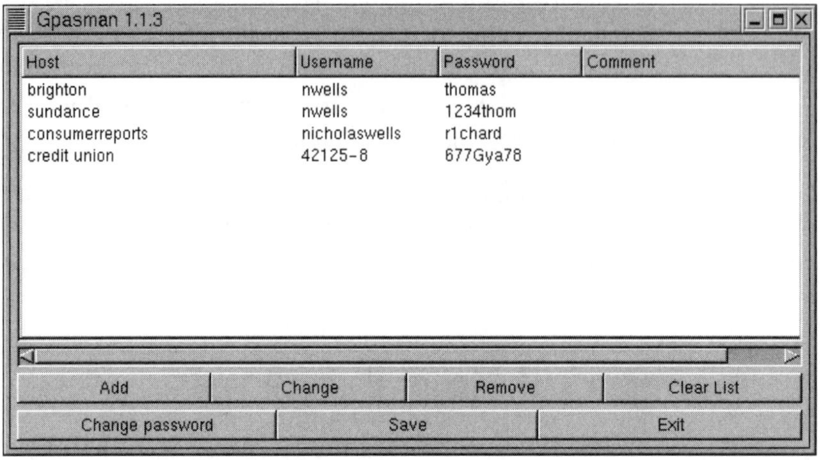

Host	Username	Password	Comment
brighton	nwells	thomas	
sundance	nwells	1234thom	
consumerreports	nicholaswells	r1chard	
credit union	42125-8	677Gya78	

Gpasman 1.1.3

Add · Change · Remove · Clear List

Change password · Save · Exit

Watch Your CPU Activity

Many convenient tools exist for Linux to display the CPU usage of your system (see, for example, the tools described in "Manage Your Files Like a Pro"). If you're using KDE, the kcpumon utility places a small graph in your panel, so you can watch your CPU activity level without having another open window on your desktop.

If you use the source code located on the CD at /Source/Desktop to build and install your own binary, kcpumon will automatically be added into your Utilities menu. The best way to use kcpumon may be to add it to your Autostart folder so that it's always running when you start KDE.

20 Other Ingenious Add-Ons

Do you use your laptop in Linux, or are you one of those people who must know your exact longitude and latitude every so often? Read on for a few additional gee-whiz programs that work with KDE or Gnome.

Connect Linux to Your PalmPilot

With the popularity of the PalmPilot, it was inevitable that someone would decide to connect one to their Linux system. Several packages now support a PalmPilot connection to Linux. You'll need to do a little work with the source code to get these working, however.

The first of these packages is pilot-link, a collection of libraries for uploading and downloading files between your Linux PC and a PalmPilot. Pilot-link is located at /Source/Desktop on the CD.

Once you have pilot-link installed, you can access your PalmPilot via your desktop.

To synchronize to your PalmPilot from Gnome, try Gnome-Pilot. The interface to Gnome-Pilot is shown in Figure 20.1. An administration tool is also under development for Gnome to PalmPilot connectivity.

FIGURE 20.1   **Gnome-Pilot can be used to synchronize your PalmPilot to your Linux system.**

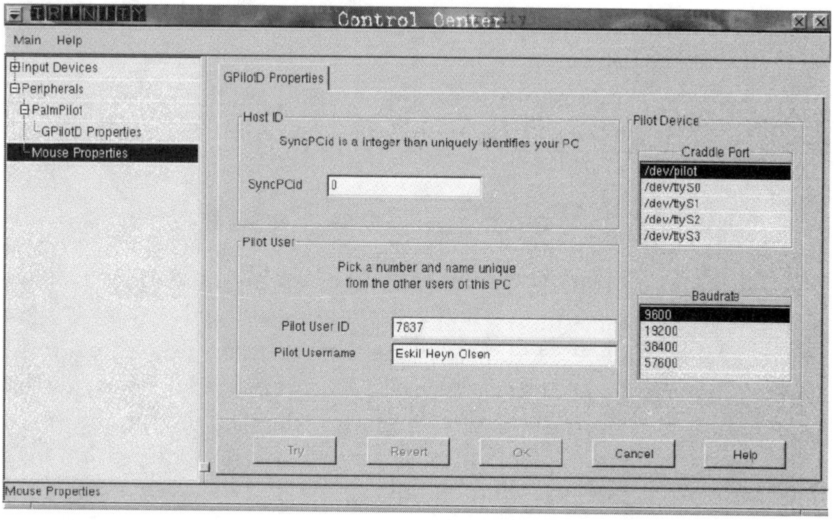

If you're running a KDE desktop, the tool you need to connect to your PalmPilot is called KPilot. It's located on the CD at /Source/Desktop. Development of KPilot continues apace, with new versions coming out regularly with additional features. The interface to KPilot is shown in Figure 20.2.

FIGURE 20.2 KPilot connects your KDE Desktop to your PalmPilot.

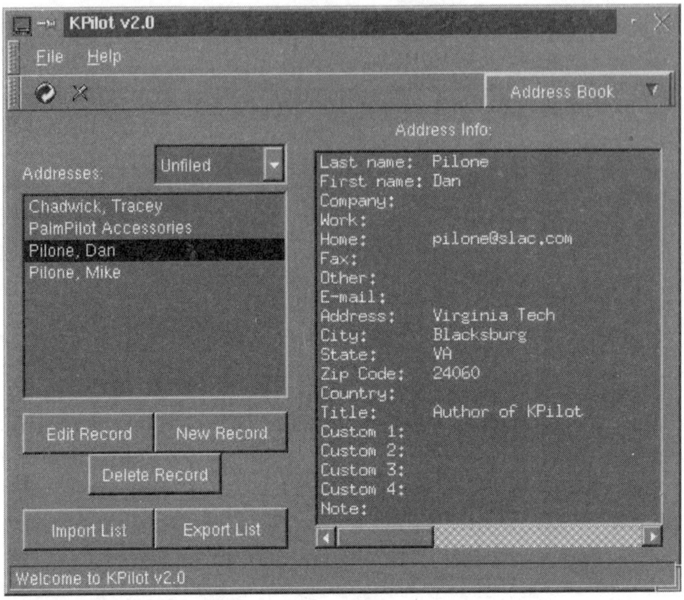

More information about Linux and the PalmPilot can be found at the Web site http://eunuchs.org/linux/palm/index.html.

Manage Your Laptop Power

If you're running KDE on a laptop, you need to use the kcmlaptop package to control your laptop functions directly from KDE. You must have the Advanced Power Management (APM) options set in your Linux kernel (so the kernel can access the appropriate laptop hardware) to use kcmlaptop. For most systems (including Red Hat 6), this requires that you recompile your Linux kernel. See your Linux documentation for details or review the documentation on the CD at /Doc/All-HOWTO-Docs/Kernel-HOWTO.html.

The kcmlaptop package acts as a control panel to manage your battery power and configure power-saving features of your laptop.

The source package (which may be needed for some Linux systems) is located at /Source/Desktop on the CD. Kcmlaptop requires KDE 1.1 or a later version.

When you install kcmlaptop, another section appears in your KDE Control Panel (and corresponding Settings menu), as shown in Figure 20.3.

FIGURE 20.3 The kcmlaptop package installs itself as part of your KDE Control Panel.

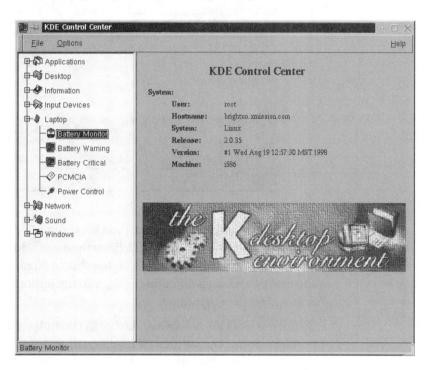

The kcmlaptop package also provides a basic status screen for your PCMCIA cards (though you can't load drivers or make any changes from this screen).

Burn Custom CD-ROMs

More and more users are seeing the need for a CD burner (a writable or read-write compact disc drive); at the same time, prices for these are falling rapidly. The KreateCD utility automates the process of creating your own CDs within KDE.

The KreateCD program is located at /Binaries/Desktop/kreatecd on the CD. When you use the source code to create your own binary, KreateCD is added to your Applications menu. The main window is shown in Figure 20.4.

FIGURE 20.4 In KreateCD you define each track that you want to burn on a new CD.

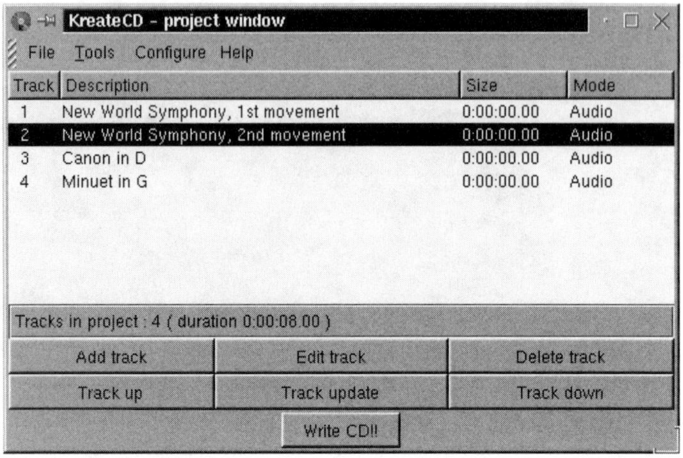

KreateCD - project window
File Tools Configure Help
Track Description Size Mode
1 New World Symphony, 1st movement 0:00:00.00 Audio
2 New World Symphony, 2nd movement 0:00:00.00 Audio
3 Canon in D 0:00:00.00 Audio
4 Minuet in G 0:00:00.00 Audio
Tracks in project : 4 (duration 0:00:08.00)
Add track
Edit track
Delete track
Track up
Track update
Track down
Write CD!!

KreateCD is organized by projects. You set up a project that includes all the tracks you want to record on a CD. Each time you add a new track to the project, you specify the type of data, the source (such as a disk file or another CD track on a different drive), and the options for the new CD. The tracks can be data or audio.

CDs use the ISO9660 file format. KreateCD includes a dialog box where you can select among the various ISO options to customize your project (see Figure 20.5). Long filenames, RockRidge extensions, Joliet extensions, and so forth are all supported.

Once you have defined all of the tracks for your CD, you can edit or arrange them as you wish. When you're done, just click the Write CD button. SCSI drive options and paths to use for data tracks can be configured as you create your project.

Find Your Place in the World (Literally)

The latest global positioning system (GPS) devices can be connected to your PC via a serial interface. The kgps utility lets you connect to your GPS device within KDE. Garmin and Rockwell GPS devices (or a compatible one) are supported by this utility, which is located at `/Binaries/Desktop/kgps` on the CD (see Figure 20.6).

FIGURE 20.5   All major ISO format options are supported in the KreateCD options dialog box.

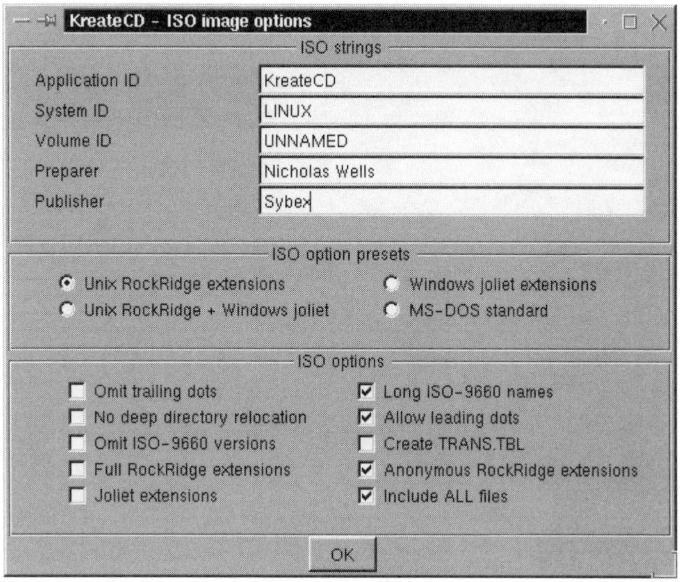

KreateCD – ISO image options

ISO strings

Application ID	KreateCD
System ID	LINUX
Volume ID	UNNAMED
Preparer	Nicholas Wells
Publisher	Sybex

ISO option presets

- (•) Unix RockRidge extensions
- ( ) Unix RockRidge + Windows Joliet
- ( ) Windows Joliet extensions
- ( ) MS-DOS standard

ISO options

- [ ] Omit trailing dots
- [ ] No deep directory relocation
- [ ] Omit ISO-9660 versions
- [ ] Full RockRidge extensions
- [ ] Joliet extensions
- [x] Long ISO-9660 names
- [x] Allow leading dots
- [ ] Create TRANS.TBL
- [x] Anonymous RockRidge extensions
- [x] Include ALL files

OK

FIGURE 20.6   Kgps can be used with your GPS device to display location information within KDE.

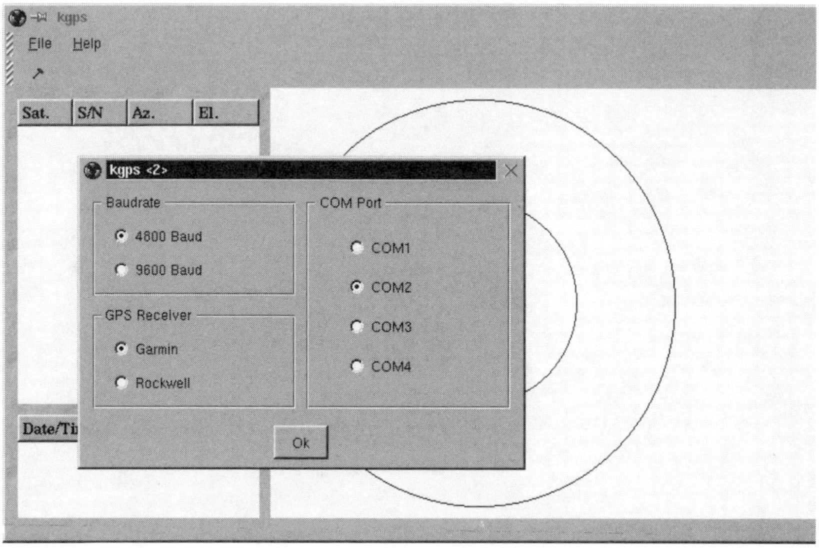

kgps
File   Help

Sat.	S/N	Az.	El.

kgps <2>

Baudrate

- (•) 4800 Baud
- ( ) 9600 Baud

GPS Receiver

- (•) Garmin
- ( ) Rockwell

COM Port

- ( ) COM1
- (•) COM2
- ( ) COM3
- ( ) COM4

Ok

Date/Ti

Satellite information, elevation, and date and time tracking are all shown in the kgps window.

Make Your Linux System a Desktop OS

With the growing sophistication of the KDE and Gnome desktops, new users to Linux are becoming accustomed to the power of a full-featured GUI. Still, the desktop you download or install by default on Linux doesn't include all the tools and toys that these other fancy new desktops have available.

This part describes add-ons for KDE and Gnome that you can integrate with your desktop. These add-ons include attractive graphical toys and practical utilities that are integrated with the desktop. The focus in this part isn't on system administration, however—it's on adding features to your desktop that you didn't know were possible to add.

 If you don't yet have a copy of KDE or Gnome installed on your Linux system, check on the CD under /Binaries/KDE1.1.1 or /Binaries/Gnome to get the software you need. Packages are provided in several formats and for several Linux distributions.

When you install Red Hat 6, you can select KDE as an option. If you do, the KDE menus are included as a submenu of the Gnome desktop. If you prefer to work in Red Hat only in KDE (leaving out Gnome), launch the switchdesk application from the Gnome desktop.

Because Gnome is the default Red Hat interface and was developed in cooperation with Red Hat, you're unlikely to need the packages in the /Binaries/Gnome directory unless you need to add an application that wasn't installed by default. For other distributions, follow the instructions in the Gnome directory to begin working with Gnome as your desktop.

Additional versions of the Gnome and KDE packages are available on the Internet sites for these desktops. If you are using a Linux version that does not use rpm (such as Debian or Slackware), you should download the packages built specifically for your system. The place to begin looking is either http://www.gnome.org or http://www.kde.org. If you decide that you prefer to use KDE as your desktop on Red Hat 6, just run the program switchdesk-kde and select KDE as your desktop in the dialog box that appears. You can run the utility again to switch back to Gnome. (Delete the file .Xclients in your home directory if the switching back and forth doesn't seem to work smoothly.)

21 Run Office Suites on Linux

The rumor is that Microsoft has a team working on Microsoft Office for Linux. While we're waiting for that to materialize, however, Linux has a collection of very good office suites that are available today. Some are commercial, some are free. Most even include the ability to exchange files with Microsoft Office packages.

Use a UNIX Standard: ApplixWare

The ApplixWare suite has been around in the UNIX world for years. Now it's available for Linux and provides a very stable and complete commercial office suite. The creator of ApplixWare, Applix, Inc. (see `http://www.applix.com`) recently announced a separate Linux division.

ApplixWare includes the following components, all available from a single master window on your graphical desktop (any graphical desktop):

- ◆ Word processor
- ◆ Spreadsheet
- ◆ Presentation graphics
- ◆ Vector graphics
- ◆ E-mail Client
- ◆ HTML authoring tool
- ◆ Database client
- ◆ Application builder (development toolkit)

The Applix word processor includes a complete set of input filters, allowing you to work with files from FrameMaker, Word 97, WordPerfect 7, and many other formats. Similar filters are provided with the other ApplixWare components.

You can try a demonstration version of ApplixWare 4.2 using the archive located at /Binaries/Office/ApplixWare on the CD. This demonstration copy doesn't include all of the ApplixWare features, but it will give you a good idea of how the system functions. It expires in April of 2000. To unpack the archive, use this command (the archive is not compressed as most of the CD archives are):

```
# tar xvf /mnt/cdrom/Binaries/Office/ApplixWare/applixdemo-v442-
x86-glibc-linux.tar
```

Follow the instructions in the top level of the unpacked archive to use the ApplixWare demonstration version. These instructions consist of reviewing the README.install file and then running the install-axdemo script.

Figure 21.1 shows a presentation being created in ApplixWare.

FIGURE 21.1   ApplixWare includes a presentation graphics tool.

Comprehensive online help is provided for each part of ApplixWare. Unfortunately, an ApplixWare demo cannot be downloaded free of charge. A commercial package is available for Linux at a low cost via their Web site or various Linux resellers.

Download a Cross-Platform Office Clone: StarOffice

Another complete commercial office suite for Linux is StarOffice, created by StarDivision in Hamburg, Germany, which was recently purchased by Sun Microsystems. StarOffice is an attempt to clone Microsoft Office in functionality, look, and feel, then to go beyond it to add additional features and Internet integration.

StarOffice can be downloaded for free on the Internet for personal use, though we are not permitted to include it on the CD. Visit `http://www.stardivision.com` to register yourself and download the StarOffice package.

The real power of StarOffice lies in two elements: First, it is a cross-platform solution. You can run an identical version of StarOffice on Windows, Linux, Solaris, OS/2, and other platforms. Second, StarOffice integrates all sorts of features into a common "desktop" from which you can start new documents, embed and share files, and access all types of Internet resources.

The features of the latest release of StarOffice include the following, all accessible from a single window:

- ◆ Text documents (word processing)
- ◆ Spreadsheet
- ◆ HTML document creation
- ◆ Web page browsing on the Internet
- ◆ E-mail (creating and receiving)
- ◆ Presentation graphics
- ◆ Vector-based drawing
- ◆ Bitmapped drawing
- ◆ A daily planner/organizer (similar to Outlook)
- ◆ Access to FTP and newsgroup sites

◆ A basic (nonrelational) database

◆ StarBasic programming to customize all parts of the system

A special tool called an Autopilot helps you create new documents in key areas, and access to Internet resources is tightly integrated into the other features. For example, when you view a Web page with StarOffice as a browser, you can immediately save that page and begin to edit it as you would any other StarOffice document. (See Figure 21.2.)

FIGURE 21.2 StarOffice includes many integrated features, accessible from a single desktop.

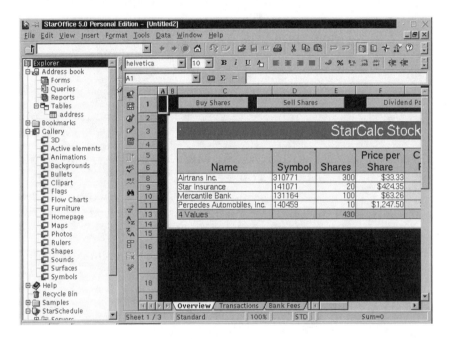

StarOffice does use a lot of system resources—you should have more than 32MB of memory for strong performance. It also requires about 150MB of disk space, although a networked installation uses only about 10MB additional for each user on the system.

Try the Free KOffice Suite

Part of the KDE project is the development of a complete office suite that is integrated with all the features of KDE. The KOffice suite isn't yet completed, but it already includes the following components that are ready to use:

♦ A word processor (KWord)

♦ An Outlook-like task organizer and daily planner (KOrganizer)

♦ A vector-based drawing program (KIllustrator)

♦ A presentations package (KPresenter)

Additional tools will include:

♦ Bitmap drawing tools (KImage)

♦ A spreadsheet (KSpread)

♦ A database with graphical interaction (Katabase)

♦ A formula designer (KFormula)

Because KOffice isn't finished yet, installing it can be a challenge. You must have the latest version of the Qt graphical libraries, compiler tools, KDE, and so forth. For detailed information, visit the KOffice Web site at `http:// koffice.kde.org`.

All of the KOffice components use a shared object system called Kparts that allows documents to be embedded in each other, something like OLE or an Object Request Broker (ORB). For example, a Kspread spreadsheet can be embedded live in a KWord document.

The KWord word processor is similar to FrameMaker in that it is frame oriented rather than page oriented. It includes auto-correction features, a collection of templates, and powerful table features. Figure 21.3 shows KWord.

FIGURE 21.3 KWord includes many powerful formatting options.

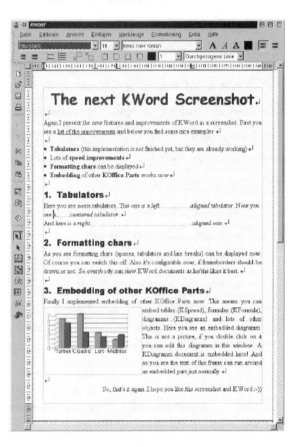

KPresent currently includes a set of templates, multiple presentation options, and the ability to embed or import numerous types of objects, bitmap formats, and graphics primitives (arcs, circles, etc.). (See Figure 21.4.)

FIGURE 21.4 KPresent can embed graphics from other KOffice packages.

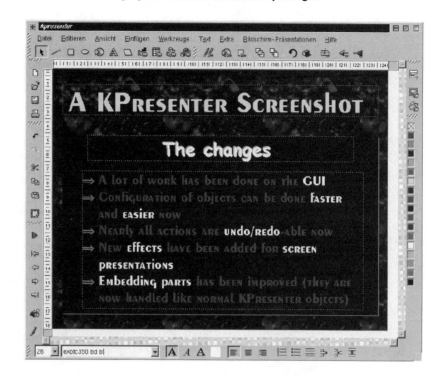

As a final example, KIllustrator lets you create attractive vector-based graphics like those shown in Figure 21.5.

FIGURE 21.5   KIllustrator provides vector-based drawing tools.

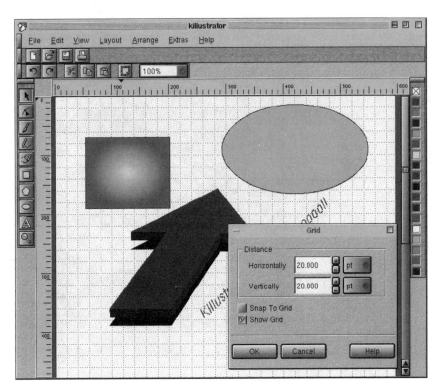

22 Run Other Office Programs on Linux

If you don't need a full suite, many word processors, spreadsheets, and other simple office-type packages are available freely for Linux. Try some of the programs described in this section, including the WordPerfect for Linux package.

The Powerful WordPerfect for Linux

Corel Corporation, which owns WordPerfect, has made a strong commitment to Linux. The WordPerfect 8 word processor is available for Linux now; other Corel suite packages are promised for the future.

As with other commercial packages, WordPerfect cannot be included on the CD here, but you can download it for free from the Corel site at `http://linux.corel.com` by registering your name and e-mail address.

In addition to the download version of WordPerfect for Linux, you can purchase a personal or server version of the product. These versions add features such as:

- A library of several thousand clip art images
- Printed documentation
- A character-based version of WordPerfect for use in host server environments
- Server license management

All three versions (including the free download) include the following:

- Cross-platform compatibility (the same file format used on WordPerfect for all platforms)
- Document management and revision control
- Complex tables with 90 built-in spreadsheet functions
- Internet publishing
- Charting and drawing tools
- Comprehensive grammar and spelling tools

Run the Wingz Spreadsheet

A powerful spreadsheet for Linux is Wingz, which is included on the CD at `/Binaries/Office/Wingz` (two versions are included for you to try). This package is shareware, meaning that if you decide to continue using it, you should send payment to the company providing the software. Wingz was developed by Informix (of database fame) but is now owned by IISG (visit `http://www.newweb.iisc.co.uk/wingz/index.html` and check the documentation in the Wingz package for details).

When you start Wingz, it doesn't look like much. The interface is plain and the features are not especially obvious. However, Wingz rewards those who look a little deeper. This package was originally renowned for its graphical capability—you can create over a dozen styles of graphs with just a click and drag.

Wingz is designed for statistical, engineering, and financial professionals and has the functionality to support those occupations. In addition, Wingz includes a powerful scripting capability. Scripts can be attached to any cell in the spreadsheet, allowing complex calculations based on numerous environmental or spreadsheet-centric factors.

Wingz is available for several platforms, including Windows, UNIX, and Macintosh, and file formats are compatible across all of these platforms. If you find this shareware version of Wingz interesting, you might even be interested in the Wingz Professional product. Figure 22.1 shows a view of Wingz.

FIGURE 22.1 **Wingz includes many powerful features that are not obvious from its plain interface.**

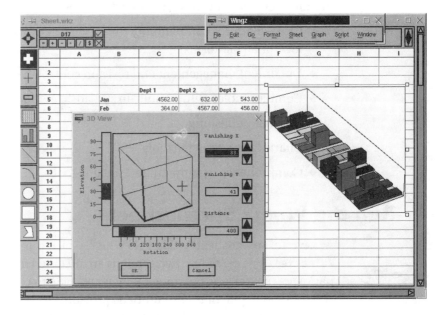

To run Wingz 1.42, follow these steps:

1. Copy the binary archive from the /Binaries/Office/Wingz directory to a location on your hard disk:

```
$ cp /mnt/cdrom/Binaries/Office/Wingz/Wingz-142.tgz /home/
nwells/part5
```

2. Unpack the binary archive:

```
$ tar xvfz Wingz-142.tgz
```

A Wingz subdirectory is created and filled with the files used by the program.

3. Set the WINGZ environment variable to indicate the path where the files are located (the path you enter here depends on where you unpacked the binary archive—the command you use won't include nwells!):

```
$ export WINGZ=/home/nwells/part5/Wingz
```

4. Change to the Wingz/bin/ subdirectory:

```
$ cd Wingz/bin
```

5. Start the Wingz program:

```
$ ./Wingz
```

Version 3.11 of Wingz is even more impressive, but it's a much larger package (requiring about 12MB on your hard disk). To use it, follow these steps:

1. Copy the binary archive from the /Binaries/Office/Wingz directory to a location on your hard disk:

```
$ cp /mnt/cdrom/Binaries/Office/Wingz/wingz-311_tar.gz /home/
nwells/part5
```

2. Unpack the binary archive:

```
$ tar xvfz wingz-311_tar.gz
```

A Wingz3 subdirectory is created and filled with the files used by the program.

3. Set the WINGZ3 environment variable to indicate the path where the files are located (the path you enter here depends on where you unpacked the binary archive—again, the command you use won't include nwells!):

```
$ export WINGZ3=/home/nwells/part5/wingz3
```

4. Change to the `Wingz3/bin/LINUX` subdirectory:

```
$ cd wingz3/bin/LINUX
```

5. Start the Wingz 3.11 program:

```
$ ./Wingz
```

View Your Word Files in Linux

Despite all this talk about alternative office suites and word processors, the most-used word processor at the moment remains Microsoft Word, which isn't available for Linux. Many of the word processors described in this part can read and write Word files, but this section describes an easier way to access those files.

Suppose you have received a Word97 file from a colleague. Rather than open a suite like StarOffice or ApplixWare, a faster and easier solution is to use the mswordview utility to immediately convert the file to HTML so you can view it in your browser.

Mswordview includes what the author calls "a ridiculous number of options" that let you customize how fonts are used, how tables are interpreted, how graphics are embedded in the HTML output, and so forth. Mswordview should be able to handle virtually anything that Microsoft Word creates.

Although mswordview includes numerous command-line options and supports a complex configuration file, none of that is needed to begin using the program. Simply use this command:

```
$ mswordview wordfile.doc
```

An HTML file of the same name (`wordfile.doc.html`, in this example) is created instantly. You don't see any other feedback, but you can open the resulting HTML file in your browser.

The executable program for mswordview is located at /Binaries/Office/ mswordview. The source code archive is located at /Source/Office/ on the CD.

23 Run Your Windows Applications on Linux

If the native Linux applications described so far in this part don't meet all your needs, try running your existing Windows applications on Linux using some of the tools described in this section. The results are not optimal, but they can fill a gap between running on a Windows machine and getting the native Linux applications that you need.

Run Old Windows Apps with Wabi

Years ago, before Java was dreamed up, SunSoft created a Microsoft Windows emulator called Wabi. It was available for Solaris and other UNIX platforms. Eventually, Caldera purchased rights to Wabi and ported it to Linux. With Wabi, Linux was able to run all the popular Windows applications, including Lotus, MS Office, WordPerfect, Quicken, and so forth.

Unfortunately, this was in the days of Windows 3.1. When Java arrived, Sun lost interest in Wabi, and, without support for 32-bit applications, so did everyone else. Caldera stopped selling the product and cannot release it publicly because Sun still owns it.

The upshot of all this is that if you need to run 16-bit Windows applications on Linux, Wabi is a great solution, if you can find a copy of it somewhere. Asking around on Linux newsgroups or checking with long-time Linux resellers are two good options to try.

Run New Windows Apps with WINE

Although Wabi was a great commercial effort in its time, the WINE project continues to develop Windows compatibility code for 32-bit applications.

WINE is not considered "finished," but it does already run some basic 32-bit Windows applications (even beyond Solitaire, which is shown in Figure 23.1 in the midst of a Gnome desktop).

FIGURE 23.1 **WINE runs basic 32-bit Windows applications, such as Solitaire, while work progresses on other office applications.**

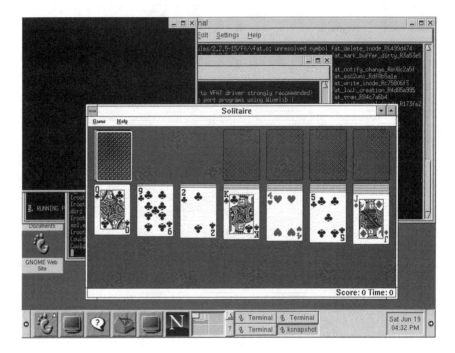

The WINE package is located at /Source/Office on the CD. It requires the Mesa graphics library, which is located in the /Binaries/Extras directory (as a binary rpm-format package).

To compile the source code and try WINE on your system, follow these steps:

1. Change to the root user so you can install the Mesa graphics library:

```
$ su
Password:
```

2. Install the Mesa graphics library from the CD (the path to your CD drive may be different):

```
# rpm -Uvh /mnt/cdrom/Binaries/Extras/Mesa-3_0-2_i386.rpm
```

3. Change back to your regular user account:

```
# exit
$
```

4. Copy the WINE package to your hard disk:

```
$ cp /mnt/cdrom/Source/Office/Wine-990613_tar.gz /home/nwells/
part5
```

5. Unpack the WINE archive:

```
$ tar xvfz Wine-990613_tar.gz
```

6. Change to the WINE directory that was created as the archive was unpacked:

```
$ cd wine-990613
```

7. Configure WINE:

```
$ ./configure
```

8. Compile WINE using this command (normally using just make works, but this format is recommended for WINE):

```
$ make depend && make
```

This step can take up to 30 minutes to complete. You should see text occasionally scrolling up your screen during the compilation process. When completed, the executable file wine is ready to use.

9. Install the WINE files to their default locations on your Linux system (you may need to become root to do this step):

```
# make install
```

10. Copy the configuration file supplied with WINE to your home directory as .winerc:

```
$cp /home/nwells/part5/wine-990613/wine.ini /home/nwells/
.winerc
```

This .winerc configuration file may need to be edited to correspond with the location where you have a Windows partition mounted in Linux. (You don't have to have Windows on your system, but that's the easiest way to configure the initial WINE setup to see it working.)

WINE is a large, complex program, and not all Windows programs will start up in WINE, much less run correctly. However, a growing number of applications function passably, and WINE developers continue to work at improving WINE so that it can run additional applications. Despite the complexity of the package, WINE is as easy to compile and run as any other Linux application. Once compiled, running a Windows program in Linux is as easy as using a command like this:

```
$ wine sol.exe
```

To learn more about the WINE project, visit their Web site at http://www.winehq.com.

Run Linux and Windows with VMWare

Beyond tools that attempt to emulate Windows functionality as a Linux process like Wabi and WINE, you can use a virtual machine emulator to actually run native Windows on Linux, including Windows 98 or Windows NT.

The program that provides this functionality is VMWare, a commercial product for Linux. You can download a 30-day trial of VMWare from http://www.vmware.com. This impressive program lets you run multiple operating systems at the same time on a single computer, using native applications from each operating system.

Turn Linux into the Ultimate Gamer

For a long time, games were the missing piece on Linux systems. But with encouragement from Linus Torvalds (creator of Linux) and a host of entertainment-hungry developers, Linux now has hundreds of terrific games available. Many commercial game vendors are porting popular titles to Linux. The games described in this section, however, are all free—and they're all included on the CD.

This part describes games that you can play on any Linux platform. Some of the games are character-based; most are graphical. Some require the KDE or Gnome environment; others can be run in any Linux system. For game enthusiasts who want additional games and information, consult the Web site http://www.linuxgames.com.

The standard game packages for KDE and Gnome, which are mentioned several times in this part, are located on the CD at /Binaries/Games/KDE and /Binaries/Games/Gnome. Other KDE and Gnome-based games are located in specific subdirectories according to the name of each game.

As you work with the files in the /Binaries/Games directories, be aware that some games may require a full install from source in order to have all the necessary graphics and libraries to run the program. In these cases, build your own binary from the package in the corresponding /Source/Games subdirectories.

24 Linux at the Arcade

In general, you can tell how old a person is by which arcade games they know best. Game creators oblige us all by continuing to port all the old games to all the new platforms. Of course, newer games are always coming along as well. Linux has plenty of both.

Lost in Space

Asteroids is the classic space game. KDE includes a great version of Asteroids in the standard KDE games package (see Figure 24.1).

FIGURE 24.1 Asteroids is a classic game that comes with the KDE games package.

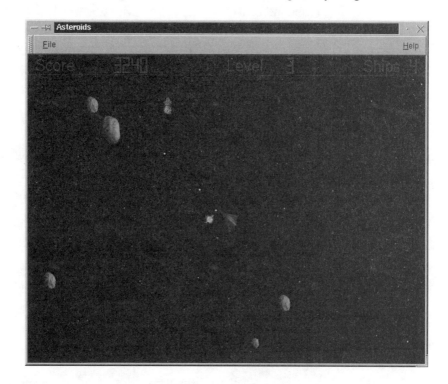

To install and run Asteroids on your Red Hat 6 system, use these commands:

```
# rpm -Uvh --nodeps /mnt/cdrom/Binaries/Games/KDE/
  kdegamesasteroids-1_1_1-1rh5x_i386.rpm
# ln -s /opt/kde/share/apps/kasteroids /usr/share/apps
  kasteroids
# /opt/kde/bin/kasteroids
```

Use the arrow keys to control the movement of your spaceship as follows:

◆ Right and left arrows rotate the ship

◆ The up arrow fires the engine (moving you forward)

◆ The spacebar shoots (only a few at a time!)

As you clear each set of asteroids, you advance to a new level with more and faster asteroids.

The game kspaceduel is similar to asteroids, except that you rotate around a planet and must constantly deal with the gravitational pull of the planet. You also battle another ship rather than just rocks (see Figure 24.2).

FIGURE 24.2 **SpaceDuel for KDE is similar to Asteroids, but gravity is constantly pulling against your ship.**

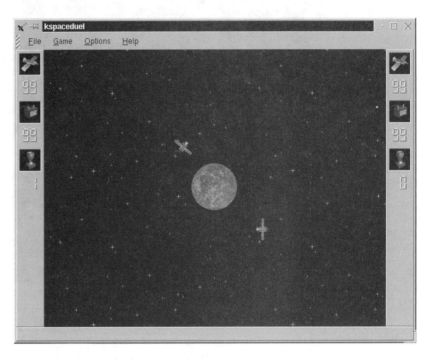

Kspaceduel requires KDE (or the KDE components installed into Gnome in Red Hat 6). The binary is located on the CD at /Source/Games/Arcade. You can build the source code on Red Hat 6 if you have installed the qt-devel rpm. The easier way, however, is to use the prebuilt binary archive in /Binaries/Games/kspaceduel. Use these commands to get it running:

```
$ cp /mnt/cdrom/Binaries/games/kspaceduel/kspaceduel-binary.tgz
  /home/nwells/part6
$ cd /home/nwells/part6
$ tar xvzf kspaceduel-binary.tgz
$ cd kspaceduel-0.3.1
$ make install
```

You may need to be logged in as root to use the make install command. Many screens full of text appear as all the components of the game are installed on your system. This archive is designed for Red Hat 6. If you are using another distribution, you should build the game from the source code package. After the files are installed, start the game:

```
$ kspaceduel
```

Kspaceduel includes a number of configuration options for how fuel is used, the speed of ships, gravitational pull, and so forth (see Figure 24.3).

FIGURE 24.3 **Kspaceduel includes configuration options for speed, gravity, energy, and so forth.**

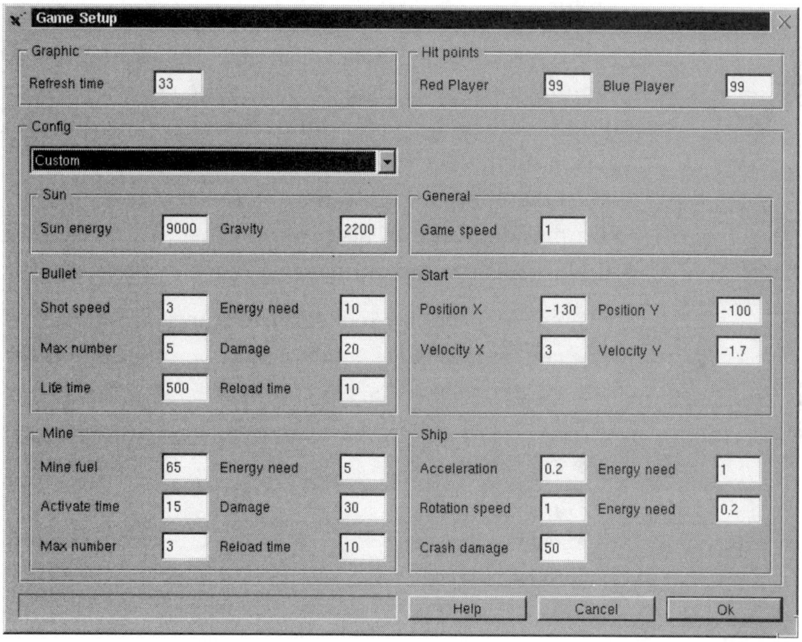

A Linux version of Space Invaders called xinvaders is included in the source directory on the CD at /Source/Games/Arcade. It doesn't require KDE or Gnome, but it may require some programming expertise to make it compile properly. Good luck.

Play Flight Simulator on Linux

The Sabre flight simulator provides a very realistic and impressive flying experience in Linux. You can select from many different scenes and airplanes and even use a demo mode to watch the simulator fly around.

A Web site dedicated to the development of Sabre is located at http://sabre.cobite.com/ and provides a user's guide and updates for the software and game play. The Web site states that at the moment, the Sabre team is working on Korean War–era fighter aircraft, such as the F-86 Sabrejet and the MiG-15. The F-84 ThunderJet and the F-51 Mustang are also available from the Sabre menu. You can even fly with a squadron if you prefer.

Sabre is located at /Source/Games/Arcade on the CD. Sabre is not an X Window program. Instead, it uses the underlying graphical tools (the svga libraries) to create something similar in look and feel to a DOS-based game. You'll need to compile Sabre before using it. The basic commands are shown here, though many screens of text appear after some of these commands. You may also want to review the INSTALL file in the Sabre subdirectory after unpacking the archive.

```
$ cp /mnt/cdrom/Source/Games/Arcade/sabre-0_2_4_tar.gz /home
  nwells/part6
$ cd /home/nwells/part6
$ tar xvzf sabre-0_2_4_tar.gz
$ cd sabre-0.2.4
$ ./configure
$ make
$ make install
$ /usr/local/bin/sabre
```

You may need to be logged in as root to use the make install command. Once you have Sabre compiled and running, the results are impressive (see Figure 24.4).

Another flight simulator worth trying is FlightGear. This project includes a separate package full of scenery and other graphics, plus a documentation package.

FlightGear requires a 3D graphics card. The complete source packages to build it are located on the CD at /Source/Games/FlightGear.

FIGURE 24.4   Sabre provides an impressive flight simulator experience on Linux.

As with Sabre, a Web site create by flight simulator enthusiasts is available at `http://www.flightgear.org/`, complete with documentation, many images, and invitations for other enthusiasts to participate in development.

Runaround Games

Many arcade games use different themes of moving around a playing field and capturing things, eating things, and so forth. One of the best known of these is Pacman. Several versions of Pacman are available for Linux.

The kpacman program (for KDE) is strikingly close to the original arcade game (see Figure 24.5). It includes the set of four ghosts, the fruits, and lots of little yellow dots. I don't know if the patterns followed by the original game are used in kpacman, however.

FIGURE 24.5   Kpacman is a Pacman clone for systems running KDE.

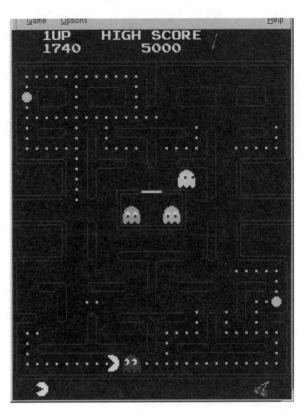

 Kpacman is located at /Binaries/Games/ on the CD. Follow these steps to install it on your Red Hat 6 system:

```
$ cp /mnt/cdrom/Binaries/games/kpacman/kpacman-binary.tgz /home
  nwells/part6
$ cd /home/nwells/part6
$ tar xvzf kpacman-binary.tgz
$ cd kpacman-0.2.4
$ make install
```

You may need to be logged in as root to use the make install command. Many screens full of text appear as all the components of the game are installed on your system. After the files are installed, start the game:

```
$ kpacman
```

Kpacman includes options that let you select a large or small playing field and change the keys you use to move around. You can even try Zacman, which has different little ghosts running around.

Another Pacman-style game for all Linux systems is Hatman. Hatman uses the svga libraries to run without using the X Window System (its appearance is almost like a DOS game). The Hatman Web site is located at `http://croftj.net/~hatsoft/hatman/`.

The Hatman menu includes a level editor and a sprite editor (sprites are the little characters on the screen). Hatman has a very nice interface, but because it runs in console mode rather than X, no screen shots are provided here. (Nor are they available on the Hatman Web site; you'll have to play the game to see it.) Use the source code on the CD at `/Source/Games/Arcade` to create your own binary.

The standard Gnome game package includes several other runaround games. One of the better ones is Gnome-Stones, which you can choose from the standard Games submenu in Gnome (see Figure 24.6).

FIGURE 24.6 In Gnome-Stones, you gather diamonds and try to avoid being crushed by rocks.

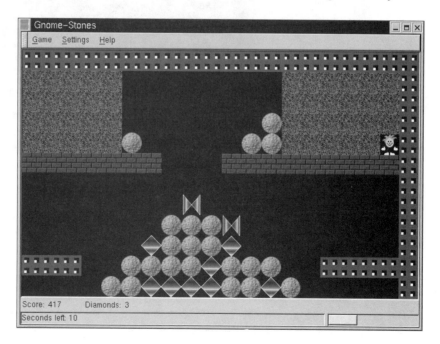

In Gnome-Stones, you explore a mine, gathering diamonds while you try to avoid the falling rocks. Once you collect all the diamonds and find the exit, you move to another, more frenetic level with more falling rocks and other objects to collect.

KDE also has several other runaround games that are not part of the default games package. These include:

◆ Ktron, shown here, in which you move around a board seeking to out-flank your opponent. Ktron is located on the CD at /Binaries/ Games/ktron.

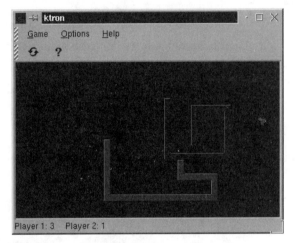

◆ Krepton, shown here, an older-style game in which you collect items while avoiding being crushed or eaten. Krepton is located on the CD at /Binaries/Games/krepton. Use these commands to install and run it (you may need to be logged in as root to use the make install command):

```
$ cp /mnt/cdrom/Binaries/games/krepton/krepton-binary.tgz
  /home/nwells/part6
$ cd /home/nwells/part6
$ tar xvzf krepton-binary.tgz
$ cd krepton-2.0
$ make install
$ krepto
```

◆ Kgoldrunner, shown here, in which you race around collecting gold in a mine while avoiding bad guys. Kgoldrunner is located on the CD at `/Binaries/Games/kgoldrunner`. Use these commands to install and run it (you may need to be logged in as root to use the `make install` command):

```
$ cp
/mnt/cdrom/Binaries/games/kgoldrunner/kgoldrunner-binary.tgz
  /home/nwells/part6
$ cd /home/nwells/part6
$ tar xvzf kgoldrunner-binary.tgz
$ cd kgoldrunner-0.1
$ make install
$ kgoldrunner
```

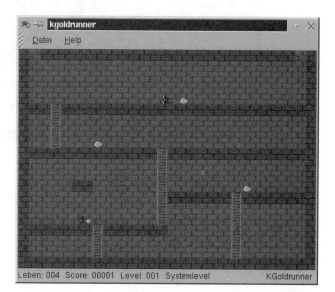

Other Arcade-Style Games

The classic Atari game Missile Command is available on Linux in the form of ICBM3D. This is a three-dimensional version of a Missile Command-style game.

ICBM3D is located at `/Binaries/Games/ICBM3D` on the CD. You can start it from any X Window System with this command (Gnome and KDE are not required):

```
$ icbm3d
```

The interface is similar to an old color-vector-style display (see Figure 24.7). You can set the level at which you want to play (1 through 99). Position where your missiles will be fired using the arrow keys, press the spacebar to fire a missile, and watch the fireworks as incoming missiles arrive and planes fly by.

FIGURE 24.7   **ICBM3D is similar to Missile Command.**

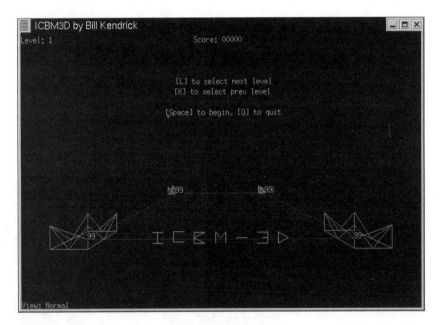

About a hundred versions of Tetris are available on various platforms. One strong version of it is SirTet on the KDE Games menu (part of the standard KDE games package). This package is part of a standard KDE installation, or you can add the KDE Games package to your system from the rpm file in the /Binaries/Games/KDE subdirectory on the CD using these commands.

```
# rpm -Uvh /mnt/cdrom/Binaries/Games/KDE/kdegames-sirtet-1_1_1
  1rh5x_i386.rpm
# /opt/kde/bin/ksirtet
```

A game of SirTet is shown in Figure 24.8.

FIGURE 24.8 SirTet is part of the standard KDE games package.

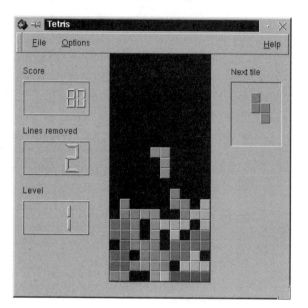

25 The Best Linux Strategy Games

For those who prefer a slower pace than the arcade (something you can do between reading e-mail messages, perhaps), strategy games provide a welcome respite.

This section describes board games, card games, and so forth for Linux. It also includes a few notes on the strategy games that are included with the standard KDE and Gnome games packages.

Play Chess

The ultimate strategy game is chess. Linux has supported the gnuchess basic chess engine from the beginning, but now a graphical interface is available to make that powerful program more interesting on your desktop.

To play a graphical chess game in Linux, you need two packages: gnuchess, which is the engine for the game, and xboard, which provides the interface. These packages are often included in standard Linux distributions. In case you don't have them, both packages are included (in rpm format) in the directory /Binaries/Games/chess on the CD. Use these commands to install them:

```
# rpm -Uvh /mnt/cdrom/Binaries/Games/chess/xboard-4.0.03
  .i386.rpm
# rpm -Uvh /mnt/cdrom/Binaries/Games/chess/gnuchess-4.0.p1793
  .i386.rpm
```

After installing these two packages, start a game of chess with this command:

```
$ xboard
```

The chessboard appears, as shown in Figure 25.1, which depicts a very sorry game of chess.

By default, the computer plays black, so you get the first move. Don't be fooled, however. The computer will win more often than not unless you're a very good player (or you make the computer play dumb).

To make a move, click and drag your mouse on one of the white chess pieces and drop it on a new square. The computer responds immediately for the first couple of moves, then more slowly as the game progresses. A timer above the board counts down for the player whose turn it is. Features include:

◆ Illegal moves are not allowed (see the message box below the timers) unless you choose Options ➢ Test Legality and uncheck this feature.

◆ Standard chess notation is used to show moves in the message window.

FIGURE 25.1 To start a game of chess, use the xboard **command.**

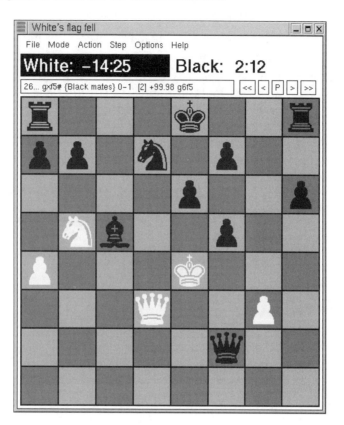

Xboard is simply an interface to gnuchess, but it does include many handy options you can use to improve your chess game. For example:

- ◆ Choose Options ➢ Show Thinking to see the computer ponder various moves (though it's a challenge to interpret the output unless you're already a chess whiz).

- ◆ Choose Step ➢ Backward to reverse the game one move and figure out a better one.

- ◆ Choose Options ➢ Highlight last move to see each move blocked out in yellow so you can more easily follow what is happening during the game.

- ◆ Choose Mode ➢ Two Machines to set up play with another person on a second computer.

◆ Back up or advance to any move of the game with the arrow buttons to the right of the message window (under the timers).

If you need something to exercise your mind when you don't have a graphical desktop, try KnightCap, a character-based chess program that you can play even from a Telnet session. The program is located at `/Binaries/Games/KnightCap` on the CD. The interface to this go-anywhere chess program is shown in Figure 25.2.

FIGURE 25.2 **KnightCap is a character-based chess program that you can play on virtually any Linux system, even without graphics.**

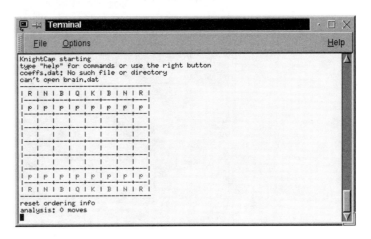

Different from chess, of course, but in the same strategic vein, both Gnome and KDE include attractive (and similar) versions of the classic tile game mah-jongg. If you're already a fan, you might recognize the play in these games as the Taipei variant played with mah-jongg tiles, rather than the traditional mah-jongg game that is similar to bridge. You can start a game in Gnome from the Games submenu. The KDE version is shown in Figure 25.3.

Card Games

Every office worker discovered long ago how addictive a good game of Solitaire or Free Cell can be. Linux has several varieties to choose from.

If you're running Gnome, the AisleRiot program is included as part of the default Gnome Games package that you can access from your Games menu. AisleRiot is a card-playing engine that includes 28 different games—if

FIGURE 25.3 Mah-jongg is included with both Gnome and KDE standard game packages.

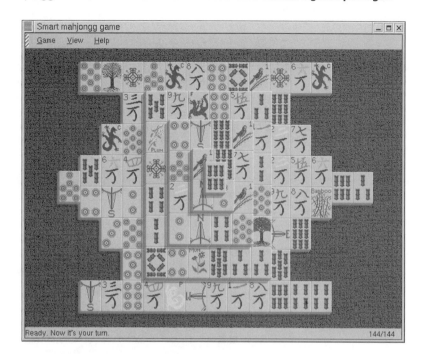

you've heard of them all, you play cards too much. Fortunately, a Hint button on the main toolbar lets you learn about each game as you play.

One of the default menu selections is a game of Klondike, which is shown in Figure 25.4. Another popular game that you can select from the Gnome Games menu is Free Cell.

The Help menu in AisleRiot provides a page describing how each of the many available games is played, including the setup, goal of play, rules, and options.

If you like to customize your display, AisleRiot lets you choose the card back, the Joker icon, and the font used for cards (see Figure 25.5). Choose Preferences from the Settings menu to see this dialog box.

If you're not running Gnome and want a simpler game of solitaire, try Sol, which is a graphical program that doesn't use a special environment like KDE or Gnome. The binary for Sol is located at /Binaries/Games/sol on the CD.

FIGURE 25.4 Klondike is only one of many games that the Gnome AisleRiot card engine can play.

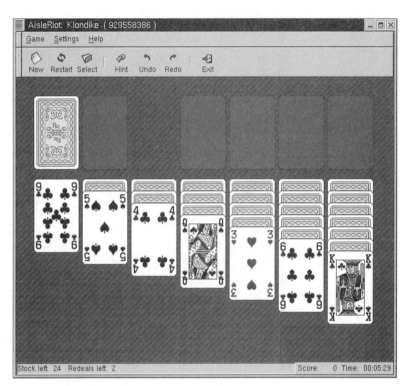

FIGURE 25.5 You can choose graphics and fonts for display of AisleRiot card games.

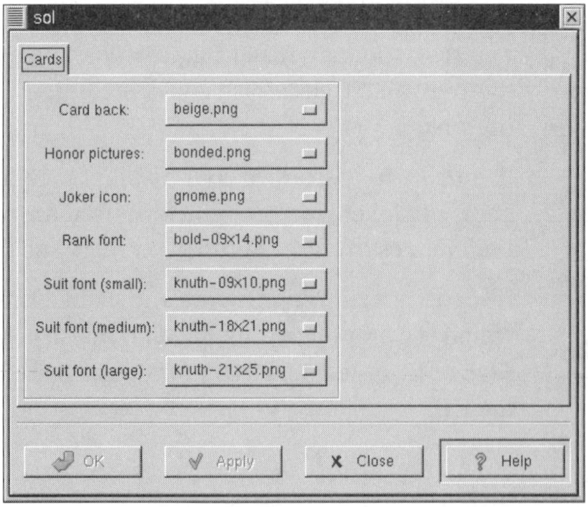

Sol only plays one game: solitaire. It doesn't include many configuration options (though you can select from a few different card backs), nor can it provide hints as you play. Simple help instructions for new players are given via the Help button, however.

The benefit of playing Sol is that you're not likely to have any problems running it because of missing libraries on your Linux system, plus it doesn't take up much space on your system (less than 0.5MB). The main window of Sol is shown in Figure 25.6.

FIGURE 25.6   It's easy to get the solitaire game Sol running on your system.

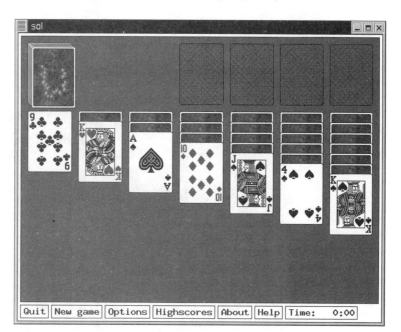

The standard KDE games package also includes two card games, both available under the Games menu. You can install the rpm package for Red Hat 6 and prepare it for use with these commands:

```
# rpm -Uvh /mnt/cdrom/Binaries/Games/KDE/kdegames-cardgames
  1_1_1-1rh5x_i386.rpm
# ln -s /opt/kde/share/apps/kpat /usr/share/apps/kpat
# ln -s /opt/kde/share/apps/kpoker /usr/share/apps/kpoker
```

The Patience game (for Kpatience, after the Xpatience solitaire game) provides nine different games, including Klondike, Ten, Napoleon's Tomb, and Free Cell. To start Kpatience, use this command:

```
# /opt/kde/bin/kpat
```

Different games are available from the Game ➢ Choose New Game submenu.

Four card backsides are available, and easy or hard (strict) rules can be selected for several of the games. Only one game (Grandfather) can provide hints as you play. The interface is shown in Figure 25.7.

FIGURE 25.7 Patience is part of the standard KDE games package. It includes nine different games with selectable difficulty levels.

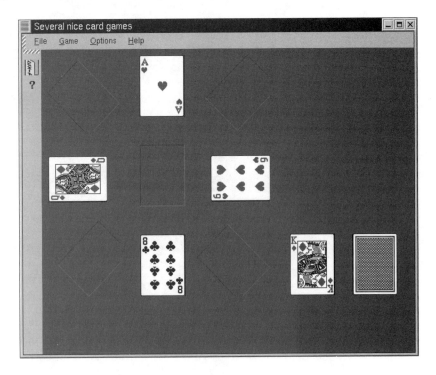

KDE also includes a more unusual card game: video poker. You can start a game with this command:

```
# /opt/kde/bin/kpoker
```

At five dollars per hand, you choose which cards to hold, drawing new cards to replace the others. Online help describes the value of various hands that you might draw. (See Figure 25.8.)

FIGURE 25.8 KDE's video poker is a different type of card game.

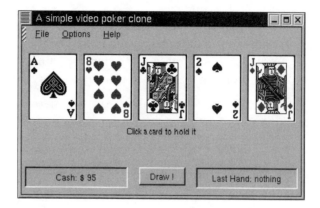

With or without a special desktop (Gnome or KDE), about the best card game engine you'll find is pysol, which provides a complete set of graphical card games in one place. Pysol is written in Python and requires that you have up-to-date versions of tcl/Tk and Python. These packages are included as rpm packages in the directory /Binaries/Extras/ on the CD, so you can install them if needed. (Red Hat 6 includes up-to-date versions in a standard installation.) To run Pysol, use these commands:

```
# cp /mnt/cdrom/Source/Games/Strategy/pysol-2_13_tar.gz
  /home/nwells/part6
# cd /home/nwells/part6
# tar xvzf pysol-2_13_tar.gz
# cd pysol-2.13
# ./pysol.py
```

Pysol comes with 17 standard card games, including:

◆ Eiffel Tower

◆ Forty Thieves

◆ Free Cell

◆ Gypsy

◆ Klondike

◆ Matriarchy

   ◆ Spider

Pysol also supports plug-in modules for additional games. Seven are part of the standard installation, including Canfield, Golf, and Grandfather's Clock.

The pysol package is easy to use because you don't have to compile it. As long as you have the necessary tcl/Tk and Python packages installed, just run the `pysol.py` script to start the game. The pysol package is included in the `/Source/Games/Strategy/` directory on the CD.

The interface to pysol is very attractive and easy to use (see Figure 25.9). A complete set of menus lets you choose many different options for each game.

FIGURE 25.9   **The card game engine pysol provides over 20 different games in an attractive interface with many options.**

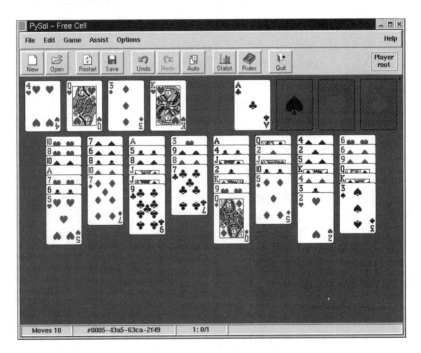

The Game ➢ Status item shows information about the game you're playing, including an ID number that can be used to go back to a game later on (see Figure 25.10).

FIGURE 25.10 The game status is always available in pysol.

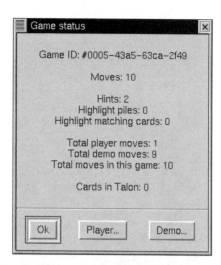

From the Game Status window (or from the toolbar), you can open a statistics window that displays each of the available card games and shows how many have been won or lost for the current user (player). A rulebook is also available from the toolbar.

Pysol includes configuration options for the card background (16 graphics), the table tile and color, how animations are done, the speed at which hints are provided, and many other options (see Figure 25.11).

Play Minesweeper on Linux

Minesweeper has caused almost as much lost productivity for Windows users as Solitaire, and so we faithfully present it here for Linux.

Gnome includes a nice implementation of Minesweeper in the standard Gnome games package. It's available from the Games menu as Gnome Mines.

Gnome Mines will look very familiar to anyone who has played Minesweeper on Windows (see Figure 25.12). To play, click on squares, trying to clear the board without landing on a land mine. Squares with numbers indicate that many mines are located somewhere in the immediately adjacent squares. You can select the size of the playing board by choosing Settings ➢ Preferences. (For real entertainment, watch the smiley face as you play.)

FIGURE 25.11 Pysol includes many configuration options for both appearance and play.

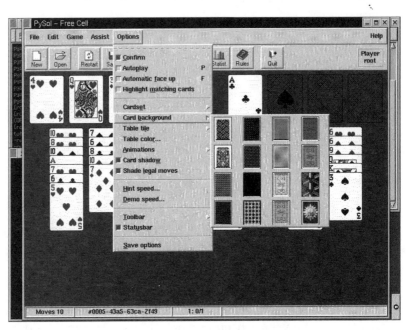

FIGURE 25.12 The Gnome Mines game is a clone of Windows' Minesweeper.

KDE's implementation of Minesweeper is even closer in appearance to the Windows version (see Figure 25.13) and includes easy to expert levels.

When you think you've found a mine, right-click on it to mark the spot. Choose Level ➢ Custom to set up the minefield as a certain size.

FIGURE 25.13 The KDE version of Minesweeper includes easy to expert levels.

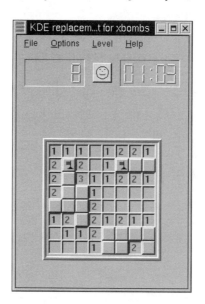

Classic Adventure

NetHack is a supercharged version of a strategy/adventure game like the old Zork or Scott Adams adventures; it's sort of like Dungeons and Dragons on screen.

NetHack is similar to gnuchess in that a game engine is used on a myriad of different systems. Linux users also have several graphical interfaces available, which makes the game much more interesting.

Several source code packages are included in the /Source/Games/NetHack directory on the CD. These include:

- ◆ The basic NetHack package

- ◆ A Gnome version of NetHack

- ◆ A KDE version of NetHack

- ◆ A Qt version of NetHack, which, though related to the KDE version by a common library, is intended for other (non-KDE) users of the Qt graphical libraries.

The short path through all of this to a game of NetHack is to go to /Binaries/Games/nethack on the CD and unpack the Qt binary package that you find in this directory. Use these commands; note that the archive is unpacked from the root directory, so you'll need to be logged in as root:

```
# cp /mnt/cdrom/Binaries/Games/nethack/qnethack-3_2_2_1_0_1_
  bin_Linux_static_tar.gz /
# cd /
# tar xvzf qnethack-3_2_2_1_0_1_bin_Linux_static_tar.gz
# /usr/games/nethack
```

Despite the attractive interface (see Figure 25.14), think of NetHack as a text-based adventure game. You choose actions such as picking things up, moving around, casting spells, and so forth.

FIGURE 25.14 **NetHack on Linux can be played via a graphical interface such as this Qt version.**

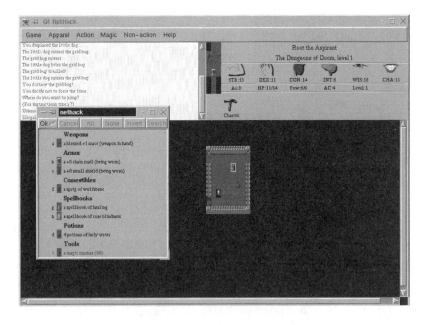

The upper-left corner of the NetHack window shows responses as you make moves. Additional dialog boxes can be opened to show more information about your situation, for example, what you're carrying (and thus can use when need arises).

For more documentation on how to play NetHack, refer to the included documentation or visit a NetHack Web site such as `http://trolls.troll .no/warwick/nethack/` or `http://kitsumi.nethack.net/software/`.

A similar game to NetHack, but played in space, is Konquest, part of the standard KDE games collection. In Konquest, you work to conquer the galaxy. You can install Konquest using the binary package on the CD with these commands:

```
# rpm -Uvh /mnt/cdrom/Binaries/Games/KDE/kdegames-konquest
   1_1_1-1rh5x_i386.rpm
# ln -s /opt/kde/share/apps/konquest
   /usr/share/apps/konquest
# /opt/kde/bin/konquest
```

Figure 25.15 shows the interface during a game of Konquest.

FIGURE 25.15 Konquest is a multiplayer space strategy game.

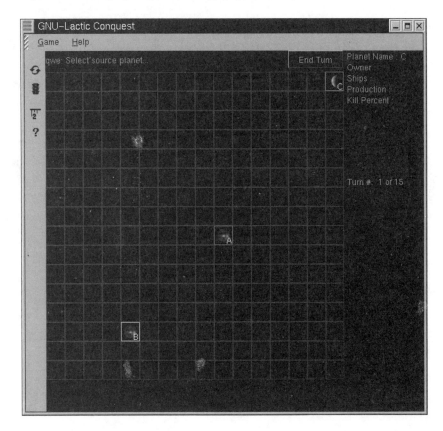

Solve Rubik's Cube on Linux

A fascinating game available for KDE is krubik. With krubik, you solve randomized Rubik's cube puzzles by rotating the cube to all sides to see the colors and dragging to rotate parts of the cube. The graphics and animation are great, even if you never want to spend the time needed to solve the puzzle.

Krubik is located on the CD at /Binaries/Games/krubik. The interface is shown in Figure 25.16, though the animation as you drag the cube around is the really interesting part to see.

FIGURE 25.16 Krubik lets you solve Rubik's cube in a KDE window. Click and drag to rotate the entire cube or one face as you solve the puzzle.

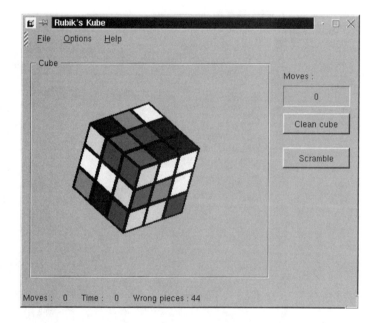

Make Your System Entertaining

Those who strive to use Linux as their desktop system for all their work may think that giving up Windows means giving up all multimedia capabilities with it. Admittedly, Linux isn't as tightly integrated with a set of auto-launching accessories for every new sound format that appears.

However, a surprising number of Linux developers are heavily into music and video. The result is a full set of audio and video programs that run on Linux. This part describes some of the best ones available. A few are standard fare on Linux systems; others are new or unexpected. Programs that require KDE, Gnome, or their libraries (Qt or GTK+) are noted in each section.

26 Make Sound Work in Linux

Running video clips in Linux (described in the next section) relies on the X Window System. Most users have X already installed and configured, so this isn't a problem.

Playing any type of sound file, however, involves a connection to special sound hardware. This isn't very difficult, but it isn't often done automatically when you install Linux.

Set Up Your Sound Card in Linux

To make a sound card function in Linux, the correct kernel modules must be added to your system. At least one of these modules must indicate how to access your sound card. Although many sound cards are supported on Linux, the SoundBlaster card is the most popular sound card in PCs, so I'll describe how to make it function in Linux. Other sound cards will probably use a procedure very similar to this one:

1. Log in as root.

2. Enter this command to load basic sound support:

   ```
   # modprobe sb io=0x220 dma=1 mpu_io=0x330 irq=5
   ```

This loads the SoundBlaster module and all the modules that go with it. If you see a warning about the sound module already being loaded, you can safely ignore it. If, however, you see an error message about the interrupt number, use the command `cat/proc/interrupts` to examine the interrupts being using on your Linux system and check the documentation for your sound card. Then try the above command again with appropriate parameters.

3. Red Hat 6 users can also try running the `sndconfig` utility that comes with Red Hat systems. This program is text-based but includes an easy-to-use interface. You can start it from any command line:

```
$ sndconfig
```

For additional information about configuring sound cards, consult the Sound-HOWTO document by pointing your browser to /Doc/Sound-HOWTO.html on the CD.

The easiest way to test that your sound works is to play a music CD. Both KDE and Gnome (and many other Linux window managers) include at least a basic CD-playing application.

In both KDE and Gnome, you can choose CD Player from the Multimedia menu. The KDE version is shown here.

Of course, if you don't hear any sound, several other things could be wrong. If you use a dual boot system and sound works fine in Windows, try using a different kernel module or parameters and read the Sound-HOWTO document. If sound doesn't work in Windows either, check the following before fiddling with Linux commands:

◆ Is the sound card installed tightly into the slot on your system board?

◆ Are the speakers plugged into the correct jack (not the microphone jack) on the sound card?

◆ Is the power connected to the speakers (many require an AC adapter or batteries)?

◆ Are the speakers turned on?

◆ Do you have several devices on your system (scanner, sound mixer, sound card, etc.) that might be using conflicting IRQ-interrupt numbers?

Try the OpenSoundSystem

If you're really interested in using sound features on Linux, consider trying the OpenSoundSystem. This is a commercial sound-driver package for Linux that includes an easy-to-use menu-based configuration utility and support for many different sound devices.

You can download an evaluation copy of this product from the 4Front Technologies Web site at `http://www.opensound.com`. The download is free after you enter some personal information. This project and company are very supportive of Linux—new drivers are released regularly for Linux. The company also sponsors the `xmms` project, which is described in Number 29, "Create a Linux-Based Music Studio."

27 Make Linux Your Personal Video Player

Thousands of video clips are available on the Web, from movie previews and promotional pieces to videos created by individuals. Linux has several utilities to let you view these video clips on-screen.

The core of playing videos on Linux is the XAnim program. This program runs on any version of Linux that uses the X Window System. It supports the following video formats, with MPEG being the most popular at the moment for Web-based video clips.

◆ MPEG video

◆ Quicktime animations (MOV files)

◆ AVI animations

◆ FLI and FLC animations

◆ IFF animations

◆ GIF89a animations

◆ DL animations (formats 1, 2, and most of 3)

◆ Amiga MovieSetter animations

◆ Utah Raster Toolkit RLE images and animations

◆ SGI Movie format files

Note that XAnim doesn't support the RealAudio and RealVideo formats. These streaming formats are proprietary. See `http://www.real.com` for details on these players and to download a free Linux version.

XAnim is included with most recent Linux distributions, such as Red Hat 6, Suse 6.1, and Caldera OpenLinux 2.2. If you're running one of these later distributions, try running `xanim` from any command line within your graphical desktop:

```
$ xanim hurricane.mpg
```

The `hurricane.mpg` movie is included in the `/Source/Video` directory of the CD. It's taken from the NASA Web site; you can see their entire gallery of multimedia at `http://www.nasa.gov/gallery/index.html`. Figure 27.1 shows XAnim playing an MPEG file. XAnim includes separate windows for controls and picture.

FIGURE 27.1 XAnim includes separate windows for controls and video playback.

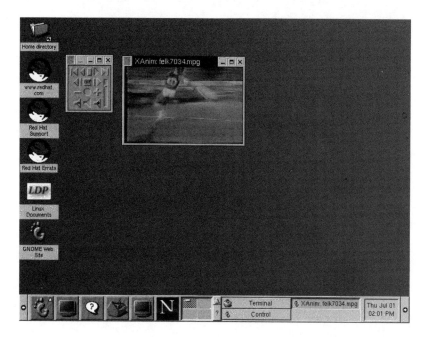

Controls for XAnim include play, pause, fast forward, reverse, and volume controls (many MPEG files don't include sound, however).

If XAnim is not installed as part of your Linux distribution, you may be able to install it from your Linux CD. XAnim is also included on the CD for this book at /Source/Video.

Because XAnim supports so many video file formats and is freely available on Linux, it has been used as the basis for other video players for the popular Linux desktops.

The GXanim program is built around the Gnome desktop and the GTK+ library. It relies on xanim as the engine to display video files.

GXanim is similar to XAnim but has a more attractive interface designed to blend with your Gnome desktop. It includes a control panel and a separate window where the video is displayed, as shown here.

A preferences dialog box lets you set options for GXanim, as shown here.

An rpm archive for the GXanim program is located at /Binaries/Video on the CD. You can use this command to install GXanim:

```
# rpm -Uvh /mnt/cdrom/Binaries/Video/gxanim-0_35-1_i386.rpm
```

A similar package for KDE is aKtion. Like GXanim, aKtion requires the XAnim package as a video engine. AKtion has a single window with both controls and video playback (though a full-screen mode is available as well), as shown here.

The source package for aKtion is located on the CD at /Source/Video; a precompiled binary for Red Hat (in rpm format) is located at /Binaries/ Video. If you use the rpm file on Red Hat 6, the program is installed in the /opt/kde/bin directory on your system, which is not where Red Hat 6 stores any other KDE files, but you can still change to that directory to use the aKtion program. AKtion includes:

◆ Full-screen playback mode

◆ A video "widget" (KXanim) that can be used to add video to other KDE programs

◆ A frame capture (press C during video playback to save the current frame to a file)

◆ Documentation in many languages (including Estonian if you need it)

If you don't have KDE or Gnome on your system, try MpegTV, located on the CD at /Source/Video or /Binaries/Video (in an rpm-format package). To install the MpegTV package, you first need to install the Xforms package. Use these commands to get started (note the --nodeps option used in the second command):

```
# rpm -Uvh /mnt/cdrom/Binaries/Extras/xforms-0_88_1-1_i386.rpm
# rpm -Uvh --nodeps /mnt/cdrom/Binaries/Video/mtv-1_0_9_10-
1_i386.rpm
```

This program plays MPEG video clips on any graphical Linux system; the controls for MpegTV are shown here.

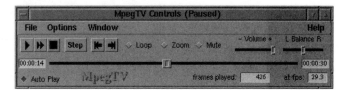

28 Tune In to Radio or TV with Linux

Several types of expansion cards exist for PCs that provide a radio or television tuner and output the signal to the PC. Several programs are available to take advantage of these cards within Linux.

These programs all rely on a feature of recent Linux kernels called Video4-Linux. This feature allows Linux to capture incoming data from a video device such as a television tuner card. The home page of the Video4Linux project is http://roadrunner.swansea.uk.linux.org/v4l.shtml.

A KDE application that lets you watch television while you're "working" is KwinTV. This program includes a separate viewing window with dialog boxes to control various items (see Figures 28.1 and 28.2), including the following:

- ◆ Scanning the TV tuner for available stations and programming
- ◆ Selecting a station from a separate dialog box list
- ◆ Using a mixer window to adjust audio quality
- ◆ Setting the video image size and input source
- ◆ Controlling the selected channel using a programmable infrared remote control that interacts with your Linux PC

FIGURE 28.1 KwinTV can scan the tuner input for available stations and programming.

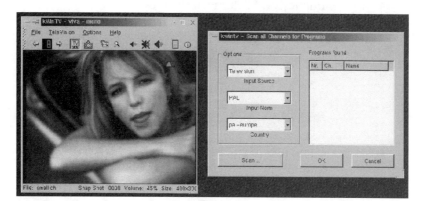

FIGURE 28.2 KwinTV maintains a channel list and includes a mixer and video streamer options dialog boxes.

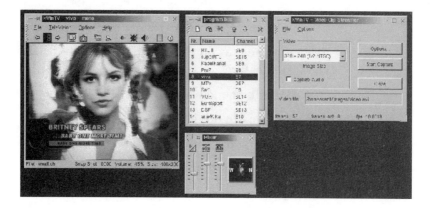

KwinTV is provided as a source code package at /Source/Video and as a binary at /Binaries/Video on the CD.

In addition to television tuner cards, cards that provide a radio signal (such as the FM band) are available. The gtuner program lets you listen to the radio as you work via an interface similar to the CD players described previously in this part.

The source package for gtuner is located at /Source/Audio on the CD. A binary file (not a complete rpm, just the executable file) is included at /Binaries/Audio. Gtuner is used with the Gnome desktop. The interface of gtuner is like a car stereo, as shown below. You can select the band, frequency, and volume of the radio.

If you prefer, you can use the slider to select a station and watch the music graphically as you listen, as shown here.

Gtuner includes a complete set of configuration dialog boxes where you can set up features such as:

◆ Sleep timer and wake up alarm

◆ Mute on exit options

◆ List of stations (memory)

◆ Support for multiple radio tuner cards

◆ A plug-in interface for expandability

A final broadcast-related program for Linux is icecast. Icecast is a streaming server for MPEG3 audio (mp3 files). Using icecast, you can broadcast an audio file from your computer (acting as a server) to any other system on your network (or the Internet, if you have sufficient bandwidth) for others to listen to. In effect, you can become a digital DJ by providing a streaming audio signal using the icecast server.

The icecast project is OpenSource software, with a home page at http://icecast.linuxpower.org/. This page includes lists of "netcast" audio. You can visit one of the pages listed and listen to music provided by an icecast server on the Internet (see Figure 28.3).

FIGURE 28.3 Many audio servers on the Internet provide music using the icecast streaming server.

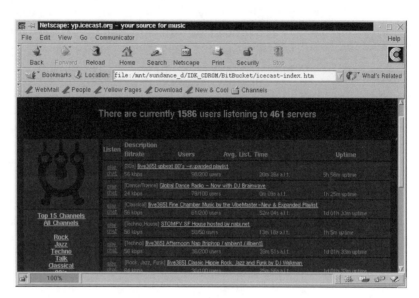

 The source code for the `icecast` server is located at `/Source/Audio` on the CD.

29 Create a Linux-Based Music Studio

Linux has dozens of great audio tools. These tools begin with a number of CD players, some of which run under any graphical Linux environment. Other programs play audio files that you download from the Internet in popular formats. Synthesizers, sound editors, and mixers are also available. Other tools convert formats or help you create music.

Play Audio Files on Linux

Audio CD players have been around on Linux for years, and they seem to be getting better all the time. In addition to the default players included with KDE and Gnome, other CD players let you enjoy your audio CDs while working within any Linux graphical environment.

Two CD players for Linux are xmcd and xfreecd, both located on the CD in /Source/Audio. An rpm binary package for xfreecd is also included at /Binaries/Audio. (The xfreecd binary is installed in /usr/local/bin by default.)

But CDs aren't the only way to collect digital music. Web sites like www.mp3.com and many others provide sample tracks or let you create and download personalized music collections. Most of these are likely to be in MPEG3 audio (.mp3 files). Linux supports these and many other audio formats including:

◆ MPEG3 (.mp3 files)

◆ WAV

◆ .au files

◆ MIDI (.mid files)

One important distinction to know in digital music is that MIDI format is a description of musical properties, while WAV and MPEG formats are digital recordings (compressed, of course). Another way to explain the difference between these formats is that MIDI is like Postscript, while WAV and MPEG are like PCX bitmapped images.

It's important to know the difference between these formats because a MIDI player (such as the one included with KDE) must be able to interpret the "instruments" described in the MIDI file to create sound waves, while playing other formats requires (in the broadest sense) dumping the audio data to the soundcard. Thus, different utilities may have very different capabilities with various audio formats.

If you want to play one of your MPEG3 audio files without even being in X, you can use the mpg123 command line program to start a file playing in the background as you work:

```
$ mpg123 chopin5.mp3
```

This program is located on the CD at /Source/Audio and /Binaries/ Audio (in rpm format).

For those with the Gnome desktop, GQMpeg provides an attractive interface similar to a CD player for your MPEG3 files, as shown here.

GQMpeg is included in /Source/Audio on the CD. A binary package in rpm format is included in /Binaries/Audio. (The binary file is installed into the /usr/local/bin directory.)

In addition to being able to play files in several popular audio formats (including MPEG3 and WAV), Xwave is an audio editor. Figure 29.1 shows Xwave with a linear tracking of a digital audio file as it is being played. With Xwave, you can cut and paste to edit an audio file.

FIGURE 29.1 Xwave allows you to graphically edit digital audio files.

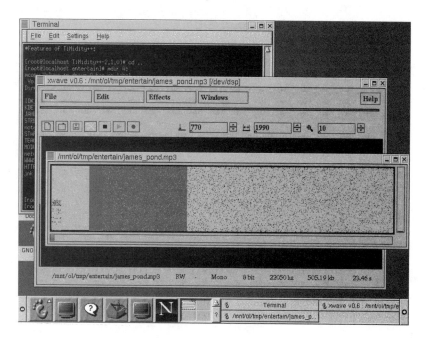

Xwave is located at /Source/Audio on the CD. A binary file is included in /Binaries/Audio, but you must copy the configuration to your system. Use this command on Red Hat 6 before running the Xwave binary:

```
# cp /mnt/cdrom/Binaries/Audio/xwave-def /usr/lib/X11/app-
defaults.
```

An ambitious project for playing audio files is the xmms project, formerly the x11amp project. Xmms, shown here, is a powerful multimedia player with a large development team.

Core features of xmms include:

◆ Seeking into audio files

◆ Separate volume and balance controls

◆ Shuffle and repeat play

◆ A spectrum analyzer and oscilloscope

◆ Graphic equalizer

◆ Support for streaming audio servers, including icecast

◆ Mouse scroll wheel support

The home page for this project is at http://www.xmms.org. The source code package is on the CD at /Source/Audio; an rpm-format binary is located at /Binaries/Audio. In order to install the xmms package, you must first install two other packages from the /Binaries/Extras directory to update those that came with your system (even a new system like Red Hat 6 needs these updates). Use these commands to prepare for and install xmms:

```
# rpm -Uvh /mnt/cdrom/Binaries/Extras/glib-1_2_3-2mdk_i586.rpm
# rpm -Uvh --nodeps /mnt/cdrom/Binaries/Extras/gtk+-1_2_3-
5_i386.rpm
# rpm -Uvh /mnt/cdrom/Binaries/Audio/xmms-0_9_1-1_i386.rpm
```

Note that if you install these upgraded glib and gtk packages, you may have trouble compiling programs that are based on the older versions. In that case, you'll want to revert to the older versions included with your original Linux distribution (check, for example, your Red Hat 6 CD).

The graphic equalizer screen of xmms is shown here.

Manage Your Sounds

Several synthesizers are available that enable you to create your own music in Linux.

Synaesthesia is a basic music synthesizer package. It's located on the CD at /Source/Audio. A binary file named xsynaesthesia is included at /Binaries/Audio.

A much more advanced project is the Analog RealTime Synthesizer (ARTS). ARTS is intended to simulate a modular analog synthesizer, creating sounds using various modules to create waveforms that can be graphically combined. Many different filters or modules are included to create different sounds. After you use the graphical interface to create a piece of music, the synthesizer "executes" the modules that you have created, sending the waveforms to the sound card.

A complete home page for the ARTS project is at http://arts.linuxbox .com/. Figure 29.2 shows how modules can be seen in the graphical display of the ARTS synthesizer.

FIGURE 29.2 The ARTS synthesizer allows on-screen manipulation of different filters, waveforms, and so forth to create music.

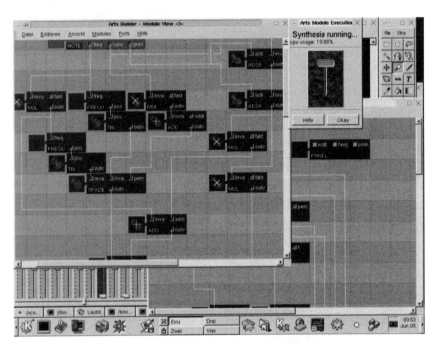

If you have many files that are in MIDI format and need to play them or convert them to WAV format, you can use the TiMidity rpm package, located at /Binaries /Audio on the CD. The program name after you install the rpm is timidity, all in lowercase.

Turn Linux into a Web Server

One of the most popular uses of Linux is as a Web server. In fact, almost any Linux product you buy will install and run a copy of Apache automatically. And Apache is the most popular Web server in the world, with nearly 50 percent of the market (if we can call it a market, when Apache is free). For details on the strength of Apache and survey statistics, visit NetCraft at `http://www.netcraft.com`.

Having a Web server installed and running, however, isn't the same as having all the power of the Web at your fingertips. Apache can do many things that are not part of a default configuration. This part describes some of the software you can add to Apache itself or use on your Web server to enhance Apache's functionality, gather additional statistical information, or prepare Apache to be used for high-traffic and high-security Web sites.

In case you don't have the latest version of Apache on your system, the source code for version 1.3.6 is included on the CD at `/Source/Apache/server`.

To learn more about Apache, visit the Web site of the Apache Project at `http://www.apache.org`, or take a look at the magazine *Apache Week*, which includes many useful articles and a searchable database of back issues, at `http://www.apacheweek.com`.

30 Extend Apache with Modules

One of the most important developments in Web server software was creating the ability to use modules in Apache. When a Web page runs a CGI script to process a form or prepare a custom HTML page, the Linux system requires some overhead (CPU time and memory) to start and manage that script as a separate program. In addition, a script can only reply to a regular browser request; it can't affect how Apache does things.

Modules extend Apache by adding functionality to the Web server itself. A module is a piece of code (written in C, C++, or Perl) that becomes part of the Web server, allowing you to customize Apache features. Of course, not everyone is up to writing a new Apache module, so this section describes some of the dozens of modules that are available for downloading to use with Apache. Many of these are included on the CD. You can use any of these modules to add features to your Web server.

Add Modules to Your Apache Web Server

Because Apache is freely distributed as source code, most serious Web-masters will download Apache and compile their own copy. This allows the Webmaster to control the exact features that are included in Apache and to use the very latest version (and so have available all possible security fixes and program enhancements).

By default, Apache doesn't include all the possible modules that are included with the source code. For example, if you want to learn about writing your own module, you should add a module called mod_example. You can add a module to Apache as you compile the source code by adding a configuration option when you make the binary program.

Modules can be added directly to the source code, or they can be added to Apache on-the-fly as a Dynamic Shared Object (DSO), which is sort of like a Windows DLL or a UNIX shared library. This means that new program functionality can be added to Apache without touching the source code or doing any programming. Just follow the steps below to insert new functionality into your Web server.

Either method (using source code or dynamic loading of a prebuilt module) makes the module available to all of the browser requests that Apache processes. Using a DSO is often easier than working with source code. By using a DSO, you can experiment with a new module, loading and unloading to see how it affects your Web server, without the need to recompile the server to try new things.

To make a DSO module part of Apache, just include this line in the configuration file httpd.conf (located in the /etc/httpd/conf directory on Red Hat 6):

```
LoadModule module_name module_filename
```

Many modules will already be precompiled on your Linux system, so you can use the LoadModule directive without recompiling Apache. For others, you'll need to create the DSO file.

When you have selected a module filename on the CD (as described later in this section) that you want to add to Apache as a shared object, use the following commands to build an Apache executable after installing the Apache source code. In each of the sets of commands that follow, replace /path/to/apache with the directory path where you want to install the Apache server software.

```
$ ./configure --prefix=/path/to/apache \
               --enable-module=example \
               --enable-shared=example
$ make
$ make install
```

These commands compile Apache with mod_example as a dynamic shared object. Mod_example should only be used to learn about Apache; it should never be used on a production Web server because it might provide information about your system to an intruder. These commands also automatically add the LoadModule line to your httpd.conf configuration file so that the shared object file is loaded each time Apache starts.

The module mod_example is part of the Apache source code, along with many standard modules and a few that aren't included by default. If you want to use all the available modules that are included with Apache, use these commands, which use all of the modules that Apache can find in the source code directory:

```
$ ./configure --prefix=/path/to/apache \
               --enable-module=most \
               --enable-shared=max
$ make
$ make install
```

Sometimes you need to add a module that didn't come with Apache. The next sections cover many useful Apache modules that you can use with the instructions that follow. These modules usually come in a source code file named mod_*modulename*.c. You can include these nonstandard modules as you build Apache by using commands like these:

```
$ ./configure --prefix=/path/to/apache \
               --add-module=/path/to/mod_modulename.c \
               --enable-shared= mod_modulename.c
$ make
$ make install
```

These commands copy the module source code to the directory `src/modules/extra/` in the Apache source code tree and activate the new module as Apache is compiled. The last option, `enable-shared`, makes the new module available as a DSO that can be loaded from the Apache configuration file.

Add Commercial Modules to Apache

Although HTTP and HTML are simply open protocols that have made the Web possible, all sorts of proprietary tools are available to make the most of what the Web can do. Many of these tools rely on Web server features that aren't part of a standard Apache server because they are built by commercial companies (whereas Apache is not commercial).

The best place to start looking for useful modules is the Apache Module Registry, operated by Covalent Technologies, Inc. on the Web at `http://modules.apache.org`. If you go to the Search page and click Search without any parameters in the search field, you'll see a list of all the modules available for Apache (see Figure 30.1).

Some of the modules are commercial products and therefore aren't included on the CD in this book. However, just knowing about them can help you get the most out of your Apache server when you need the special features that these commercial products offer.

The ColdFusion product from Allaire Corp. provides Web-based applications on a number of platforms, including HP-UX, Solaris, and Windows NT. Allaire has announced support for Linux, beginning with a stub that allows Linux-based Web servers to serve ColdFusion applications that are hosted on other servers (such as HP-UX).

You can learn more about the ColdFusion Apache module and the Linux stub by linking from the Apache Modules Registry or visiting `http://www.allaire.com/`.

Another tool for Web application development that already runs on a Linux Apache Web server is TalentSoft's Web+ product. You can learn more about it by visiting `http://www.talentsoft.com` and downloading a limited version to try out.

If you work with Microsoft's Frontpage product and have the Microsoft Frontpage Extensions, you should check out the module that enables the

FIGURE 30.1 The Apache Modules Registry includes links to dozens of useful additions for your Web server.

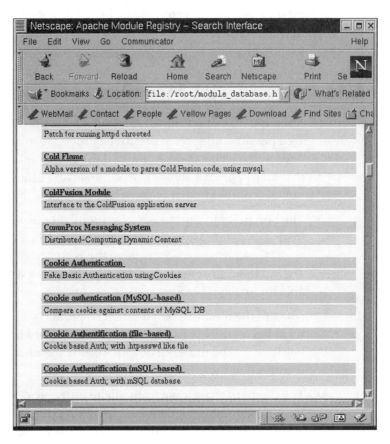

Frontpage extensions in Apache. See the link in the Apache Module Registry for information.

Another Microsoft project, Active Server Pages, is being supported by an OpenSource development project to allow use of the many Active Server Page–related tools and code on Linux. The code for Linux is still under development. You can check its status and download the latest version of the Linux-Apache ASP module from `http://www.activescripting.org/`.

For those needing security enhancements to Apache, the Raven SSL module (also from Covalent Technologies, Inc.) provides 128-bit strong cryptography for Apache. This is a commercial product, but you can download a 30-day trial for evaluation by visiting `http://www.covalent.net/raven/ssl/`.

Another authentication enhancement is the RADIUS authentication module, which is included as source code on the CD at `/Source/Apache/modules`.

Many Apache sites include scripts that process forms or create customized HTML pages as browsers request data. These scripts can bog down a Web server, making response times unacceptable. The VelociGen module from Binary Evolution, Inc. uses capabilities similar to the standard `mod_perl` module to allow you to embed Perl scripting language commands right in your HTML pages. These and other scripts on your system can then be served back to browsers nearly as fast as static HTML pages. To learn more about this commercial product, visit `http://www.BinaryEvolution.com/`.

Add New Authentication Options to Apache

Apache includes several authentication systems for verifying the identity of a user who wants to download a file from your Web server. These include the standard method of using a special file of usernames and passwords that have been especially created for use with Apache and your Web pages.

Many times, however, you have other authentication systems that you want to merge with your Web server, making access to Web pages contingent upon a user's other accounts or access on your network.

Apache modules are available to authenticate users connecting to your Web server via several mechanisms, such as NDS and Samba. This section describes some of these modules, most of which are included on the CD.

When using authentication systems, it's very important to remember that a standard connection between a Web server and a browser is not encrypted. If you use the authentication modules listed here to exchange authentication information, you should probably use a secure Web server so that all exchanges (such as username and password information) are encrypted. The Stronghold version of Apache is a commercial product with encryption. You can also use a free version of Apache that includes Secure Sockets Layer (SSL) support. Visit `http://www.apache-ssl.org` to download the server. Because of United States export restrictions, all downloads and mirrors for this program are located outside the U.S.; it also cannot be included on the CD for this book.

Authentication via the NIS system is available in an Apache module, though the code is still experimental. You can experiment with it yourself (it's on the CD at `/Source/Apache/modules`), but don't use it on a production Web server yet. Check on the Apache Module Registry for more stable versions first.

TO AUTHENTICATE USING...	TRY THIS MODULE
An m-sql database of users	mod_auth_cookie_msql
A MySQL database of users	mod_auth_cookie_mysql
A PostgreSQL database of users	mod_auth_pgsql
An LDAP server	auth_ldap
DCE	mod_auth_dce
A Kerberos server	mod_auth_kerb
A Windows NT PDC or other Samba server	mod_auth_smb
A NetWare bindery (or emulated) server	mod_auth_nds
A Lotus Notes server	mod_auth_notes (not on the CD)
An external script that examines browser information	mod_auth_external
Other, more specialized protocols	Visit the Apache Module Registry at `http://modules.apache.org`

Other authentication systems use cookies (which Apache manages via the `mod_usertrack` module). By using the additional modules `mod_auth_cookie_msql` or `mod_auth_cookie_mysql`, you can integrate the cookie-checking authentication with records stored in an SQL database (mSQL or MySQL). A valid user must then be stored in the database, according to specifications that you establish. These two modules, along with a README file, are located on the CD at `/Source/Apache/modules`.

A similar package lets you authenticate to user information stored in a Postgres database. This module, `mod_auth_pgsql`, is also located at `/Source/Apache/modules`.

An LDAP server can be used to authenticate users visiting your Web site via the `auth_ldap` module. A source code package for this module is included on the CD in the directory `/Source/Apache/modules`.

If you have DCE on your system, you can use this method to authenticate users via `mod_auth_dce`. The source code package is located on the CD at `/Source/Apache/modules`.

Kerberos is a popular and powerful security mechanism that you can also use for Apache authentication if you have a Kerberos server set up on your local network. The module `mod_auth_kerb` is also located at `/Source/Apache/modules`.

For those with existing network infrastructure, the goal of Web-based authentication is often to map incoming user requests to existing user accounts on the local network. This is particularly useful for employees that use the Web to access company or personal data while travelling. Several authentication modules allow Apache to test incoming requests against local network resources.

If you're using a Windows NT or other SMB-based network, including a Samba-based infrastructure on Linux, you can use `mod_auth_smb` to authenticate incoming Web requests against the users allowed by your Primary Domain Controller (PDC). A README file and source code for this module are both located on the CD at `/Source/Apache/modules`. This module is marked as alpha-quality code, though it has been tested extensively by the module developer.

NetWare servers are growing in popularity again. Using `mod_auth_nds` you can authenticate Web requests against the user database on a NetWare server. This module is located on the CD at `/Source/Apache/modules`.

Note that `mod_auth_nds` uses the ncpfs version of the NetWare protocol tools to access a NetWare server. (This package is included on the CD in `/Source/Extras`.) Unfortunately, this doesn't provide NDS access—only NetWare 3.*x* bindery access is supported. Extensive work by both Novell and Caldera Systems (under license from Novell) has not made available a NetWare API for Linux. The result is that, while authentication to an NDS server would be a relatively small project, it is not yet available.

If you use Lotus Notes, a preliminary module is available to support authenticating Web requests to your Notes user database. This module can be downloaded and used free of charge, but it cannot be redistributed so it is not included on the CD. For information, visit `http://www.oceangroup.com/download.html`.

On the Apache Module Registry site, you can find additional authentication modules for less common systems.

For those with authentication needs that aren't addressed by all of these options, `mod_auth_external` allows you to define a script (external to Apache) that defines whether a user is authenticated or not, based on the information returned by the client. The source code and a README file for this module are located on the CD at `/Source/Apache/modules`.

The trade-off for the flexibility of using `mod_auth_external` (beyond the need to write your own authentication script) is that Apache must start the script as an external program to handle any request that needs authentication services. For situations like this, consider using the `mod_fastcgi` module (also included on the CD at `/Source/Apache/modules`), which attempts to keep scripts "alive" in memory to reduce the performance hit of running CGI scripts. You can learn more about the FastCGI project by visiting `http://fastcgi.idle.com/`.

Explore Other Useful Modules

Many other useful modules are available for Apache. One of the latest trends in making Apache more configurable without sacrificing performance is embedding programming languages either into Apache itself or into HTML pages. These and a few other interesting modules are described in this section.

VelociGen is a commercial product that embeds Perl or tcl scripts into an HTML Web page. Similar OpenSource modules are also available. The first is embperl. This OpenSource project builds on `mod_perl` to allow Perl code to be embedded in your HTML pages. You can learn more about this project by visiting `http://perl.apache.org/embperl/`. The source code for the embperl module is included on the CD at `/Source/Apache/modules`.

If you prefer to write scripts in tcl, check out `libapache_mod_dtcl`, also located on the CD at `/Source/Apache/modules`. This module lets you embed tcl scripts in an HTML page, with a tcl server to preprocess the scripts within Apache.

And, for those who have become Python fans and prefer its object-oriented nature, PyApache lets you include Python scripts within an HTML page. This module is located on the CD at /Source/Apache/modules.

Scripts are nice, but some developers insist on working in C. By using mod_cint, you can embed C source code within an HTML Web page. The code is processed as the page is sent out by Apache. This complex tool is included on the CD at /Source/Apache/modules, and it requires a supporting library package called libcint, which is on the CD at /Source/Extras.

Two handy modules can help you control connections on your Apache server. Mod_bandwidth and mod_throttle, both located on the CD at /Source/Apache/modules, support configuration directives to manage a connection speed to one or all users. With these, you can indicate the bits per second that a connection is permitted to use and even see graphical tracking of user activity based on bandwidth usage.

For something a little lighter, mod_gifcounter makes it easy to add a page counter to any Web page. It's located on the CD at /Source/Apache/modules.

Many other modules are described, with links, in the Apache Module Registry. These modules provide many types of clever functionality that you can add to your Web server or use as a template to develop your own Apache modules. Some of the other module topics include:

- On-the-fly decompression of Web pages using gunzip
- Advanced session management and tracking
- Extended support for various languages, including Chinese, Russian, and Japanese
- Web page counters
- Java tools

31 Make Apache a Proxy Server

A proxy server provides security for Web requests leaving your network. Rather than have every person on your local network actually connect to Web servers all over the world, they can connect to a proxy server, which receives their requests and then forwards each one as if it came from the proxy server. When a response arrives, the proxy server returns the information to the client browser.

Using a proxy server provides several advantages over having everyone on your network connect directly to outside Web sites:

◆ The proxy server can cache frequently accessed pages, saving network bandwidth when many people access the same sites regularly.

◆ The proxy server can be configured to block access to certain external sites or restrict access by certain users on the local network. All access can be blocked at certain times without adjusting each person's PC configuration.

◆ Users inside your network have a harder time creating inadvertent security holes because they are connecting to an internal server—the proxy—rather than an external Web server.

◆ Outgoing network bandwidth is managed from a single location.

With all of these advantages, many organizations use a proxy server to allow employees to browse the Web. One of the most popular proxy server programs is called Squid.

The Squid proxy server is highly configurable. Because it provides services for outgoing Web requests, it is sometimes run on a separate computer from the Apache server that handles incoming Web requests. This isn't necessary, but it can make security a little easier to manage. Squid is included on the CD at /Source/Apache/server.

Apache itself, however, can also be used as a full-featured proxy server. While it may seem strange at first, Apache can serve Web pages for your organization at the same time it retrieves Web pages for browsers on your network. How does this work?

If you use a feature of Apache called `mod_proxy`, you can configure the browsers in your organization to point to the Apache server as a proxy for HTTP requests. When a request arrives at the Apache server that is marked as `proxy:`, Apache forwards the request on to another Web server (after checking that your configuration allows access). When the reply comes back from the remote Web server, Apache returns the document to the browser as if it came from the internal Web server.

Mod_proxy is not installed by default when you use Apache, but it is included with the standard package of Apache source code, so you can recompile Apache and begin using `mod_proxy` immediately. (The Apache source code package is located on the CD at `/Source/Apache/server`.)

Why use a combined Web server and proxy server with Apache? A few good reasons are

◆ When you are confident about your skills in setting up Apache configuration, it's much easier to maintain one program than two.

◆ Security concerns are reduced by only needing to track updates for one program.

◆ Squid is popular and proven, but Apache still has a larger user base testing it and more developers working on it, and it's probably a more stable program.

Once you have `mod_proxy` set up on your Apache server, you can enable it with a single Apache configuration directive in `httpd.conf`:

```
ProxyRequests on
```

If you want to use some of the other features of the Apache proxy module, read about these additional directives in your Apache documentation (or visit a site like `http://www.apacheweek.org` and search for articles on "proxy"). Each directive in the following table is shown as an example with a description of what the example will accomplish. Complete syntax information provided on the Apache Web site at `http://www.apache.org/docs/mod/mod_proxy.html`. Other configuration options are available (besides those listed here—see the Apache Web site) to help make your Apache proxy server efficient, reliable, and secure.

PROXY DIRECTIVE EXAMPLE	DESCRIPTION OF RESULTS
`ProxyBlock espn`	Blocks access from within your network to any Web site with the string "espn" in the URL. (Isn't that cruel?)

PROXY DIRECTIVE EXAMPLE	DESCRIPTION OF RESULTS
ProxyPass /intranet/espn www.espn.com	Maps requests for an external server (www.espn.com in the example) to a local directory, effectively creating an internal mirror of the site as documents are requested.
CacheRoot /www/proxy/cache	Establishes a root directory for caching documents that the proxy server feature retrieves and enables document caching.
CacheSize 102400	Sets the amount of disk space allowed for proxy cached documents to 100MB. (The parameter is in KB.)
NoCache www.fidelity.com	Instructs not to cache any documents from the listed domains or IP addresses. Use this for documents that are updated frequently and those that may contain personal information that shouldn't be stored (browser headers may also affect what is cached).
CacheMaxExpire 24	Defines how long, in hours, before all cached documents expire (and must be retrieved again from their source Web server).

32 Fine-Tune Your Apache Configuration

The copy of Apache that comes installed by default on your Linux system is probably great for viewing online documentation and serving up a few personal or business Web pages, but Apache is capable of much more. However, the default configuration used by most Linux vendors isn't designed to support the next amazon.com site. This section lists tips for tuning Apache for better performance.

Support Massive Web Traffic

Apache running on a fast Linux system can easily fill 10MB of outgoing bandwidth (see http://www.mindcraft.com for a few survey details.), but this isn't enough for many busy Web sites. In these cases, you can use multiple parallel Web servers, but you also want to get the most performance you can out of each server.

Performance limits on Apache can be related to either the operating system that Apache is running on, or to the configuration of Apache and its modules. Some keys to improving the performance of your Web site are provided in this section.

When you start Apache, that process begins receiving Web requests on the network, but it doesn't respond to them itself. Instead, it starts other copies of Apache responding to the requests, each copy of Apache being controlled by the master copy that was started first.

In order to handle thousands or millions of requests in a day, many copies of Apache run at the same time. You can adjust the following directives to control how many copies of Apache are used and how they behave. To use the higher values suggested in this list, you should have a powerful server (a dual-Pentium II 450 with 256MB is a good starting place).

MinSpareServers This is the number of copies of Apache that is always kept running. Set this number higher if your Web traffic is irregular ("spikey") so that spare servers are always available to handle sudden bursts of traffic. A default value of 5 might be increased to 25 for a busy server.

MaxSpareServer   This is the maximum number of copies of Apache that will be started on your system. This number imposes a limit on the resources used by Apache as it tries to handle all incoming requests. Each additional server uses about 1MB of memory. A busy server might have this directive set to 100.

MaxClients   This is the maximum number of distinct clients that can connect to the Web server (to all copies of Apache). Each client can have multiple simultaneous requests, but once this limit is reached, another client requesting a document will be put on hold until Apache has finished handling requests for one of the current clients. The value of this directive might be set to 256 or higher. You should also check the HARD_SERVER_LIMIT in the `httpd.h` file to update how much traffic Apache will allow. This prevents Apache from crashing your system when it runs out of resources.

MaxRequestsPerChild   This is the maximum number of requests that a copy of Apache will handle before being closed and another copy of Apache is started to replace it. This is done to prevent a long-running copy of Apache from causing problems because of system memory leaks. On Linux, where memory leaks are not a problem, set this directive to 0 to avoid the overhead of killing and restarting processes on a busy server.

SendBufferSize   This is the size of the TCP buffer used to send outgoing data. If you have a fast connection to the Internet (such as a T3 line), setting this value higher than the default will improve server performance.

HostnameLookups   By setting this directive to Off, Apache will log the IP address of incoming requests rather than the domain name. This saves a lot of time for each request. Apache includes tools to update log files by looking up hostnames "offline" so you're not using your Web server capacity.

With a few fine-tuned directives, the most time-consuming part of servicing a Web request is running the scripts and server-side programs that are needed to prepare a dynamic HTML page. To increase your throughput, try these techniques:

◆ If your scripts are written in Perl, Python, or tcl, try one of the modules mentioned in the last section (especially `mod_perl`) that builds a script interpreter into Apache. These can dramatically improve performance when running these scripts.

◆ For all types of scripts, try the module FastCGI, which is included on the CD at /Source/Apache/modules. This module makes scripts run much faster by keeping them in memory between the times they are called.

◆ If you have static HTML pages that are requested frequently, use the mod_mmap_static module (part of the standard Apache code, though it's not included by default). This module keeps HTML pages loaded into memory so they can be returned to a client without reading the hard disk.

◆ Use a separate database server on your local network to spread the processing load of database lookups. Be certain you have a very fast internal network, however, or this may cause a bottleneck between the Web and database servers.

If you're up to working with the Apache source code, additional performance improvements are available by tweaking the system for a higher load. Detailed instruction for doing this are found at http://www.apache .org/docs/misc/perf-tuning.html. This document is included on the CD at /Source/Apache/server, but check the URL for the latest version.

If you've checked all of these things, see if a network analyzer indicates that you still have unused network bandwidth and incoming Web browser requests that could use it (meaning that the Apache server is the bottleneck on the system). The suggestions given in the following list may allow Linux to handle more Web traffic:

◆ Adjust the number of processes allowed by Linux. Sometimes the number of Apache processes needed to service Web requests outstrips the preset limit in Linux. You can change this value in the Linux source code and then recompile your Linux kernel.

◆ Adjust the number of file handles that Linux allows. Each copy of Apache uses a couple of file handles. If they're all used up, Apache can't do anything until some are released by another copy of the program.

More hints for tuning Linux performance are available at http://www .tunelinux.com. Specific hints for working with different parts of the system (kernel, file systems, etc.) are provided on this site.

33 Track Your Web Site Traffic

Each time a browser accesses your Web site, an event is logged to the Apache access log. On Red Hat 6 systems, this file is `/etc/httpd/logs/access_log`. The location may vary on other Linux systems but the filename is generally consistent. The information in the access log includes the IP address of the client browser, the date and time of the request, and the HTTP command (which includes the filename being requested).

Even on a site without much traffic, the access log often has a lot of data. On larger sites, it must be rotated regularly (daily or weekly) to avoid filling the hard disk with a record of Web page accesses. A few lines from the access log might look like this:

```
192.168.100.4 - - [25/Mar/1999:15:16:53 -0700] "GET
  / HTTP/1.0" 200 1879
192.168.100.4 - - [25/Mar/1999:15:16:55 -0700] "GET
  /head.gif HTTP/1.0" 200 17446
192.168.100.4 - - [25/Mar/1999:15:16:55 -0700] "GET
  /mmback.gif HTTP/1.0" 404 204
192.168.100.3 - - [25/Mar/1999:15:17:06 -0700] "GET
  / HTTP/1.0" 200 1879
192.168.100.2 - - [01/Jun/1999:21:06:03 -0600] "GET
  /01ch.html HTTP/1.0" 200 11254
192.168.100.2 - - [01/Jun/1999:21:06:18 -0600] "GET
  /02ch.html HTTP/1.0" 200 187091
```

The contents of the Apache log can be configured using the CustomLog and LogFormat directives, but the previous lines show the Common Log Format (CLF), which is used by default on Apache and most other Web servers. Several Apache modules let you log other information as well.

Having all this information recorded is valuable for several reasons, such as tracking who is accessing your site and which pages are most popular. The information isn't easy to use in its raw format as shown here, but many tools are available to process this data and report about it in summary form so that useful composite information can be seen. For example, a summary of your Web site statistics might show you:

◆ Which files are most often downloaded so that you can take steps to speed up access to those files

◆ Which countries are accessing your site the most so that you can tailor content to that area

◆ The time of day that Web traffic is the lightest so that you can plan any scheduled downtime or maintenance for then

◆ One domain that appears to be trying to explore or mirror your entire site without permission so that you can block access to that domain

Of course, Web statistics also provide raw information about how many hits your server has responded to, how many megabytes of data were transferred, and so forth. Be careful about using this type of raw data to draw too many conclusions. With all the proxy servers, animated gifs, and other complicating factors, simple numbers like hit rates don't mean that much any longer. Sophisticated commercial tools exist to provide more meaningful end-user tracking via cookies or other mechanisms. Use the tools described here to track more general user trends and for system administration planning.

One of the oldest Web log analysis tools is wwwstat, which is located on the CD at /Source/Apache/statistics. Using wwwstat, you can compile an HTML page that includes information such as:

◆ Summary information for each calendar period

◆ Total amount of Web traffic divided by request date

◆ Total amount of Web traffic divided by hour of the day

◆ Reports on which domains client requests are coming from

◆ Reports on how many times each directory and file on your site was requested

Although wwwstat has been around for years, it still produces very useful output. To learn more about using wwwstat and view a list of supporting documentation and utilities, visit http://www.ics.uci.edu/pub/websoft/ wwwstat/.

Wwwstat creates an HTML file, but the data can be converted to graphical form by using the tool gwstat, which is located on the CD at /Source/ Apache/statistics. A sample of the many types of graphs that gwstat can

create is shown in Figure 33.1. The home page for gwstat is `http://dis.cs.umass.edu/stats/gwstat.html`.

FIGURE 33.1 Output from wwwstat can be converted to graphs using gwstat.

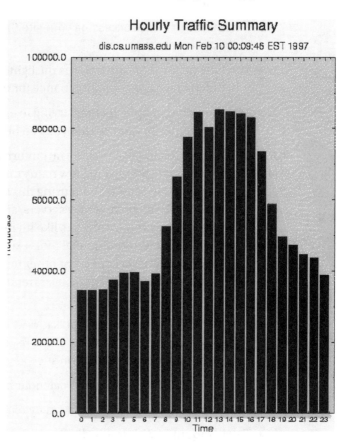

More graphically inclined Webmasters might prefer starting immediately with the 3Dstats package, located on the CD at `/Source/Apache/statistics` (an HTML installation page is also included in this directory).

3Dstats uses the same access logs as wwwstat, but it creates three-dimensional VRML models of the server's load by month, day, or hour. Using a VRML viewing, you can move through the graphs, examining them from different viewpoints and exploring specific areas in more detail.

A sample screen of 3Dstats taken from the home page at `http://www.netstore.de/Supply/3Dstats/` is shown in Figure 33.2.

FIGURE 33.2 3Dstats creates 3D virtual reality models of your Web statistics. You can explore these models with a VRML viewer.

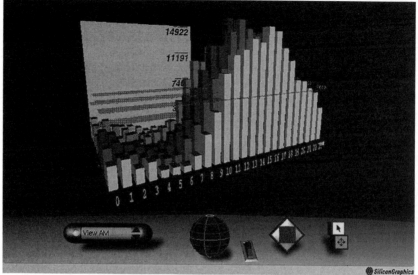

Both wwwstat and 3Dstats use the common log format but can be configured to include different parts of the log data or to work with modified log formats.

The tool that claims the title of most popular log analyzer, however, is Analog. Some of its features include:

- ◆ Very fast processing of even very large log files (many gigabytes)
- ◆ Many configuration options, including the ability to configure the log format used by your copy of Apache
- ◆ Output in any of 30 different languages
- ◆ 27 different reports

The output of Analog is an HTML page that looks similar to the wwwstat output, but Analog includes small bar graphs in the Web page. Analog is included on the CD at /Source/Apache/statistics. You can also visit the home page for Analog at http://www.statslab.cam.ac.uk/~sret1/analog/, where you can read the full documentation, see a list of helper applications (scripts, graphing tools, etc.), and view sample output pages.

34 Host Multiple Web Sites on One Server

Apache has the ability to serve documents for multiple domains (or *hosts*) as if they were coming from separate Web servers. For example, you might have one copy of Apache responding to requests for `http://www.booksahoy.com` and `http://www.childrenscorner.com`, or whatever domain names your Web sites are using. Apache can serve documents for as many of these virtual hosts as you can keep track of.

Two types of virtual hosting are possible:

◆ IP-based, in which your computer has more than one IP address assigned to it (using IP aliasing or multiple network cards). Each domain name is associated with one IP address.

◆ Name-based, in which all domain names come to your single IP address but are interpreted by Apache based on the request itself.

The configuration directives in `httpd.conf` (the main Apache configuration file, located in the `/etc/httpd/conf` directory on Red Hat 6) apply to the default Web site, or the one that is associated with the hostname of your Linux server itself. But you can configure your name server (using DNS) to send requests for several domains to your Linux system. Just have the administrator of your DNS server set up another domain name that points to your IP address.

When a browser connects to your Web server, it does so based on your IP address. The information that the browser sends to the Web server, however, normally includes a line stating what domain name is being requested. If you're using name-based virtual hosting and the browser doesn't include this information, Apache can't tell which virtual host to use, since the IP address alone doesn't contain this information. In these cases, Apache usually uses either the default (nonvirtual host) document root or the first virtual host.

Once you have your DNS server set up so that requests for multiple domains arrive at your Linux Web server, set up a virtual host in your

Apache configuration with a separate document root for the HTML files that apply to each virtual host.

If you are using name-based virtual hosting, your configuration might start to look something like the following overly simple example. Note that a virtual host container can include nearly any of the Apache directives, including <Directory> containers that apply to areas within the document tree for that virtual host. The <VirtualHost> containers begin with the directive NameVirtualHost, which defines the IP address that these requests will arrive on (this is controlled by your DNS server configuration).

```
NameVirtualHost 192.168.100.3


<VirtualHost www.childrenscorner.com>
ServerAdmin webmaster@brighton.xmission.com
DocumentRoot /www/childrenscorner/docs
ServerName www.childrenscorner.com
ErrorLog /www/childrenscorner/logs/error_log
TransferLog /www/childrenscorner/logs/access_log
</VirtualHost>


<VirtualHost www.booksahoy.com>
ServerAdmin webmaster@brighton.xmission.com
DocumentRoot /www/booksahoy/docs
ServerName www.booksahoy.com
ErrorLog /www/booksahoy/logs/error_log
TransferLog /www/booksahoy/logs/access_log
    <Directory /www/booksahoy/docs>
    Options None
    AllowOverride None
    allow from all
    </Directory>
        <Directory /www/booksahoy/docs/upgrades>
        AuthType Basic
        AuthName Upgrades
        AuthUserFile /www/booksahoy/conf/upgrade-users
        # require valid-user
        require user nwells jkoch ed
        AddHandler server-parsed shtml
        Options +Includes
```

```
                    # Options IncludesNOEXEC
                    </Directory>
              </VirtualHost>
```

If you were using IP-based virtual hosting with IP aliasing, each of your <VirtualHost> containers would begin like this example:

```
<VirtualHost 192.168.100.30>
ServerAdmin webmaster@brighton.xmission.com
DocumentRoot /www/lawresearch/docs
ServerName www.lawresearch.com
ErrorLog /www/lawresearch/logs/error_log
TransferLog /www/lawresearch/logs/access_log
ScriptAlias /scripts /www/lawresearch/scripts
</VirtualHost>
```

Virtual hosts are an important feature of Apache. No additional software is needed, and no special configuration is required for Apache; just add the <VirtualHost> containers to your configuration file once DNS is correctly set up. Although much more could be said about virtual hosts, this introduction should get you started.

35 Graphically Configure Apache

By now, you've probably explored the Apache configuration files and seen how complicated they can become, especially when virtual hosts, directory containers, and security limits are included in them. A graphical tool called Comanche (Configuration Manager for Apache) is available to configure Apache, though it is not part of the Apache project itself. Consider Comanche a tool for learning Apache configuration and managing small to medium Web sites. I wouldn't recommend it yet for large or complex sites, though it is a full-featured program.

Comanche is written in tcl, so it's not especially fast, but it looks good, and as a configuration tool it doesn't need to be really fast. It's located on the CD at /Source/Apache/comanche. An rpm is also included in the same directory. Though it's stored in the /Source directory, Comanche is a script and so doesn't need to be compiled.

If you're running Red Hat, the easiest way to install Comanche is with the rpm command. Comanche requires that you first install the itcl package from your Red Hat CD. It's also included in the /Binaries/Extra directory on this book's CD. (You'll need to log in as root for these two rpm commands.) First install itcl.

```
# rpm -Uvh /mnt/cdrom/RedHat/RPMS/itcl-3.0.1-29.i386.rpm
```

Then use this command to install Comanche from this book's CD:

```
# rpm -Uvh /mnt/cdrom/Source/Apache/comanche/comanche-9904061_
   noarch.rpm
```

After installing the Comanche package, start it from a graphical command line:

```
$ comanche
```

The initial window is shown in Figure 35.1.

FIGURE 35.1 Comanche opens with a single folder named eComanche.

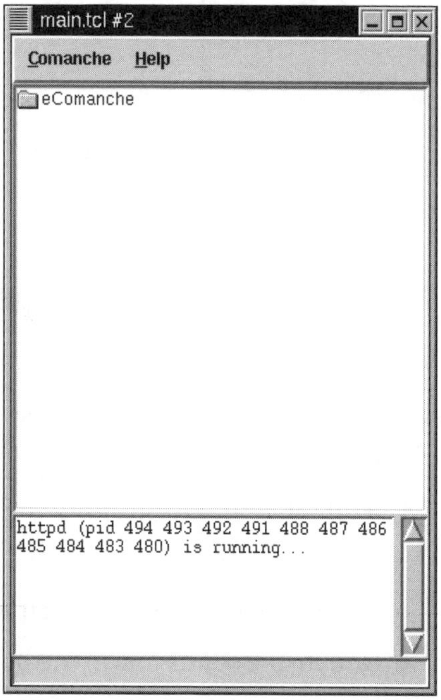

Double-click the eComanche folder to see the Apache Machine icon. Configuration options (such as virtual hosts) are arranged in a tree structure under the Apache Machine icon. A status box at the bottom of the window shows you that the Apache httpd daemon is running.

Double-click Apache Machine to see two items: Server Management and Default Web Site. Double-click Default Web Site to see directories that are defined for the current Web site (see Figure 35.2).

FIGURE 35.2 **Each configuration section of Apache is shown as part of the Comanche tree display.**

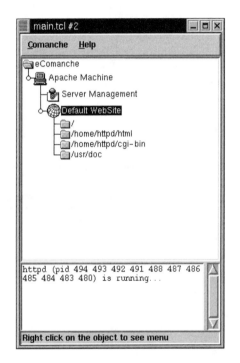

By right-clicking the Server Management item, you can do any of the following:

- ◆ Stop the Web server
- ◆ Start the Web server
- ◆ Restart the Web server (which rereads all configuration information)
- ◆ Update the status line in the bottom of the Comanche window

When you right-click the Default WebSite item and choose Properties, you see a dialog box with many pages of information that you can graphically configure. Anytime you see a yellow dot to the left of an item, you can double-click that item to open a tree beneath it. A total of 14 pages of configuration data are provided for the Default WebSite.

Some of the configuration options in the Properties dialog box are straightforward, such as the Logs window, where you can enter the filename for each of the logs that Apache can create (see Figure 35.3).

FIGURE 35.3 In the Logs window, you define a filename where each Apache log is stored.

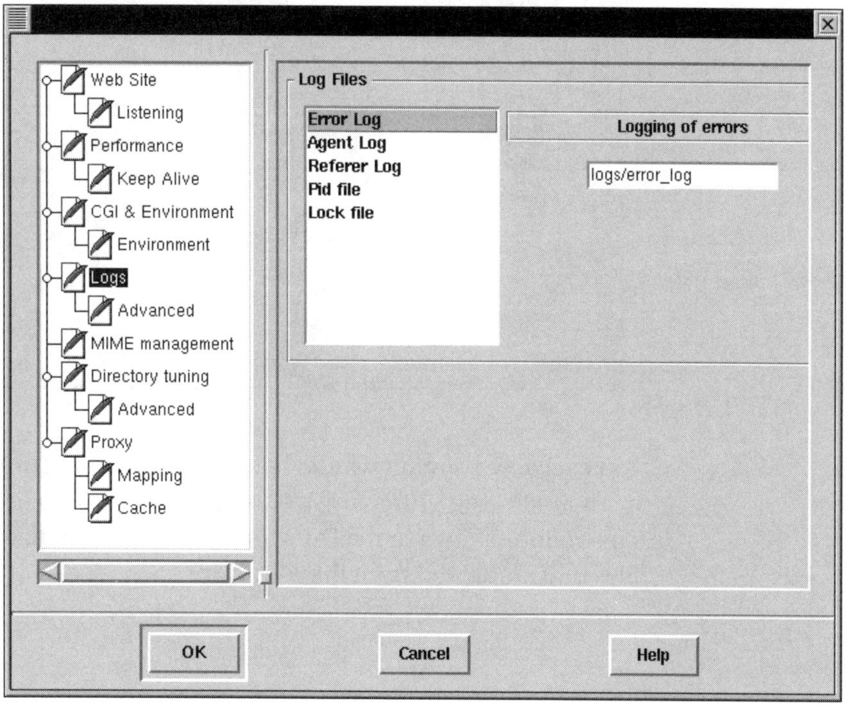

![Dialog box titled with tree navigation on left showing Web Site, Listening, Performance, Keep Alive, CGI & Environment, Environment, Logs (highlighted), Advanced, MIME management, Directory tuning, Advanced, Proxy, Mapping, Cache. Right side shows Log Files with Error Log, Agent Log, Referer Log, Pid file, Lock file, and Logging of errors field with logs/error_log. Bottom has OK, Cancel, Help buttons.]

Other windows, such as the Proxy window (shown in Figure 35.4) or the Directory Tuning/Advanced window, require that you already understand something about what Apache can do and how to configure it.

FIGURE 35.4 In the Proxy window, you can enable the Apache proxy server and set basic proxy options.

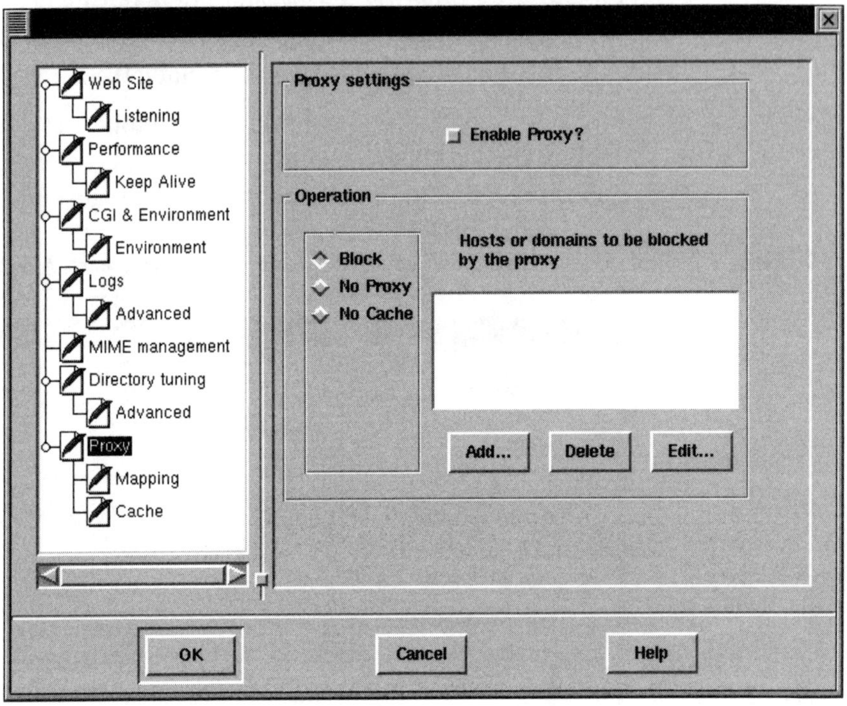

You can view a similar window (though with fewer configuration options) by right-clicking a directory icon under Default WebSite (see Figure 35.5). The options shown in the Directory Configuration dialog box apply only to files that are served from that directory.

FIGURE 35.5 A Directory Configuration dialog box includes options that apply only to files in one directory and its subdirectories.

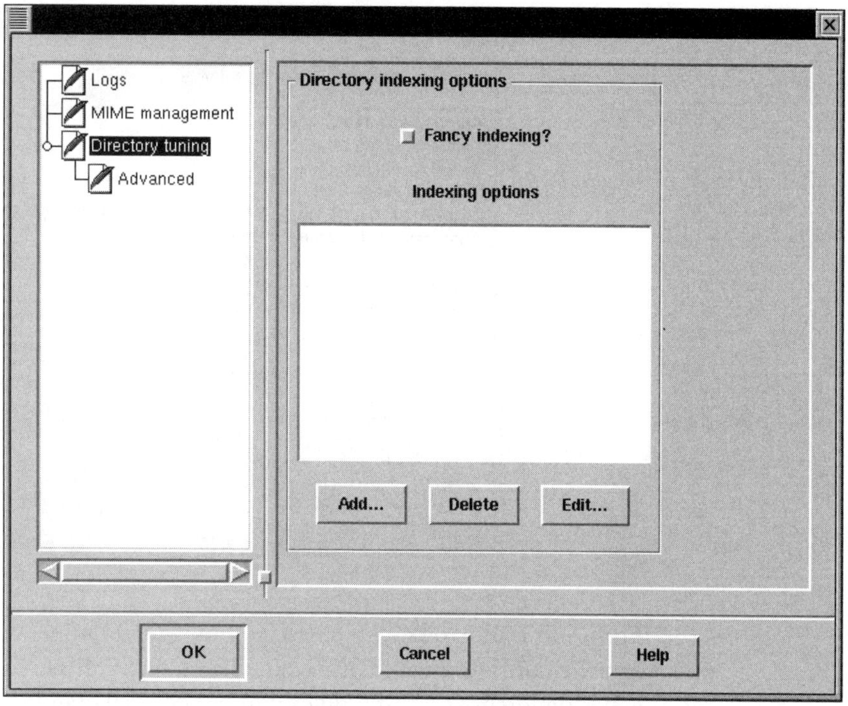

After setting up configuration information in the Properties dialog boxes, right-click the Server Management icon and choose Save Config to update the Apache configuration files. Then choose Restart from the same menu to make your new configuration take effect.

If you're curious about how Comanche interprets the Properties dialog boxes to prepare an Apache configuration file, choose the ConfView option from the right-click menu of either Default WebSite or one of the directory items. A window appears (see Figure 35.6) showing you each of the configuration lines that will be placed in the Apache configuration.

FIGURE 35.6 You can view the configuration lines that Comanche will use for Apache, based on your responses in the Properties dialog boxes.

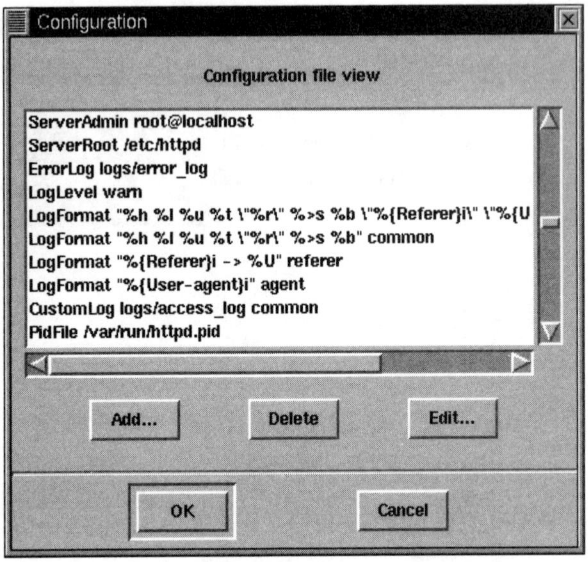

From this dialog box, you can manually add, change, or delete lines for the Apache configuration. This bypasses the ease-of-use provided by the Properties dialog boxes, but it gives you full control over what configuration options are used.

Another great feature of Comanche is the ability to add configurations for new virtual hosts, directories, or locations. To add a new virtual host to your Web site, right-click the Apache Machine item, then choose New ➤ Virtual Host. Enter the name of the new virtual host, and it appears as a new container in your Comanche main window.

To add a configuration for an additional directory or location within any host (default or virtual), right-click the hostname (such as Default WebSite or a virtual host that you have added). Then choose New ➤ Directory or New ➤ Location. When you enter the path to the directory or location, it appears as a separate item in the host container (see Figure 35.7).

FIGURE 35.7 Virtual hosts and additional configurations for directories and locations are easy to add in Comanche.

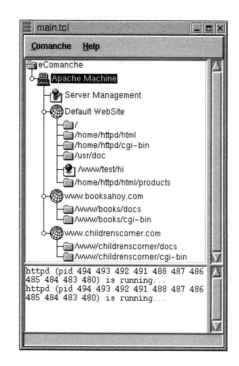

After adding virtual hosts, directory or location items, you can right-click and choose Properties to set up the configuration for that item. Remember to save the configuration and restart Apache to make the configuration take effect.

Turn Your System into a Super-Server

Networking computers together is a very big topic. Entire books (much larger than this one) have been written on the subject. Once you have your basic network up and running, however, you may not think about how to rearrange it to improve performance, increase security, or make it easier to maintain from day to day.

This part describes how to enhance what your Linux network can do. Many of the features described are part of your standard Linux product—you just didn't know all the tricks it could do until now.

36 Connect in New Ways

Whether you're using a single desktop Linux system or running a complete Linux-based network, once you have your network connection established, you probably don't think much more about it. In this section, you'll see several ways that Linux can connect to a network. One might be the one you're using—or the one you should consider using.

Connect without Managing IP Addresses

The bane of running a LAN with Internet connectivity is managing the IP addresses of numerous clients. Anytime a configuration change is required, the TCP/IP information on each host must be laboriously and individually updated.

By using the Dynamic Host Configuration Protocol (DHCP), clients are assigned an IP address each time they connect to the network. If IP address configurations must be changed, they can be changed on the DHCP server— one time—and the results are propagated to all clients automatically.

Linux can act as a DHCP client, receiving an assigned IP address from a DHCP server. Linux can also act as a DHCP server, assigning IP addresses to clients on your network based on a pool of addresses and configuration information that you provide. Check with your system administrator about the availability of a DHCP server on your network.

The source code package for DHCP is located on the CD at /Source/ System Tools. But every Linux distribution should include a copy of DHCP that you can easily install and use. If you're using a distribution like Caldera OpenLinux 2.2, DHCP can even be configured during installation, so these steps are not needed.

As an example, the commands to install the DHCP client daemon on Red Hat 6 (after mounting your CD drive) would be:

```
# cd /mnt/cdrom/RedHat/RPMS
# rpm -Uvh dhcpcd-1.3.17pl2-1.i386
```

After installing the DHCP client, you can reboot your system (or restart the networking protocols using your initialization scripts in /etc/rc.d/init.d). Then check your network configuration using the ifconfig command. If you see 0.0.0.0 as your IP address, wait a few moments for the DHCP server to assign an IP address to your system. If you still don't appear to have an IP address, contact your system administrator or check the configuration of the DHCP server. The output of ifconfig should look something like this (your IP address is the inet addr: field for the eth0 Ethernet interface):

```
lo        Link encap:Local Loopback
          inet addr:127.0.0.1  Bcast:127.255.255.255  Mask:255.0.0.0
          UP BROADCAST LOOPBACK RUNNING  MTU:3584  Metric:1
          RX packets:302 errors:0 dropped:0 overruns:0 frame:0
          TX packets:302 errors:0 dropped:0 overruns:0 carrier:0 coll:0

eth0      Link encap:Ethernet  HWaddr 00:20:AF:EE:05:45
          inet addr:24.128.53.102  Bcast:24.128.53.255  Mask:255.255.254.0
          UP BROADCAST NOTRAILERS RUNNING MULTICAST  MTU:1500  Metric:1
          RX packets:24783 errors:1 dropped:1 overruns:0 frame:1
          TX packets:11598 errors:0 dropped:0 overruns:0 carrier:0 coll:96
          Interrupt:10 Base address:0x300
```

Setting up your Linux system to act as a DHCP server to all the hosts on your network is a little more complicated than setting up a DHCP client, but not overly so. When Linux is your DHCP server, it will provide IP addresses to all the DHCP clients on your network, including Windows PCs and any other system that uses DHCP to query the server for an IP address.

The DHCP server package is included in every Linux distribution; it is also part of the package included in the /Source/System Tools/ directory on the CD.

For example, to install the DHCP server daemon on Red Hat 6, use these commands after mounting the Red Hat CD in your CD-ROM drive:

```
# cd /mnt/cdrom/RedHat/RPMS
# rpm -Uvh dhcpd-2.0b1p16-6.i386.rpm
```

After installing the DHCP server program, a few configuration steps are required before the server will respond to DHCP client requests. Follow these steps to configure the DHCP server:

1. Execute the route command, checking to make sure a route of 255.255.255.255 is included. This may have been set up by the command that installed your DHCP server. (If you have Windows clients using DHCP on the same network as your Linux system, the 255.255.255.255 route must be included in Linux to prevent errors on the Windows systems.)

```
# /sbin/route
Kernel IP routing table
Destination   Gateway   Genmask     Flags Metric Ref Use Iface
127.0.0.0     *         255.0.0.0   U     00     0   lo
```

2. If necessary, use one of the following commands to add the 255.255.255.255 route to your system. Try the first command; if it gives an error, try the second.

```
route add -host 255.255.255.255 dev eth0
route add -net 255.255.255.0 dev eth0
```

3. Configure the /etc/dhcp.conf configuration file. A sample file is shown here:

```
default-lease-time 600;
max-lease-time 7200;
option subnet-mask 255.255.255.0;
option broadcast-address 192.168.1.255;
option routers 192.168.1.254;
option domain-name-servers 192.168.1.1, 192.168.1.2;
option domain-name "mydomain.org";
```

```
subnet 192.168.1.0 netmask 255.255.255.0 {
    range 192.168.1.10 192.168.1.100;
    range 192.168.1.150 192.168.1.200;
}
```

This sample file causes the DHCP server to assign IP addresses from the range 192.168.1.10 to 192.168.1.100 or from 192.168.1.150 to 192.168.1.200. Each client IP address is valid for 600 seconds (or the time the client requests, to a maximum of 7200 seconds). After that time, the client must request a new IP address. The DHCP server also provides information for the client's subnet mask, broadcast address, router/gateway settings, and DNS server.

If you need to assign a specific IP address to a certain client (based on the hardware MAC address of the client's Ethernet card), add lines such as these:

```
host haagen {
    hardware ethernet 08:00:2b:4c:59:23;
    fixed-address 192.168.1.222;
}
```

 For more information about DHCP, consult the DHCP HOWTO document at /Doc/DHCP.html on the CD. This document includes additional configuration ideas and troubleshooting tips. The DHCP protocol is found in the Internet document RFC 2131, which you can peruse at http://www .freesoft.org/CIE/RFC/2131/index.htm.

Use Multiple Addresses on One Network Card

Although it might seem strange given the growing scarcity of IP addresses, organizations that have extra addresses sometimes find it useful to assign more than one IP address to a single network card.

Multiple IP addresses are always used for a computer that has more than one network card, such as an Internet gateway with two Ethernet cards. There are other situations, however, when two Ethernet cards are not needed but two IP addresses are still helpful as a means of separating traffic that comes to one computer for two logical "sites."

For example, suppose you have a Web site and an FTP site for your organization. You also want to host both a Web and an FTP site with a different domain name. If you use a separate IP address for the second site (`www.two.com` and `ftp.two.com`, for example), you can more easily configure and track activity to this site.

Using two or more IP addresses on one network card is called IP aliasing. Linux supports IP aliases with a kernel module. If the kernel module is not built-in or dynamically loaded in your kernel, you can add it with this command:

```
# insmod ip_alias
```

If you're running Red Hat 6, IP aliasing is built-in—you don't need to load a module. With IP alias support in the kernel, you can configure IP alias addresses either manually or using a graphical tool like `LinuxConf` in Red Hat.

To manually configure an IP alias, use the standard commands to set up a network interface. IP aliases are noted with a colon and number after the physical device. For example, if your Ethernet card is `eth0`, the first IP alias (thus the second IP address for the Ethernet card) is `eth0:0`; the second alias (the third IP address) is `eth0:1` and so forth.

To add an alias, use these two commands, changing the device and address information to fit your system:

```
# ifconfig eth0:0 192.168.100.21 netmask 255.255.255.0
   broadcast 192.168.100.255
# route add -host 192.168.100.21 dev eth0:0
```

If the commands are successful, the `ifconfig` command shows the additional network interface and the `route` command shows the additional host route:

```
# ifconfig
lo        Link encap:Local Loopback
          inet addr:127.0.0.1  Bcast:127.255.255.255  Mask:255.0.0.0
          UP BROADCAST LOOPBACK RUNNING  MTU:3584  Metric:1
          RX packets:28 errors:0 dropped:0 overruns:0
          TX packets:28 errors:0 dropped:0 overruns:0

eth0      Link encap:Ethernet  HWaddr 00:20:AF:3D:80:8E
          inet addr:192.168.100.2  Bcast:192.168.100.255  Mask:255.255.255.0
          UP BROADCAST RUNNING MULTICAST  MTU:1500  Metric:1
          RX packets:14 errors:0 dropped:0 overruns:0
```

```
          TX packets:9 errors:0 dropped:0 overruns:0
          Interrupt:10 Base address:0x300

eth0:0    Link encap:Ethernet  HWaddr 00:20:AF:3D:80:8E
          inet addr:192.168.100.21  Bcast:192.168.100.255  Mask:255.255.255.0
          UP BROADCAST RUNNING  MTU:1500  Metric:1
          RX packets:0 errors:0 dropped:0 overruns:0
          TX packets:0 errors:0 dropped:0 overruns:0
#
# route
Kernel IP routing table
Destination      Gateway     Genmask          Flags  Metric  Ref  Use Iface
192.168.100.21   *           255.255.255.255  UH     0       0    0 eth0:0
192.168.100.0    *           255.255.255.0    U      0       0    1 eth0
127.0.0.0        *           255.0.0.0        U      0       0    0 lo
```

You can make the IP alias settings permanent using a configuration tool like LinuxConf in Red Hat 6 or by editing the configuration scripts in the /etc/sysconfig directory.

Securely Share One Internet Connection

It's fairly easy to use Linux as a gateway to the Internet for your LAN, even over a modem. Just configure both network interfaces (such as eth0 and ppp for a LAN to modem gateway) and update the kernel routes using the route command (this requires that IP forwarding be enabled in your Linux kernel, of course). (For information on IP forwarding, see this document on the CD: /Doc/All-HOWTO-Docs/NET-3-HOWTO.html.) Two potential problems with this solution are

◆ Your ISP notices that you're connecting 50 people to the Internet with your single $15 per month connection and they are not pleased.

◆ You are concerned that you face a security risk because everyone on the Internet can see the IP addresses of every computer on your LAN.

True, your ISP shouldn't care what you do, so long as you abide by established time and bandwidth policies. And the simplest of blanket firewalls will prevent anyone from reaching the computers on your LAN.

But a more elegant solution, one which provides more flexibility for your internal users and better security in both directions, is to use a Network

Address Translation system (NAT) to make all of your traffic to the Internet appear as if it came from a single IP address. On Linux, this is commonly called IP masquerading.

Some vendors sell little black boxes that are nothing but NAT systems to allow an entire LAN to connect to the Internet through a single modem. Many of these boxes, of course, are running Linux.

Using IP masquerading is conceptually similar to using a Web proxy, but it's done at the IP address level. This means that hosts within your LAN can connect to anything on the Internet (that is, anything that you allow through the firewall that you have surely set up by now). How does this work? The following steps show the process at a simplified level.

1. A packet of data destined for the Internet arrives at the Linux gateway from within your LAN. The packet includes a field with the IP address of the host on your LAN.

2. The IP masquerading code in the Linux kernel makes a note of the request ID and changes the IP address of the host on the LAN to the IP address of the Linux gateway.

3. The packet is forwarded to the Internet normally (as if originating from the gateway, however).

4. When a response packet arrives at the Linux gateway from the remote host, the IP masquerading code sees that the packet is a response to a request from a LAN host.

5. The destination IP address is changed from the Linux gateway to the host on your LAN, and the packet is routed within the LAN so that it reaches the host that originated the request.

In this scenario, the host on your LAN isn't set up differently to use IP masquerading and in fact can't tell that the request was handled in this way. In addition, the remote host on the Internet doesn't know anything about the "real" host making the request. Everything appears to have come from the Linux gateway.

Since it's much easier to protect one machine (the Linux gateway) than each machine on your LAN, this system is inherently more secure. By configuring a strong firewall on the Linux gateway and adding a Web and FTP proxy server, your Linux system acts as a powerful virtual traffic cop for all the traffic that goes to and from the Internet from within your LAN.

No additional software is needed for IP masquerading. Support for this feature is an optional setting in the Linux kernel and requires that you recompile your kernel for most, but not all, Linux systems. Because of this, details for setting up IP masquerading are not provided here, but distribution-specific information should be available from your Linux vendor. The HOWTO document is also included on the CD at /Docs/IP-Masquerade .html. This extensive document should get you up and running unless you run into problems that require technical support from your vendor.

37 Enhance Your Network Security

In the first few parts of this book, you learned about tools that show how your network is being used. In this part, you'll discover some tools to monitor and enhance your network security. Most network security revolves around a few basic concepts. The trouble is that some system administrators prefer to hope that no one will bother their systems. More often than not, this is a vain hope. By learning a few concepts and implementing even one or two security measures, you can greatly increase the security of your network.

You're probably familiar with IP addresses and domain names. To reach a distant computer on the Internet (or even a local IP-based network), your computer sends a data packet with the IP address of your system and the IP address of the system you want to communicate with. Routers may pass the packet on to other networks to reach its final destination.

Before these IP addresses can be used for the network packet, the domain name that you normally enter (such as www.yahoo.com) must be converted to an IP address either by using a static file on your Linux system or by querying a domain name services computer (a DNS server). Converting the domain name to an IP address is a separate operation from contacting the server you really want to reach, but in most cases you can't do the latter without contacting the DNS server first.

The other part of the networking packet that you should know about is the port number. Each service on the Internet uses a port number to listen and respond to queries. The data packet that contains the IP address of your system and the destination system includes the port that your system is connecting from (which is chosen from any port available and isn't that important) and the port that you want to connect to. The port you connect to on the server is where the security concerns arise.

Here are the major steps that occur when you use a browser to connect to a Web server—in this example, the Sybex server. (This example is a bit simplified because several connections may occur at the same time, user authentication and cookies may come into play, and so forth, but it illustrates the point well.)

1. You enter a URL in your browser:

   ```
   http://www.sybex.com/catalog/index.shtml
   ```

2. Your browser takes the server name that you entered and sends a request to the DNS server that you have configured on your LAN or ISP. You can think of the request as something like this

   ```
   "What's the IP address of www.sybex.com?"
   ```

3. With the IP address from the DNS server, your browser establishes a connection using a network packet that includes information such as

   ◆ Your IP address

   ◆ A port number on your system (a fairly random number—whatever is available)

   ◆ The IP address of www.sybex.com (which is 206.100.29.83)

   ◆ Port 80 (the default for Web servers)

4. If the Sybex server allows your browser to establish a connection on port 80, your browser sends this HTTP command over the connection:

   ```
   HTTP/1.1 GET /catalog/index.shtml
   ```

5. The Web server responds with the data in the index.shtml document.

This is all straightforward. Most of the network services that we use operate just like this example, including FTP, e-mail (SMTP, IMAP, and POP), and Telnet sessions.

Now turn the situation around and assume that you're running the Web server in the example. The security problems arise when someone outside your network attempts to connect to your server either from an IP address that you don't want using your server (a spammer, for example) or by using a port number that you didn't intend to have active.

If an intruder can find a port where a connection is accepted, additional access may be gained by consistent tinkering, sending random data, and so forth.

The utilities in this section are designed to watch for holes in your network armor, plug those vulnerable spots, and notify you when someone is attempting to gain unauthorized access to your system. Using some of these utilities requires that you know much more about Linux networking than this simple introduction provides. However, most of the utilities have copious documentation to help you learn about their features and the networking areas that they apply to.

Scan for Network Intruders

One method that potential intruders use to access your network is attempting to connect using different port numbers, hoping that they can discover an access point.

By using the portsentry utility, you can scan the network packets addressed to your computer to determine if someone is trying to scan for a connection.

Portsentry has many useful features, including the ability to automatically begin blocking traffic from someone who appears to be scanning for a security hole. One potential disadvantage of portsentry is that you must do a lot of configuration before you compile the program (hence, no binary is provided on the CD). The source code is located at /Source/System Tools on the CD. Using portsentry, you can configure and check for the following:

◆ A list of TCP ports to check for activity or to check all ports within a certain numeric range (stealth scanning is also supported)

◆ A list of ports that should not be watched (that is, should allow normal traffic)

◆ A list of hosts that should be blocked

◆ A specific command to execute based on the address of an incoming attacker (use the command to block the attacker's IP address via the firewall, for example)

◆ A message to post back to the attacking system

To use these features in `portsentry`, check the `README.install` file in the source code package for details on setting up the `portsentry.conf` file before compiling the program.

A different approach to security is taken by the Security Administrator's Integrated Network Tool (SAINT). (Yes, they made up the name to match the acronym they wanted to use.) SAINT is located at `/Source/System Tools` on the CD.

SAINT is a Perl script that you can interact with from either the command line (which is powerful but less attractive for screenshots), or via a Web browser. By using the Web browser, you can use SAINT to set up a list of hosts (other computers) to scan for potential security problems (see Figure 37.1).

Where `portsentry` is used to check your system for attackers doing a port scan, SAINT is used to scan other systems (like an attacker). SAINT is a diagnostic tool that will tell you if potential security breaches exist on a system. The idea is to use it on systems that you manage, not on those of other people.

The SAINT script sets up a copy of a Web server on port 1038 of your system and uses that Web server to process Web forms so that you can check site security from a browser and see the results immediately. For example, Figure 37.2 shows the form where you select a target site and determine the level of security scanning to perform.

After a scan has been performed on a target host, you can review information in your browser, including

◆ Vulnerabilities organized by type or danger level

◆ Host information, arranged by service, domain, subnet, and so forth

◆ Trusted hosts and their counterparts

FIGURE 37.1   **SAINT can use a Web browser interface to scan systems for security problems.**

Many of the scanning features of SAINT can be configured from your browser as well. Figure 37.3 shows the Configuration Management form. Documentation and troubleshooting screens are also part of SAINT.

Protect Users from Themselves

Users are often unaware of the efforts of others to use their accounts as an unauthorized access point. By using the sbscanner script, you can check for a number of common problems that might compromise the security of a user account on your system.

Sbscanner is a shell script; you don't need to compile it. The complete package is located at /Binaries/System Tools/sbscanner on the CD.

FIGURE 37.2 Multiple security scanning options are supported by SAINT.

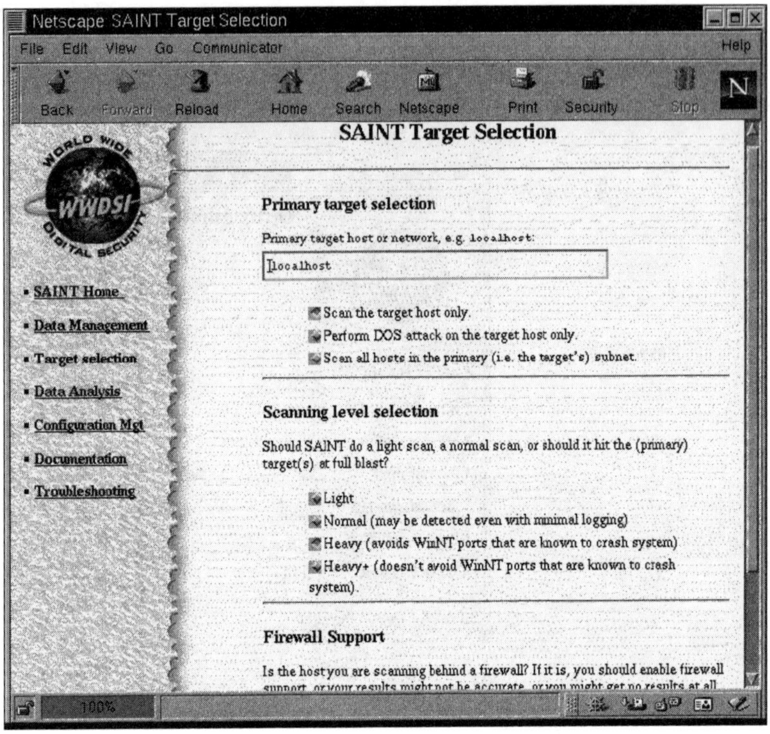

Sbscanner checks for the following potential problems. See the README file for a complete list:

◆ Anonymous FTP problems

◆ Accounts without a password

◆ Promiscuous mode networking (which allows all packets on the network to be viewed)

◆ RHost files (used for logging in or copying files from a remote host)

◆ Programs in /home with the Set User ID bit on (allowing a user to gain additional access by running a program)

◆ X Hosts allowed to connect

◆ Permissions on vital subdirectories

◆ Permissions on the system log file (to prevent erasing evidence of break-ins)

FIGURE 37.3   The features that SAINT uses to scan for security problems can be configured within your Web browser.

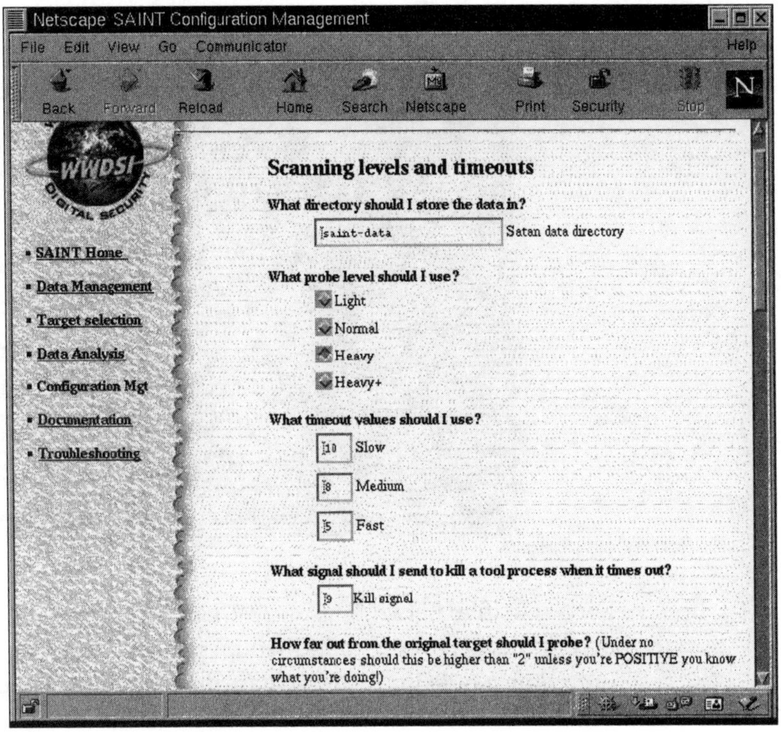

- ◆ MD5 sums of common files (to prevent substituted binaries)
- ◆ Other suspicious files

To run sbscanner, log in as root and use this command:

```
# ./sbscanner
```

As the script runs, it prints messages informing you of its progress through each test, as shown in Figure 37.4.

Set Up a Linux Firewall

When a local network is connected to other networks (or the rest of the world via the Internet), a router is used to pass network data packets between the two (or more) networks. By setting up a firewall, you can control very precisely which data packets are passed between the networks. This is one of the best ways to protect your system against intruder attacks.

FIGURE 37.4 The sbscanner **script checks your system for a variety of common security problems.**

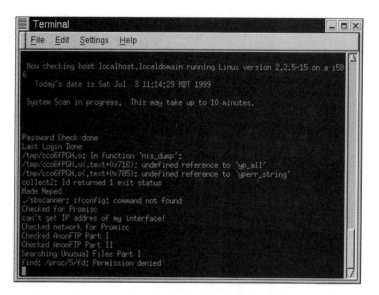

```
Now checking host localhost.localdomain running Linux version 2.2.5-15 on a i58
6
    Today's date is Sat Jul  3 11:14:29 MDT 1999

System Scan in progress.  This may take up to 10 minutes.



Password Check done
Last Login Done
/tmp/cco6fPGH.o: In function `nis_dump':
/tmp/cco6fPGH.o(.text+0x718): undefined reference to `yp_all'
/tmp/cco6fPGH.o(.text+0x785): undefined reference to `yperr_string'
collect2: ld returned 1 exit status
Made Neped
./sbscanner: ifconfig: command not found
Checked for Promisc
can't get IP addres of my interface!
Checked network for Promisc
Checked AnonFTP Part I
Checked AnonFTP Part II
Searching Unusual Files Part I
find: /proc/5/fd: Permission denied
```

For a sensitive network, all access can be denied with only a few small exceptions according to individual situations (this is sometimes called punching a hole in the firewall to allow a person special access). For more general-purpose networks, a looser firewall can be set up that lets most traffic pass through but is ready to be tightened if problems arise from inside or outside the network.

So why not use the most restrictive rules on every firewall? As with all security, the more secure a system is, the more difficult it is to administer it and the more hassle it causes to those who are authorized to use it.

Linux includes all the firewall features you're likely to need. In fact, if you spend the time to set up a strong Linux firewall file, most sites won't need to purchase commercial firewall software. Unfortunately, setting up a Linux firewall file is not an easy task; it's certainly not one that can be covered in detail in this book.

Because the IP networking functions of Linux are a core part of the kernel, Linux makes both a secure and a fast firewall. In versions of the Linux kernel before 2.2, the Linux firewall features were configured using a command called ipfwadm. This cryptic but powerful command allowed you to set up rules within the kernel. These rules determined which packets were passed on for normal processing and which were dropped without further action.

The firewall feature (ipfwadm) must be enabled in your Linux kernel before using the ipfwadm command. This may require recompiling your kernel, depending on the Linux system that you're using. The commands to add firewall rules to the kernel are placed in a firewall configuration file that is executed each time the system starts up. A few sample lines showing ipfwadm commands are shown here:

```
# Let Squid do its thing with http
ipfwadm -O -a accept -P tcp -S $IFEXTERN $UPPORTS -D $ANYWHERE
   www -W $WAN
ipfwadm -I -a accept -P tcp -k -S $ANYWHERE www -D $IFEXTERN
   $UPPORTS -W $WAN
# and with https
ipfwadm -O -a accept -P tcp -S $IFEXTERN $UPPORTS -D $ANYWHERE
   443 -W $WAN
ipfwadm -I -a accept -P tcp -k -S $ANYWHERE 443 -D $IFEXTERN
   $UPPORTS -W $WAN
# Allow LAN users to ftp to Internet hosts via Squid
ipfwadm -O -a accept -P tcp -S $IFEXTERN $UPPORTS -D $ANYWHERE
   ftp -W $WAN
ipfwadm -I -a accept -P tcp -S $ANYWHERE ftp -D $IFEXTERN
   $UPPORTS -W $WAN
# ftp-data channel
ipfwadm -O -a accept -P tcp -S $IFEXTERN $UPPORTS -D $ANYWHERE
   ftp-data -W $WAN
ipfwadm -I -a accept -P tcp -S $ANYWHERE ftp-data -D $IFEXTERN
   $UPPORTS -W $WAN
```

In the latest Linux kernels, a revised firewall system called IP Chains is used. This system is an improvement in both performance and security over the previous ipfwadm system. Similar tools are used to manage IP Chain-based firewalls (for examples, see the next section).

The IP Chains package used to administer the firewall features of the latest Linux kernel is included on the CD at /Source/System Tools/.

Manage Your Firewall in KDE or Gnome

Even if you haven't learned everything about how firewall features work in the Linux kernel, you can use the kfirewall utility to set up basic rules to protect your network (see Figure 37.5). This program lets you see the actual firewall rules that it creates based on your selection from a graphical interface. By reviewing the rules, beginners can learn more about firewalls and experts can check that they're accomplishing their goals.

FIGURE 37.5 With kfirewall, you can graphically configure rules to protect your network.

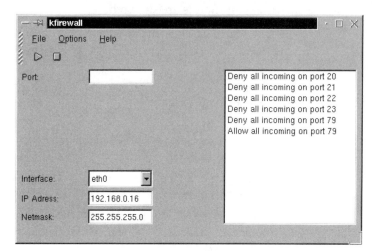

Kfirewall is used within the KDE desktop. It works with the IP Chains feature of the Linux kernel (version 2.2 or later). You cannot use kfirewall if you're using the older ipfwadm firewall system. You must be logged in as root to use kfirewall.

Kfirewall is located at /Source/System Tools/ on the CD. An rpm-format binary is also included at /Binaries/System Tools/kfirewall. When you install kfirewall, it is added as an item on your KDE menus.

As you graphically add and delete rules for which packets are allowed into and out of your network, you can also check the Rules dialog box (see Figure 37.6) to see a summary of what action will be taken on your network traffic. The home page for kfirewall is http://megaman.ypsilonia.net/kfirewall/info.html.

A similar program for Gnome (or those using the GTK+ graphical libraries) is the GTK+ Firewall Control Center, gfcc. The source package for this program is located at /Source/System Tools/; an rpm-format binary is included at /Binaries/System Tools/gfcc. Figure 37.7 shows the main window of gfcc, where you can begin defining firewall rules for incoming, forwarded, and outgoing packets.

FIGURE 37.6   Kfirewall can display a summary of rules based on your graphical selections.

```
— –⋈ current ipchains rules                                      · □ ×
Chain input (policy ACCEPT):
target   prot opt   source        destination      ports
DENY     tcp  ------ anywhere        192.168.0.0/24      any ->  ftp-data
DENY     udp  ------ anywhere        192.168.0.0/24      any ->  20
DENY     tcp  ------ anywhere        192.168.0.0/24      any ->  ftp
DENY     udp  ------ anywhere        192.168.0.0/24      any ->  fsp
DENY     tcp  ------ anywhere        192.168.0.0/24      any ->  ssh
DENY     udp  ------ anywhere        192.168.0.0/24      any ->  ssh
DENY     tcp  ------ anywhere        192.168.0.0/24      any ->  telnet
DENY     udp  ------ anywhere        192.168.0.0/24      any ->  23
Chain forward (policy ACCEPT):
Chain output (policy ACCEPT):



               Refresh              Close
```

FIGURE 37.7   With gfcc you can define rules for incoming, forwarded, and outgoing IP packets.

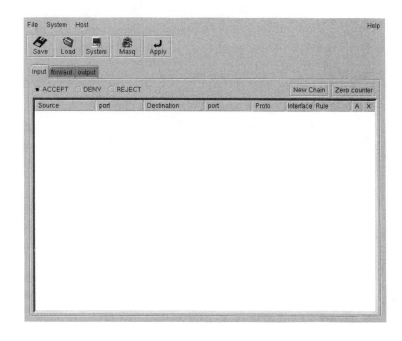

Each rule that you define in gfcc can include specifications to prevent denial-of-service attacks. The source and destination IP address and port are included in each rule as well (see Figure 37.8).

FIGURE 37.8 Each rule defined in gfcc can include all of the fields shown in this definition dialog box.

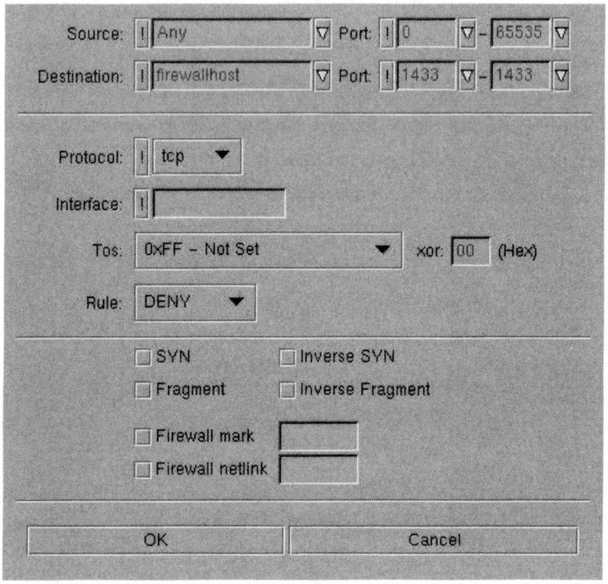

Clone
Windows NT

Every operating system has strengths and weaknesses; hence, you choose different tools for different tasks. More and more, however, I seem to be choosing Linux for just about everything. In this part, you'll learn how to use features that come with Linux that allow it to connect to your NetWare and Windows NT servers (and your Windows 95/98/2000 systems as well).

In case you already have NetWare and Windows NT servers on your network, you'll learn how to connect to those servers using their native protocols. To the NetWare or NT server, your Linux system will appear just like another Windows client, which makes it easier to interact with systems that don't know about Linux yet.

38 Clone a Windows NT Server on Linux

The ability to have your Linux system appear to others on your network as if it were a Windows NT server can make it much easier for others to accept that you are using Linux—because they won't know that you are.

Using the Samba server and its associated utilities, Linux will appear to other Windows systems (95, 98, 2000, and NT) as if it were just another Windows system. Your Linux computer appears in the Windows Network Neighborhood windows, you can share files and printers, maintain per-user password security, define shares, and so forth.

The Samba server is a project aimed at making the SMB protocol that's used by Windows available on many other systems so they can all share resources. Currently Samba is available on dozens of different Unix systems in addition to Linux. All of these systems can share files and printers with each other and with "real" Windows systems. You can learn more about the Samba project and read more detailed documentation about the information in this section by visiting the Samba organization's Web site at http://www.samba.org. Mirror sites are located worldwide.

Running a Samba server on Linux has a distinct advantage over using a real Windows NT server: Linux rarely crashes. Others on your network may not know that the Windows NT server that provides file and print sharing is actually a Linux system—they may even praise you for never having the downtime that other Windows users complain about.

Set Up a Samba Server

The Samba server suite is included with most distributions of Linux. If you didn't include the Samba package when you installed Red Hat 6 (check by using the command `rpm -q samba`), you can add it to your system from the Red Hat CD using this command:

```
rpm -Uvh /mnt/cdrom/RedHat/Rpms/samba-2.0.3-8.i386.rpm
```

In addition, the `/Binaries/Samba` directory contains rpm-format archives for various systems that you can install on your copy of Linux. Source archives are also included at `/Source/Samba` on the CD.

Depending on your Linux distribution, you may be able to set up Samba to begin working using a tool like LinuxConf (Red Hat), YAST (Suse), or COAS (Caldera OpenLinux). Once the Samba package has been installed, however, the Samba server normally starts running each time you boot your system.

The catch is that when Samba runs, if it doesn't find a valid configuration file, it stops running. You can tell whether the Samba server is running by using the following command, which searches the list of processes running on your system for those that include the letters *bd*:

```
$ ps aux | grep .mbd
root      556  0.0  2.1  1312   652  ?  S    13:46   0:00 smbd -D
root      558  0.0  1.9  1104   608  ?  S    13:46   0:00 nmbd -D
```

The two lines that show the Samba server are those ending with `smbd` and `nmbd`. These are the samba SMB server daemon and the NetBIOS daemon (which the SMB daemon uses).

If these programs are not yet running on your system, follow the configuration steps in this section. After the configuration is set up, restart the Samba server using the steps shown and run the `ps` command above to check that the server is running.

The configuration file for Samba is located in `/etc/samba.d` (for Open-Linux), in `/etc` (for Red Hat), or in a similar location, depending on your Linux distribution. When you install the binary files that match your distribution name from the CD, they will look in the correct location for your version of Linux.

The file `smb.conf` or `smb.conf.sample` is normally installed as part of the Samba package. You can begin using Samba once you have set up this file. A basic configuration may be set up already (as on Red Hat 6), but you should check the configuration as described here before using Samba.

The Samba configuration file (`smb.conf` or `smb.conf.sample`) includes a configuration line for almost every possible Samba option—and there are many options. Some of the tasks that you can perform with a Samba server include the following:

◆ Restrict connections to your server to a certain set of IP addresses

◆ Define printers on Linux that can be accessed from Windows systems

◆ Set up how the Linux Samba server announces itself to other SMB systems (such as Windows clients on your network)

◆ Use WINS for name resolution on your network

◆ Have the Linux Samba server act as a Primary Domain Controller for your network (this feature is still experimental, however)

Fortunately, a comment is included with each of the possible commands in the `smb.conf` file. (Comments are the lines that begin with "#" or with ";".) You can read the descriptions and uncomment any features that you want to try. A basic configuration for Samba includes information about how to authenticate users and what parts of your Linux system to share with clients.

In the following listing, I've pulled out all the noncomment lines from a very basic `smb.conf` file so you can see what it contains without all the comments. Your best option is to use the default configuration file that is installed with Samba on your Linux distribution. If you want to try this example directly, it's included on the CD as `/Binaries/Samba/smb.conf.compact`. The sample configuration file that follows provides for printer sharing, per-user home directory sharing, and a public area that all users can access (features that are probably part of your default setting, such as the one in Red Hat 6):

```
[global]
    workgroup = WELLS
    server string = Toshiba-Caldera-Linux-Samba Server
```

```
    printcap name = /etc/printcap
    load printers = yes
    printing = lprng

    security = user
    encrypt passwords = yes
    smb passwd file = /etc/samba.d/smbpasswd

    socket options = TCP_NODELAY
    dns proxy = no

[homes]
    comment = Home Directories
    path = %H/Public
    browseable = yes
    writable = yes
    create mask = 0750

[printers]
    comment = All Printers
    path = /var/spool/samba
    browseable = no
    guest ok = no
    writable = no
    printable = yes
    create mask = 0700

[public]
    comment = Public Stuff
    path = /home/public
    browseable = yes
    public = yes
    writable = yes
    printable = no
    write list = @users
```

A few additional steps must be performed with other Samba-related files before you can run to your Windows systems to have a look. Notice that the [homes] and [public] section define subdirectories on your Linux system.

These subdirectories must exist, or a connection intended for that resource will fail. To prepare my system to use this configuration file, I had to create the two directories that the configuration file refers to: /home/public and /home/nwells/public. You may need to log on as root to create the /home/public directory, but be certain that the Public directory is owned by the person whose home directory it is in.

Now, take a look at the [global] section to see how a few key settings there operate. The /etc/printcap file is named as the source for printers. This setting makes all logical printers on your Linux available to Windows users. You can also specify a certain Linux printer definition as the only one available for Windows users. (This is a good idea, because it allows you to manage print jobs from Windows systems independently.)

Set the workgroup line to match the Windows Workgroup that you want this system to be a part of. It should normally be in all capital letters. Set the server string line to a descriptive string about this server. I like noting the machine type and that it's a Linux server, but you can leave that part out if you prefer. (Set the string to "Windows NT Server" if you'd like to hide the fact that people are using Linux.)

The only troublesome part that remains is to configure the user security for your Samba server. Because the SMB protocol is used by systems ranging from Windows 95 to Windows 2000, differences in how passwords were implemented can cause headaches when you connect machines of many different types to your Samba server. Using encrypted passwords is always a good idea, but you may have to make a change in the Registry of some clients to enable them to use encrypted passwords. If all of your clients use unencrypted passwords, you can choose not to use them on the Samba server.

To set up the passwords so that Windows users can access the server, you must prepare an smbpasswd file, as defined in the smb passwd file line:

```
smb passwd file = /etc/smbpasswd
```

If you are running Red Hat 6, uncomment this line in your /etc/smb .conf file.

One way to set up the Samba password file is by using a few of the Samba utilities to copy your Linux user database (/etc/passwd) to the smbpasswd file. The command to do this is either mksmbpassword or convert_smbpassword, depending on your version of Samba.

To add individual users to the Samba password file, use the `smbadduser` command with a username from your Linux system. For example, I already have a user named nwells on Linux, so I can add that user to the `smbpasswd` file using this command:

```
# smbadduser nwells:nwells
```

The name after the colon (also nwells in this example) is the user account name for Windows systems, which might differ from the Linux username. After you enter this command, you are prompted to enter a password (twice) for Samba access for this user (coming from a remote client).

For any user that is part of the `smbpasswd` file, you can use the `smbpasswd` command (the command and the file have the same name) to change the password for a user.

```
# smbpasswd nwells
New SMB password:
```

You must enter the password twice to confirm it. The password is updated in the `smbpasswd` file.

The important part of setting up these users is that a matching username and password exist on both the Linux Samba server (in `smbpasswd`) and on the Windows client that attempts to connect to the server. Don't bother with the `smbusers` file that you see in the same directory. It's intended to map Linux users to Windows users, but it isn't used in this example configuration.

Your configuration is now complete. To make it take effect (and to start the Samba server if it didn't start because of a missing configuration file), use this command for Red Hat Linux:

```
# /etc/rc.d/init.d/smb restart
```

Or, for OpenLinux, use these commands:

```
# /etc/rc.d/init.d/samba stop
# /etc/rc.d/init.d/samba start
```

Similar commands should apply to all Linux systems. Go to the `/etc/rc.d/init.d` directory on your Linux system and look for a script named `smb` or `samba`. Scripts in this directory are used to stop and start system services.

Finally, run the `ps` command given previously to see if the `smbd` and `nmbd` processes are running.

Test the Samba Server

With the Samba server running, you should be able to view your Linux system from a Windows client (95, 98, NT, or 2000).

Before you can access the Linux Samba server, you should be certain that the Client for Windows Networking is installed in the Configuration tab of the Network dialog box in your Control Panel. If you can see other Windows systems in the Network Neighborhood from your Windows computer, then the Windows client is working fine.

The easiest way to access Linux Samba resources is to log in to your Windows system with a username and password that match what you configured in the smbpasswd file on Linux. Otherwise, you will have to enter the password when you attempt to access a resource on the Samba server.

To access the Linux Samba server, follow these steps:

1. On your Windows desktop, double-click the Network Neighborhood icon (this icon only shows up after your Windows networking has been set up in the Control Panel).

2. If the Linux Samba server and the Windows client are in the same workgroup, the Samba server should appear in the Network Neighborhood window, as shown in Figure 38.1 (note the server string on the left side of the figure—Brighton is actually a Linux system).

FIGURE 38.1 **A Linux Samba server appears in the Windows Network Neighborhood.**

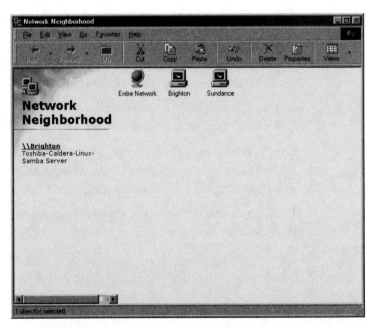

3. If the Linux Samba server is in a different workgroup, double-click the Entire Network icon and then the icon for the workgroup that the Samba server is a part of.

4. The name of the Linux Samba server is the same as the hostname of your Linux system (Brighton in these example screens).

5. If you cannot locate the Linux Samba server, choose Find ➤ Computer on your Windows Start menu and enter your Linux hostname (see Figure 38.2). Because of latency in how Linux and Windows broadcast their availability, a newly active Linux Samba server may not show up automatically in Windows for a while. You can also try pressing F5 in a Windows Explorer window to force a refresh.

FIGURE 38.2 **With new Linux Samba servers on your network, it may be necessary to use the Find Computer dialog box.**

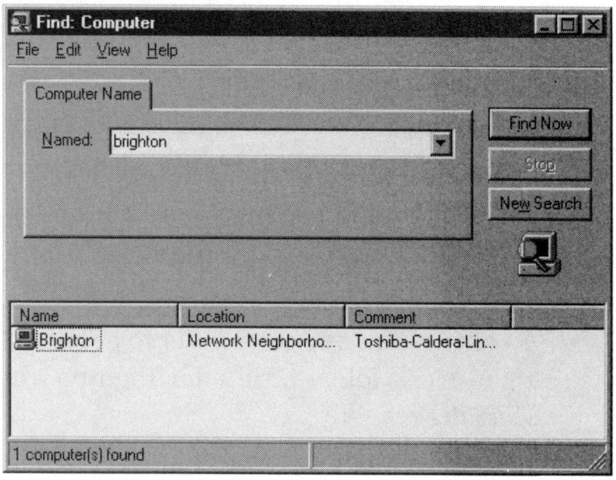

6. Once you have located the Linux Samba server, double-click its icon. The shares available on the Samba server are shown as individual icons (see Figure 38.3).

FIGURE 38.3 Each shared resource on the Linux Samba server appears as an icon in Windows.

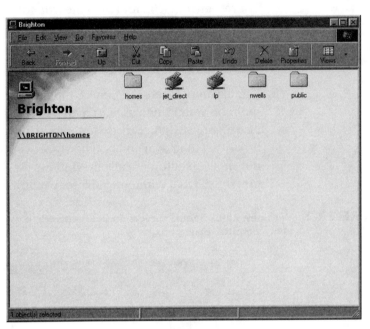

7. You can now open folders, drag and drop files to copy them, and perform other standard Windows operations on these resources that are actually located on your Linux server.

To map a Windows drive letter to a shared Linux Samba server resource, right-click a folder within the Brighton window and choose Map network drive.

In order to use the printers shown as part of the Samba server, you must add the definition for them to your Windows system by performing these steps:

1. Choose Settings ➢ Printers on the Windows Start menu.

2. Double-click the Add Printer icon in the Printers window.

3. In the Add Printer Wizard, choose Network printer.

4. In the Network path or queue name field, choose Browse and use the browsing window to select the printer definition under the Linux Samba server (see Figure 38.4).

FIGURE 38.4   You must add a printer definition in Windows before you can access a printer via the Linux Samba server.

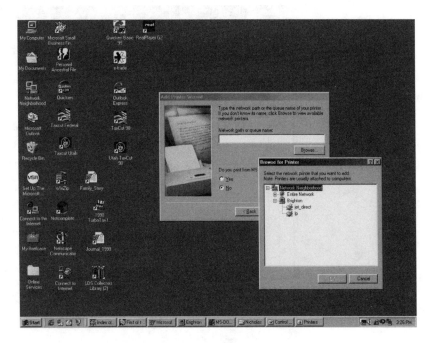

5. Select the printer model to which the Linux Samba server is printing.

6. Print a test page if you wish.

Use Graphical Configuration Tools

Given that the number of configuration options available in the Samba server continues to rise, it's fortunate that many graphical tools are now available to help configure the server without resorting to hand editing the configuration files as I've just described.

These tools are not part of the Samba suite, but they can be used to prepare or update the smb.conf file graphically.

At least one of these tools is included with a standard Linux system. The LinuxConf toolset in Red Hat Linux includes fairly comprehensive Samba set-up dialog boxes (see Figure 38.5).

As the figure shows, many fields are available for configuration, but you must know what to enter in the fields—no help is given in the form of a

FIGURE 38.5 LinuxConf includes dialog boxes to set up Samba server options.

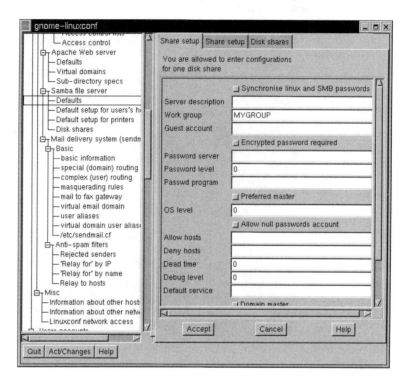

drop-down list for each field. The Help button brings up a full description of each field, however, so this can be a good way to learn about the Samba options.

Screens are provided in LinuxConf for the default settings (similar to the [global] section of the smb.conf file), as well as for disk shares and user home directory configuration. Despite its faults, having such tools available is a great step up from always having to hand edit the configuration file.

The KDE Control Center has a default window to view all active connections to the Samba server. This window simply displays the output of the smbstatus command, which you can run from any command line.

In addition to these tools for Red Hat and KDE platforms, several other utilities can help with Samba configuration. The gtksamba utility provides an attractive interface for users of the Gnome desktop in which you can set the values of parameters in the different sections of the configuration file (see Figure 38.6).

FIGURE 38.6 GTKsamba lets you set up Samba by entering parameter values for different sections of the configuration file.

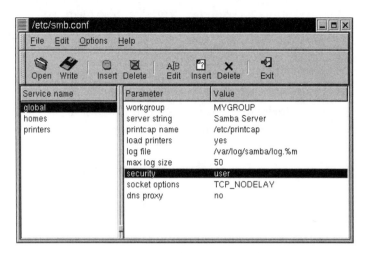

Despite the nice interface, the utility can be a little obscure. Even more than with LinuxConf, you must already know how to configure Samba before this utility will be of much help.

The GTKSamba program is located on the CD at /Binaries/Samba. You can run it with this command:

```
$ ./gtksamba
```

The source code for this package is included in the /Source/Samba directory.

39 Access Windows NT Servers from Linux

Samba gives you a powerful way to use Linux as a file and print server that all of your Windows clients can access, but many networks already make extensive use of Windows NT servers. Samba lets you connect to these Windows NT servers and other Windows systems as a client.

Using these features, you can use Windows NT as a shared file server, access shares on any Windows client (that you've been granted access to), print to a Windows printer, and so forth. These features also apply to any other system running a Samba server. For example, one Linux system can act as a client to another Linux system running as a Samba server.

As with setting up a Samba server, the surest method of accessing other SMB systems such as Windows NT is on the command line, as explained in the following sections. Graphical utilities to assist with the process are shown afterwards (see Figure 39.1).

Connect to an SMB File Server

To connect to an SMB server, including a Samba server running on any platform, use the smbclient utility. This command line utility has an interface that combines commands from the command line FTP client and a standard Linux shell. Table 39.1 shows several of the most-used commands.

TABLE 39.1 Most Used Commands for the smbclient Utility

smbclient Command	Description
help	Prints a list of all smbclient commands.
ls	Lists the files in the current directory on the remote server.
get filename	Downloads a file from the remote server, copying it to your local current working directory.
put filename	Uploads a file to the current remote directory (this requires permission to write files on the remote server).
!command	Executes a Linux command while still in the smbclient interface (for example, use !pwd to see your Linux working directory).
exit	Closes the smbclient utility.

To use the smbclient command, you need to know the name of the server you wish to connect to and the username that is valid on that server. Enter this command:

```
$ smbclient -L servername -U username

Added interface ip=192.168.100.3 bcast=192.168.100.255
  nmask=255.255.255.0
Server time is Tue Jul  6 12:44:34 1999
Timezone is UTC-6.0
Password:
Domain=[WELLS] OS=[Unix] Server=[Samba 1.9.18p8]
security=user

Server=[BRIGHTON] User=[nwells] Workgroup=[WELLS] Domain=[WELLS]

Sharename      Type        Comment
---------      ----        -------
homes          Disk        Home Directories
IPC$           IPC         IPC Service (Toshiba-Caldera-Linux-
                           Samba Server)
jet_direct     Printer
lp             Printer
nwells         Disk        Home Directories
public         Disk        Public Stuff

This machine has a browse list:
Server                 Comment
---------              -------
BRIGHTON               Toshiba-Caldera-Linux-Samba Server
This machine has a workgroup list:
Workgroup              Master
---------              -------
WELLS
$
```

When a password is requested (as on the sixth line down in the listing above), use the password for your user account on the SMB (Windows) system that you're connecting to.

As shown above, this command lists the available shares on the server that you indicated. It provides a good test to see if you can reach the SMB server. You can even leave off the -U parameter to learn about the server's public shares.

If you already know the name of the share you want to connect to, you can skip the above step and use the following command to make the connection and begin accessing the SMB system as a file server.

```
$ smbclient //sundance/d -U nwells
Added interface ip=192.168.100.3 bcast=192.168.100.255
  nmask=255.255.255.0
Server time is Tue Jul  6 12:47:04 1999
Timezone is UTC-6.0
Password:
security=share
smb: \>
```

The format is the SMB standard that begins with two forward slashes and one slash separating the server and share names. If you see the prompt, you have successfully connected to the remote SMB server. You can try some of the commands listed in Table 39.1 as you download and upload files to the SMB file server.

In addition to the basic commands in Table 39.1, many common Linux commands work in smbclient. If you have permission to create and update files on the remote server, you can use any of them, including mkdir and rmdir, rm, and del. In many cases, more than one command is provided for a function (such as ls and dir).

The smbclient utility is a great tool for connecting to remote SMB servers, including Windows NT servers, but it isn't very tightly integrated with other work that you're doing in Linux. Also, many people prefer to manage their file systems graphically, and smbclient falls short there.

Several solutions are available to correct these shortcomings. The first option you have is to use a graphical utility such as Kwin for KDE or TkSamba (which is written in tcl/Tk and should run on any Linux system).

These utilities provide a graphical interface for uploading and downloading files, much as popular FTP clients do. For example, in TkSamba, shown in Figure 39.1, you can select servers and shares, establish a connection, and then select files to work with.

FIGURE 39.1   **TkSamba can be used to graphically connect to a Samba server for file sharing.**

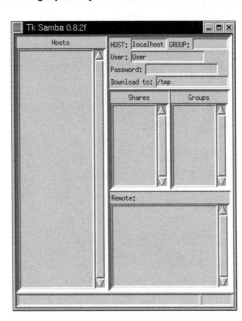

 TkSamba is included in the /Binaries/Samba directory. You can run it using this command:

```
$ ./TkSmb
```

The complete package is in the /Source/Samba directory. Because it is written in a scripting language (tcl), little is required to get it running. Using the INSTALL script in the complete package is a good way to get all the required components installed in the right locations on your system. These commands will do it (using a subdirectory I've created for tools in this part):

```
$ cd /home/nwells/part10
$ tar xvzf /mnt/cdrom/Source/Samba/TkSmb-0_8_2f_tar.gz
$ /home/nwells/part10/TkSmb-0.8.2f/INSTALL
```

Check the directories listed in the dialog box that appears and click the Install button to continue. (If you use the default locations, you'll need to be logged in as root.)

Integrate SMB into Your Linux File System

Although graphical tools can make it easier to access files on an SMB file server, you can also use other Samba utilities to completely integrate the SMB file server with your Linux file system.

If you've used the mount command before, you know that it makes another file system behave like part of your root file system. For example, when you use this command

```
# mount /mnt/cdrom
```

you can go to the /mnt/cdrom directory and access the contents of your CD-ROM drive as if they were just another part of your file system.

More complete mount commands are sometimes required, depending on how your system is set up. For example, you might access a remote NFS file server using a command like this:

```
# mount -t nfs  sundance:/home/nwells  /mnt/sundance
```

This command indicates the type of the remote file system, the remote server and path, and the locate path to use as a mount point (an access point). Of course, you must have permission to access the sundance server via NFS.

NFS works well for sharing files across Unix systems; with the Samba suite available on so many platforms, SMB is a good solution for almost all file sharing across platforms. The Samba suite of utilities includes a package called smbfs, for the SMB file system. Using this package, you can mount remote SMB file systems just as you do remote NFS file systems or local file system devices (like CD-ROM drives).

To use the smbfs features, you must have this package included on your system (it is usually included when you prepare the Samba server). You must also have support for the SMB file system loaded into your kernel. Support may be built in, or it may be included as a loadable module. If smbfs support is included as a loadable module, the following command will show it as part of your system:

```
$ lsmod | grep smbfs
smbfs60
```

If you're not certain that support for SMB file systems is available on your Linux system, enter the following command to attempt to load support into your kernel as a module.

```
$ insmod smbfs
```

Now you're ready to use the special mounting command to integrate an SMB file system into your Linux directory structure. The command is very similar to the smbclient command, but it may require additional parameters.

```
$ smbmount //sundance/c /mnt/sundance -U nwells
Password:
```

As with smbclient, enter the password for your account on the SMB server. If this command is successful, you can use the cd command to go to the mount point that you specified (/mnt/sundance in the example) and begin accessing the remote SMB file system as if it were part of your local file system.

In some cases, additional parameters may be required to make smbmount (or even smbclient) function properly. For example, you may see a message that states "my hostname too long as a netbios name." In this case, you can add your client's hostname to the command like this:

```
$ smbmount //sundance/c /mnt/sundance -U nwells -c brighton
```

The man pages for smbclient and smbmount are included with the Samba package that you install from the CD.

Once you have used the smbmount command successfully, you can use all of the standard Linux tools to work with the files on the SMB server (as long as you have permission to perform the operation you want to perform). Figure 39.2 shows a standard KDE file manager window open to a Windows 98 file system that was mounted using smbmount.

FIGURE 39.2 **SMB file servers can be accessed via standard Linux utilities after mounting with smbmount.**

![KDE file manager window showing /mnt/sundance_c/WINDOWS directory listing]

file:/mnt/sundance_c/WINDOWS/

| File | Edit | View | Bookmarks | Cache | Options | | Help |

/mnt/sundance_c/WINDOWS

My Document	Bubbles.bmp	-rwxr-xr-x root root	2118 20:01 11.05.98
Nicholas	CALC.EXE	-rwxr-xr-x root root	94208 20:01 11.05.98
Program Files	CDPLAYER.EXE	-rwxr-xr-x root root	106496 20:01 11.05.98
QUICKENW	CDROMR.EXE	-rwxr-xr-x root root	132096 14:55 17.09.98
RECYCLED	CFGMOD.EXE	-rwxr-xr-x root root	42812 12:44 22.12.94
SOFTSTUF	CHARMAP.EXE	-rwxr-xr-x root root	17408 20:01 11.05.98
TAX98	CLEANMGR.EXE	-rwxr-xr-x root root	131072 20:01 11.05.98
TaxCut96	CLIPBRD.EXE	-rwxr-xr-x root root	18432 20:01 11.05.98
WINDOWS	CLOUD.GIF	-rwxr-xr-x root root	11306 20:01 11.05.98
tmp	CLSPACK.EXE	-rwxr-xr-x root root	53248 20:01 11.05.98
sundance_d	CMD640X.SYS	-rwxr-xr-x root root	24626 20:01 11.05.98
win	CMD640X2.SYS	-rwxr-xr-x root root	20901 20:01 11.05.98
	COMMAND.COM	-rwxr-xr-x root root	93880 20:01 11.05.98
	CONFDENT.CPE	-rwxr-xr-x root root	4357 20:01 11.05.98
	CONFIG.TXT	-rwxr-xr-x root root	17468 20:01 11.05.98

Many additional utilities are provided with the Samba suite to help you access SMB file and print servers. The following table summarizes these utilities:

SAMBA UTILITY	DESCRIPTION
addtosmbpass	Adds a username to the smb password file (follow this by using the smbpasswd command to set a password for the user).
nmblookup	Queries for information about a server name using the NetBIOS protocol.
smbadduser	Creates an association between a Linux user and a user listed in the smbpasswd file (an SMB user); this utility affects the smbusers file and is for use with name mapping features.
smbprint	Submits a print job to a print queue located on an SMB server.
smbtar	Similar to Linux tar; backs up and restores Windows directories to a Linux file (or tape archive).
smbtestparm	Examines the contents of the smb.conf configuration file, providing messages for any erroneous or potentially error-causing configuration items.
smbstatus	Shows all SMB client connections (when the Linux system is acting as an SMB server).

40 Run a NetWare Server on Linux

In addition to the many Windows servers that you might want to connect to from Linux, thousands of NetWare servers are used around the world, most often for file and print sharing. You can connect to these with Linux as well.

Use NetWare for Linux

Years ago, Novell had a product called NetWare for Unix. This product was licensed to the major Unix vendors such as IBM, Hewlett-Packard, Digital, and so forth, so that they could provide a NetWare server on their Unix systems. In this environment, the NetWare server ran as a standard Unix process, though it required some special handling to provide a NetWare file system on top of a Unix file system.

Caldera Systems recently licensed NetWare 4.1 from Novell and ported it to Linux. Now you can run a real NetWare server on Linux—and none of the clients on your network will be able to tell that it's not a standard NetWare 4 server. Features of NetWare for Linux include

- NetWare 4.10b-compatible file services
- Seamless access from Windows 95, Windows 3.1, DOS, Linux, Macintosh, and UnixWare clients
- The ability to forward NetWare print jobs to Linux-hosted printers (requires the `nwclient` program discussed in the next section)
- Fully capable NDS server (version 611)
- Streams updates to the Linux kernel

The NetWare for Linux product is commercial software, licensed from Novell, so it isn't included on the CD. You can, however, download a free copy of it from the Caldera Systems Web site at `http://www.calderasystems.com/products/`. You must provide some information about yourself to complete the download. The download version is complete, including several thousand pages of Novell documentation, updated to reflect the Linux platform. The only catch is that the product only supports three users (unless you purchase additional licenses).

If you like using NetWare for Linux, you can purchase (online, if you wish) additional user licenses to extend your copy of NetWare for Linux. A CD-ROM can also be ordered if you don't want to download the large program files.

NetWare for Linux is a full-featured server product, but like NetWare for Unix, it doesn't allow you to load NetWare NLMs. File system performance will also be reduced compared to a native NetWare server running on the same hardware because of the emulation used within the Linux file system.

The major benefits of using NetWare for Linux include the following:

◆ Only one computer is needed to act as a file and print server as well as an application server.

◆ Integration of Linux-based Internet connectivity with NetWare clients is seamless because NetWare for Linux uses native IPX/SPX protocols.

◆ Linux poses no reduction in stability compared to a native NetWare server.

◆ In a network with existing NetWare servers, NetWare for Linux makes it easier to integrate Linux into the existing environment.

◆ In future releases of Novell products, adding NDS to Linux will make system administration of a Linux PC possible through the distributed NDS resource database.

All of these benefits assume, of course, that you're not trying to learn how to administer both NetWare and Linux from scratch. If you only know one of these two powerful but complex systems, you should probably stick with that one.

Use a Free NCP Server

NetWare for Linux is a commercial product. A free version of an NCP file and print server is also available. This program is called `mars-nwe`.

Although `mars-nwe` is intended to be a Linux replacement for a NetWare file server, it falls a bit short. In particular, unlike the NetWare for Linux product, `mars-nwe` is a bindery-only product—no NDS support is provided. Overall, the `mars-nwe` project doesn't seem to have the momentum behind it that many of the more impressive developments do (such as Apache, WINE, and the KDE and Gnome desktops).

 The `mars-nwe` server source is included in `/Source/NetWare`; I recommend, however, that you download the NetWare for Linux product and give that a try instead.

41 Access NetWare Servers from Linux

You may not need to create a NetWare file server running on Linux, but if you already have NetWare servers on your network, you can still access them from Linux.

Caldera Systems created a NetWare client for Linux as part of their NetWare development. This client allows you to connect to a native NetWare server to share files and printers. Some of the features of this client software are as follows:

- ◆ It's based on IPX/SPX, so the native NetWare server sees Linux as a regular DOS client. Nothing needs to be added to the NetWare server.

- ◆ The NetWare client integrates into the Linux file system. Just go to the /NetWare directory to automatically see servers and NDS trees on your network.

- ◆ The client is fully NDS-aware.

Utilities are provided for file and print sharing, allowing you to print directly to a NetWare print queue (bindery or NDS-based) and access NetWare volumes.

Utilities are also provided to let you administer a NetWare server from Linux. These utilities are both command line and graphical. One advantage of the command line NetWare utilities is that you can write scripts to perform NetWare administration tasks and then schedule the scripts to run at any time. For example, you could automatically check your file system at 2 A.M. each morning. Or, you could create a set of new user accounts after everyone leaves the office for the day (including you).

These utilities include the following:

- ◆ Changing a password
- ◆ Viewing or setting file rights
- ◆ Viewing or setting object or property rights
- ◆ Viewing or changing properties of a bindery or NDS object

◆ Creating a new NDS or bindery object

◆ Viewing a NetWare print queue

◆ Deleting a job from a print queue

Note that all of these functions are client-oriented. A complete set of server-side utilities is included with the NetWare for Linux server product.

To get the NetWare client, go to the Caldera Systems Web page at `http://www.calderasystems.com/products/` and begin to download the NetWare for Linux server. Part of that package is the NetWare client. After registering, you can choose to download only the NetWare client portion.

As with the NetWare server, a free version of the NetWare client is available. This package, called `ncpfs`, is included on the CD as a source code rpm and as a gzipped tarball at `/Source/NetWare`. The binary package (in rpm format) is located at `/Binaries/NetWare`. This package provides bindery-emulation (NetWare 3) access to NetWare servers from Linux.

By using `ncpfs`, you can mount a NetWare volume in Linux much as `smb-mount` allows you to mount an SMB file share. The NetWare client from Caldera is more full-featured and is automounting, but for those who prefer to avoid commercial software, `ncpfs` is a good choice.

Use Linux as a Business Server

When you set up a Linux system in an office environment, you may need a special set of tools to make it into a business server. These might include things like financial tools, virus scanners for incoming e-mail, and software to create a fax server on Linux. This part describes these Linux tools, some of which are free and some of which are commercial or shareware.

42 Check E-mails for Viruses

Sadly, e-mail viruses are in the news more and more. Linux is not adversely affected by most of these because the viruses propagate themselves as DOS/Windows programs or macros to popular Windows applications. If users were careful not to open attachments that looked suspicious in any way or were from unknown persons, the growth of viruses would decrease dramatically. However, that doesn't appear likely to happen. And while Linux itself is rarely affected by viruses, many times viruses are stored on a Linux e-mail server before being downloaded to an unsuspecting client.

The tools in this section can help you check e-mail attachments on your local system or at the e-mail server before they are downloaded and infect a client system. All three of these packages are included on the CD, but they have different licenses, which are noted as each is described.

The AntiVir program comes from the German company H+BEDV Detentechnik GmbH. It is easy to use and can be run as part of a script to check e-mail attachments for all users on a Linux mail server.

The program is in binary format. Two files are included on the CD, both located at /Binaries/Business. The archive avlglibc uses the latest C libraries for Red Hat 6, OpenLinux 2.2, Suse 6, and so forth; for older versions running version 5 of the C libraries (this would be the case for OpenLinux 1.2, Red Hat releases before 5, and so forth), use the archive avllib5. After unpacking the program archive, run the install.sh script to prepare the binary program:

```
# ./install.sh
```

Answer Y to the query to create a symbolic link; this creates a link in the /usr/bin directory so that the AntiVir program can be executed from any command line.

Once the AntiVir program is installed, it can be run from a command line, specifying the directory to check for viruses. Because the standard storage area on a Linux server for incoming e-mail messages is /var/spool/mail, you might use this command to check e-mail on your Linux mail server:

```
# antivir "/var/spool/*" -s
```

The quotation marks are important. By using them, the wildcard "*" is passed to the AntiVir program rather than being expanded by the shell before starting AntiVir.

Output from AntiVir is shown on the console. You can redirect that output to a file using standard Unix redirections (the > or | characters).

AntiVir can be used free of charge for private use. Some of the features of the program, however, are not available until you have registered with the software vendor and received a license key. This is still free, but it lets the vendor know who is using the software. Instructions for obtaining the license key via e-mail, as well as descriptions of additional AntiVir features, can be found in the README file. When you have a license key, you can use the following options:

◆ Don't follow symbolic links outside the current file system

◆ Don't follow any symbolic links

◆ Use quiet mode (suppress verbose output)

Another virus checking program is the McAfee VirusScan Validate program. This is a commercial product that is released for Linux as shareware. If you decide this product meets your needs and want to continue using the product after your 30-day trial, you should contact McAfee at http://www.mcafeemall.com and arrange to pay the fee of $200. Details are included in the README.1st file.

In the meantime, let's have a look at what the program offers. The archive nlxb318e.tar is located on the CD at /Binaries/Business. This archive includes two subdirectories, one for the a.out binary and one for the ELF binary. (Use the ELF binary unless you're running a copy of Linux that's more than two years old.)

Once you have unpacked the archive, run the `install-vscan` script for the version you choose to run (a.out or ELF) to install the Linux virus-scanning program:

```
# ./install-vscan
```

The uvscan binary file is installed in the `/usr/local/bin` directory. This is the program file that actually scans for viruses. To execute it, simply include the file name you wish to scan (or a wildcard to check all files in a directory). Uvscan can check both Linux and Windows files for viruses:

```
# /usr/local/bin/uvscan *
```

Some of the command line options available with uvscan include

◆ Clean infected files, if possible

◆ Delete infected files

◆ Check files based on their file extension

◆ Ignore compressed files

◆ Descend into subdirectories

◆ Look for macro viruses with varying levels of sensitivity

You can see all of the options by using this command:

```
# uvscan --help | less
```

One of the more interesting options is `--virus-list`. This option causes uvscan to print the list of virus variants that it can search for. I counted 12,478 items in the list (many are simple numeric codes, but you'll recognize some of the names).

43 Do Calculations in Linux

To some people, a computer is nothing but an expensive calculator. Yet, unless they already have a spreadsheet open, most people still run for their handheld calculator when they need to work with some figures. This section describes a few of the fancy calculators that are available for Linux.

Many of these are specialized tools for financial wizards, computer science majors, chemists, and so forth. Being none of these myself, I'll let you explore the more esoteric Greek symbols on your own.

Perform Financial Calculations

A good financial calculator is a must when you don't have a spreadsheet open (or if you don't know all the right formulas). Linux can run a simple mortgage computation or a quantitative financial analysis of your equities.

Mcalc is a simple but attractive mortgage calculator that prepares an amortization table (a schedule of payments showing principle and interest each month). The schedule is saved to disk, but it's also viewable on screen. Figure 43.1 shows the interface of mcalc.

FIGURE 43.1   Mcalc **uses a simple but effective interface to show mortgage amortization tables.**

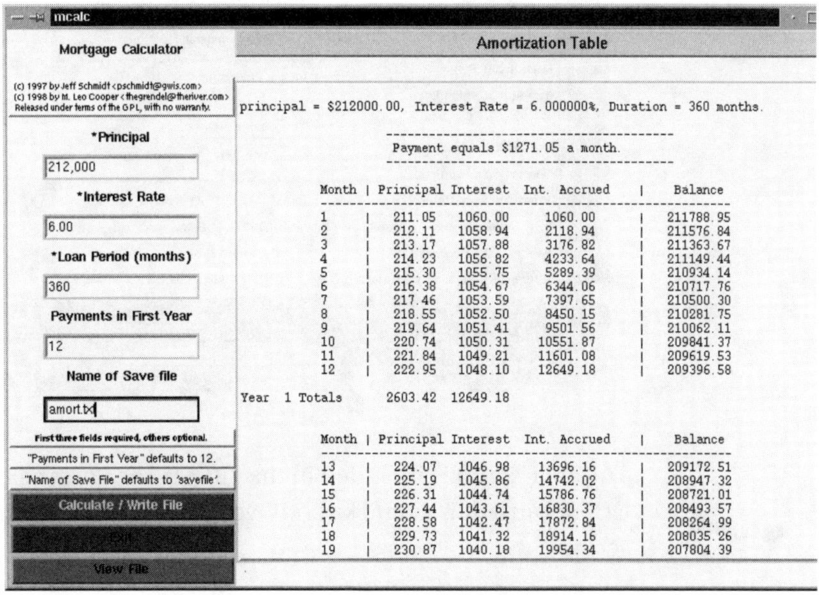

You can use the file that mcalc creates within other programs, such as a spreadsheet or word processor. The mcalc program is written in tcl/Tk but also has a C component, so the standard make command is used to prepare the source code to run. (You can also just run the ./mcalc program

immediately after unpacking the archive.) `Mcalc` is located on the CD at
`/Binaries/Business`.

Another mortgage calculation tool written in tcl/Tk is `mort`. This program
lets you enter additional principal payments and see the effect on your
total payment time and interest payments. You can run multiple scenarios
and track the results in a separate window (see Figure 43.2).

FIGURE 43.2 Mort **lets you track the effect of additional principal payments.**

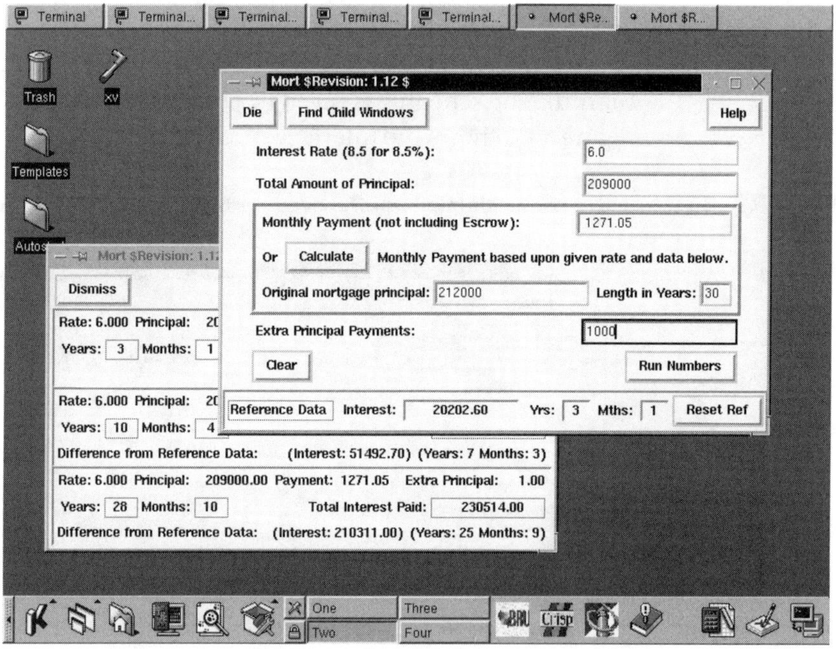

The `mort` script is included in the `/Binaries/Business` directory on the
CD. Because it is a tcl/Tk script, you don't need to compile it; just run the
script:

```
$ ./mort
```

If the program won't run, you may need to change the first line of the file to
point to your wish tcl/Tk interpreter. For example, change the line from

```
#!/usr/local/bin/wish
```

to

```
#!/usr/bin/wish
```

Analyze Your Stocks

If you find all this discussion of mortgage calculations a little boring, you should try the `tsinvest` package to do some serious financial analysis of your stock portfolio.

`Tsinvest` runs a simulation to determine the optimal gains that you can achieve from a portfolio of multiple equity investments. The program determines which equities to invest in from a set that you provide by calculating the instantaneous Shannon probability and statistics for all of the equities. A statistical estimation technique is then used to estimate the accuracy of the calculated statistics for the equities.

This is serious investment work. You may want to consult the `tsinvest` home page at `http://www2.inow.com/~conover/ntropix` for more information. The `README` file included with the package is also a good source of information (though it assumes you are familiar with some stock trading terms and techniques). `Tsinvest` is located on the CD at `/Source/Business`.

Information about the stocks that you want to analyze is stored in the `stocks` file in the `tsinvest` directory. A set of old stock data is included in the source code package as a sample for analysis. The format of the stock information is described in the documentation. Additional stock information can be obtained from `http://www.ai.mit.edu/stocks.html`. A few lines of the stock information are shown here:

```
960430    TRW     93.875
960430    TSNG    9.625
960430    TTC     31.875
960430    TUG     5.250
960430    TWMC    5.000
960430    TWN     23.125
960430    TWX     40.875
960430    TX      85.500
960430    TXN     56.500
960430    UAL     215.500
960430    UK      45.500
960430    USG     26.125
960430    USRX    156.500
```

A man page for tsinvest is also included in the tsinvest directory. A few sample commands taken from the README file are shown in the following table:

COMMAND	DESCRIPTION OF ACTION
$ tsinvest -d 1 -i -s -t stocks	Analyzes the portfolio in the stocks file with an algorithm that is similar to human "graph watching."
$ tsinvest -d 2 -i -s -t stocks	Analyzes the stocks in the stocks file with a "high volatility" algorithm, similar to "noise trading."
$ tsinvest -d 5 -i -s -t stocks	Analyzes the stocks with a "persistence" algorithm.
$ tsinvest -v	Prints the command line options available in the program.

Perform Scientific Calculations

Some programs for Linux focus on imitating popular handheld calculators, such as the old Hewlett-Packard HP-67 or TI-30. Others branch out with their own designs. These calculator programs are programmatically very simple; most can be prepared from the source code with the single command:

```
$ make
```

Binary files are also provided on the CD for most of these programs, as noted in each description that follows.

Several of the programs described in this section use the Reverse Polish Notation (RPN) system. This system is likely familiar to you if you've used any of the popular HP calculators (other than the business-oriented models). If you've never seen one, an RPN calculator is odd: it has no "=" button. Instead, you use Enter to "push" numbers into a series of registers, then press operations keys (like "+" or "1/x") to perform actions on the numbers in the registers. One of the registers is the display. I'll walk through a couple of sample calculations with an RPN calculator to demonstrate.

The HP-67 is an old RPN calculator that includes many useful functions. It's a character-mode application. The source package is located at /Source /Business on the CD. The source package includes the binaries as well, but you can just use the two binary files, hp67 and hp67.static, in /Binaries /Business.

After unpacking the archive, run the program hp67 (or hp67.static if you have trouble with the libraries on your system). You can also compile the program from source code if you prefer:

```
#  ./hp67
```

The calculator appears as a full-screen (80x25) character display (see Figure 43.3).

FIGURE 43.3   **The HP-67 emulator includes many functions in a simple character-mode interface.**

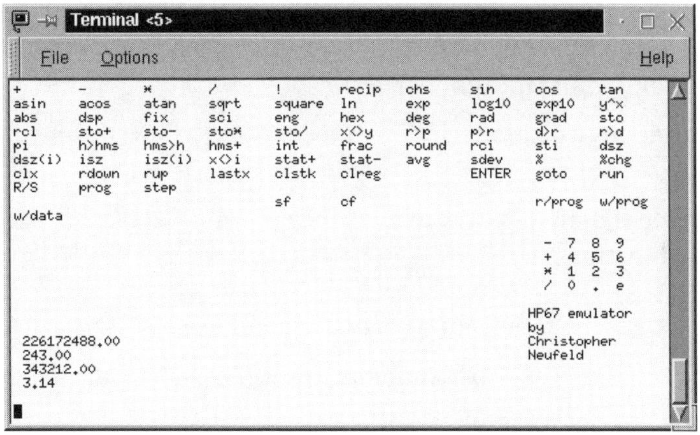

To begin using the calculator, type in a number and press Enter. The number moves to a line above. Then type a second number and press Enter. This number also moves up one line, and the first number scrolls up. To add these two numbers together, press the "+" key. The two numbers are added and placed in the lower line.

If you think of each line as a register, the function of the plus sign can be stated as "add together the contents of the X and Y registers and place the result in register X." This method gives you a lot of flexibility when completing involved or complex calculations. It also makes it easier to keep track of exactly what numbers are part of the calculation (once you become familiar with it).

The HP-67 emulator includes 10 registers. You can see them scroll up the screen as you work or shift down as operations are completed. To complete any of the operations, type in the descriptive name and press Enter. For example, to compute the cosine of the bottom register, type **cos** and press Enter.

The pcalc calculator is used from the command line. It is a programmer's calculator, intended mostly to help with doing simple math operations with hexadecimal, octal, or binary numbers. Pcalc is located on the CD at /Source/Business. The binary program is located at /Binaries/Business.

To use pcalc, you enter a command line that includes the expression you need to calculate. Output from every calculation is shown in decimal, hexadecimal, and binary formats. Here are a few examples. To convert a number between formats, just enter the number, as shown in the following table:

TASK	COMMAND IN PCALC	RESULTS
Convert a number between formats (just enter the number)	$ pcalc 0x300	768 0x300 0y1100000000
Add together two hexadecimal numbers	$ pcalc 0x1234 + 0x3e	4914 0x1332 0y1001100110010
Complete square root, trig, or similar functions	$ pcalc sqrt 625	25 0x19 0y11001

Other features of pcalc include:

- Mixes different bases (hex, decimal, etc.) in one expression
- Defines variables
- Uses standard math constants (such as *pi* and *e*)
- Uses built-in math functions like sin, cos, exp, and log.
- Uses calculation scripts—files composed of multiple lines of pcalc instructions.

The pcalc README file includes more details about the features of this programmer's tool.

Another RPN calculator is Dcalc. Dcalc uses a character-mode interface similar to the HP-67 emulator. It is shown in Figure 43.4.

FIGURE 43.4 Dcalc **is an RPN calculator that uses a full-screen character display.**

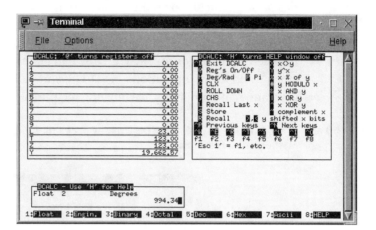

Dcalc is located on the CD at /Source/Business and /Binaries/Business. While other calculators usually include storage registers, Dcalc shows these registers on-screen above the standard working registers. The registers and the help window can each be turned off if you prefer to work with a clearer screen.

To exit Dcalc, press Q and confirm by pressing Y.

A graphical program that is included with nearly every Linux distribution is xcalc. (It is included at /Binaries/Business in case you don't have it installed on your Linux system.) Figure 43.5 shows the interface to this basic scientific calculator. (Notice that an "=" sign is included!)

FIGURE 43.5 Xcalc **is a scientific calculator that is included with nearly every Linux distribution.**

A more refined graphical scientific calculator is `kcalc`, part of the KDE Utilities package (included on the CD at `/Binaries/KDE`). This calculator is available in the Utilities menu on a standard KDE installation, or on the Utilities submenu under KDE Menus if you're using Gnome on Red Hat 6 and have installed the KDE portion. KCalc, shown in Figure 43.6, includes memory storage and logical operations (AND, OR, and so forth), in addition to the common math functions like tangent, reciprocal, and exponential.

FIGURE 43.6 Kcalc **is included with the KDE Utilities package. It includes hexadecimal and mathematical features.**

Looking at the other end of the spectrum, the `mpc` algebraic calculator is perfect for those fans of the `vi` text editor who don't want anything but a command prompt interfering with their work.

The `mpc` calculator is located at `/Binaries/Business`. When you start it, you see nothing but a ":" prompt. At this prompt, you enter expressions to calculate, as shown here.

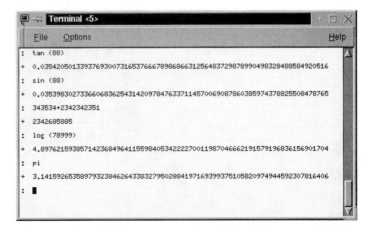

As you can see, the default precision shown should be enough for most calculations (73 significant digits). Unfortunately, no commas are used as thousands separators.

For more information about how to use the mpc calculator, enter the command **help**. To end the program, enter the command **quit** or **exit**, or press Ctrl+C.

44 Create a Linux Fax Server

One of the most useful devices in your office is probably your fax machine. By using some simple software and your modem, Linux can act as a fax server, replacing or augmenting the capabilities and capacity of your current fax machine.

Depending on the features of your modem, a Linux fax server can receive faxes for multiple users on your system, delivering them to each individual. It can also allow anyone on your network to fax a document through a single modem connected to your Linux computer.

In addition to fax server software, which controls your modem and may be able to manage incoming and outgoing faxes for multiple users, separate fax viewing utilities are available. These permit users to view a file in the fax graphics format on screen, printing the document only when needed or saving the file for future reference.

Most of the freely available fax server programs (and some of the commercial ones) are based on the HylaFax package. This package is powerful but not especially easy to use; hence, many developers have used it as a base but attempted to build an easy-to-use interface on top of it.

The HylaFax package is included as source code on the CD at /Source/ Business. Two binary packages are also included: a Red Hat package in rpm format (you can try it on other platforms as well) and a generic Linux binary in tar.gz format. These are located at /Binaries/Business. The easiest way to get HylaFax installed if you're using Red Hat 6 or another

Linux system that supports rpm is by using the following command. (I've found the `--nodeps` option on the rpm command helpful in some cases, but I didn't include it here because it's best not to use it if you can help it.)

```
rpm -Uvh /mnt/cdrom/Binaries/Business/hylafax-4_0p123rh5_
    i386.rpm
```

If you use the generic Linux binary package (`/Binaries/Business/hylafax-i386-linux-v4_0p12-1_tar.gz`), be aware that it is designed to be copied to your root directory and unpacked while you're logged in as root. This copies all the files into the correct system directories, but it's a little unusual for a tar archive.

Once you have HylaFax installed, you can use a front-end package like Tkhylafax, located at `/Source/Business` on the CD. This tcl/Tk script provides a graphical front end to the most basic capabilities of HylaFax. To run Tkhylafax you must run the make program, even though the program is a script. In some cases, you may even need to change the execute permission on the script. Try these commands:

```
cp /mnt/cdrom/Source/Business/tkhylafax-3_2beta_tar.gz /home/
    nwells/part11
cd /home/nwells/part11
tar xvzf tkhylafax-3_2beta_tar.gz
cd tkhylafax
make
chmod a+x tkhylafax
./tkhylafax
```

Other faxing tools include Khylafax (for KDE) and Efax, both located on the CD at `/Source/Business`, and Gnokii, which is an interface for Nokia cell phones with faxing features. The Gnokii program is provided in source and binary format. Source code in tar and rpm format is located at `/Source/Business`; the binary, in rpm format, is located at `/Binaries/Business`.

NOTE The Nokia tool, the G3 fax viewer, and FaxMail are provided "as is" for users to try, so be aware that they will require some tinkering.

The G3 fax viewer lets you view faxes that have arrived at your Linux system in a fax format (these sometimes have the file extension .001, for example). Not only does G3 let you view the faxes that you have received as graphical files, but it also lets you print them out to PostScript. Once a fax has been converted to PostScript, it can be printed on paper or used in many other programs that can use PostScript files.

The G3 fax view and PostScript converter is located on the CD at /Source/ Business.

FaxMail enables you to send faxes from your Linux computer via e-mail, with the resulting message being delivered to a fax number that you enter. You can attach files to the e-mail message, include other documents, and so forth. The entire e-mail message is automatically converted to PostScript and sent to the fax machine you indicate.

Figure 44.1 shows the main screen of FaxMail. The program is included on the CD at /Source/Business.

FIGURE 44.1 FaxMail **lets you send a message and other attached files via e-mail to a recipient's fax machine.**

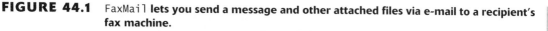

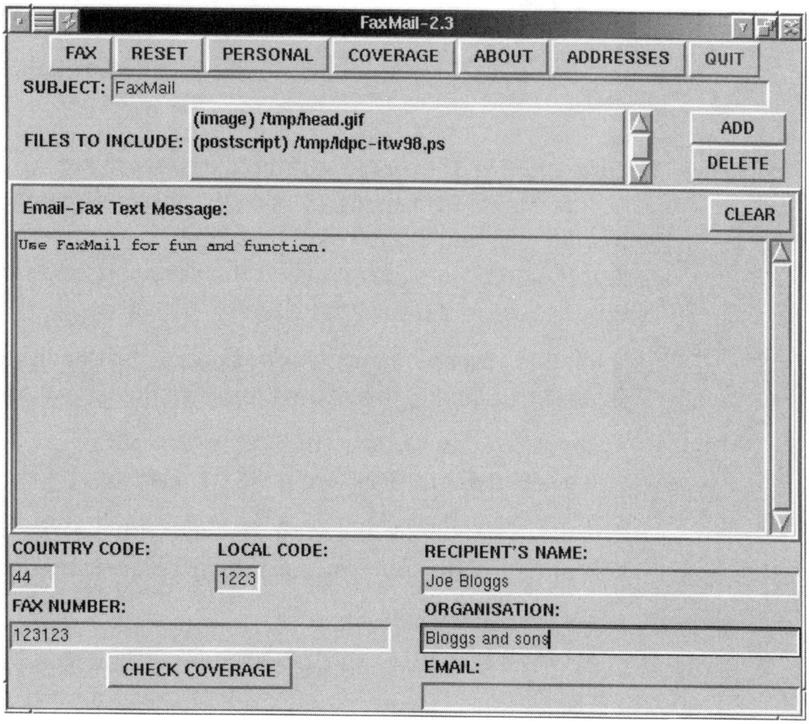

Although `HylaFax` is a well-known and popular package for sending faxes in Linux via your modem, the `Mgetty+Sendfax` package is also useful for this purpose. It is located on the CD at `/Source/Business`. The `TkFax` package provides a graphical interface to the `Mgetty+Sendfax` back end.

You can both send and receive faxes using `Mgetty+Sendfax` and the `TkFax` interface. The `TkFax` program is a tcl/Tk script and is located on the CD at `/Binaries/Business` (see Figure 44.2).

FIGURE 44.2 TkFax **provides a graphical interface to the** Mgetty+Sendfax **package.**

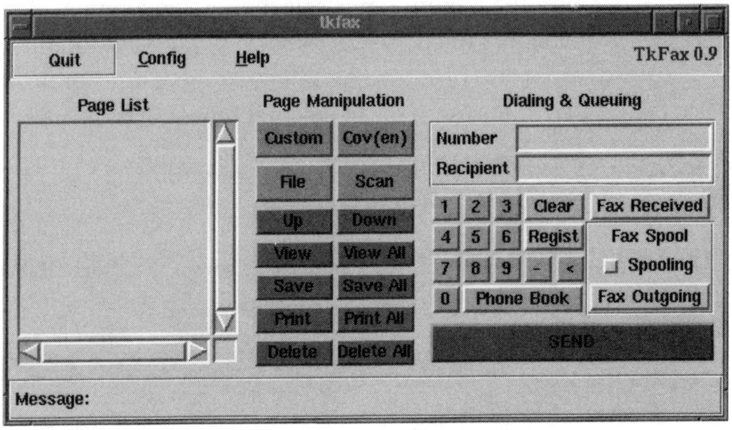

To get the `TkFax` program running, unpack the archive (which is named `tkscanfax-0_91_tar.gz`). The script files are set up to expect that you'll put the program in the `/usr/local/lib` directory. If you don't want to do that (I didn't), you'll need to edit the `tkfax` and `tkscan` files so that they only appear in the current directory instead of `/usr/local/lib`.

To do this, just open the `tkfax` or `tkscan` file (depending on whether you're scanning or faxing) in a text editor. Find the lines that look like this:

```
set fax(libdir) /usr/local/lib/tkscanfax
set c(libdir) /usr/local/lib/tkscanfax
```

Change them to look like the following, with a period to indicate the current directory (the one you start the program from):

```
set fax(libdir) .
set c(libdir) .
```

Because users often need to scan a document before using faxing software to send it from their Linux system, the TkScan program is also included with the TkFax package. This scanning package uses a standard scanner interface, though it probably won't work with all Linux-compatible scanners. The main window of TkScan is shown in Figure 44.3. Both TkFax and TkScan are scripts and so do not need to be compiled before running them.

FIGURE 44.3 TkScan **lets you scan in documents (or anything else) to be faxed using Linux faxing tools.**

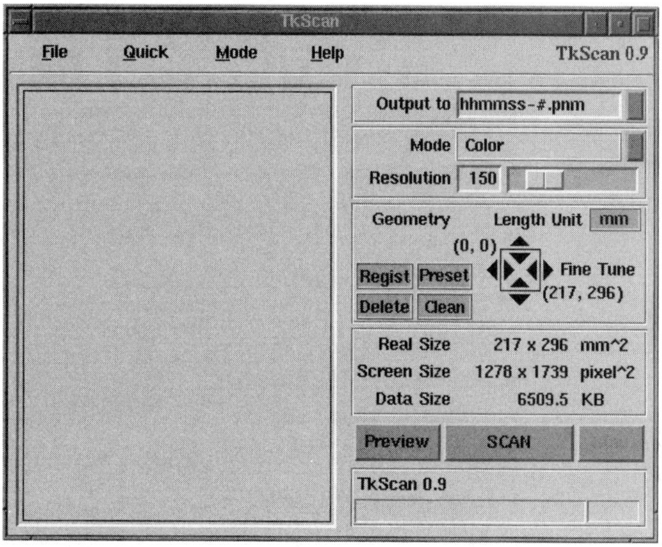

For more information about these two programs, you can check the home page for TkFax and TkScan at http://muon.kaist.ac.kr/~hbkim/linux/tkscanfax/.

One final faxing tool is xfax, a graphical program that allows you to both send faxes through a back end like Mgetty+Sendfax and view incoming faxes on-screen.

 Xfax is located on the CD at /Source/Business. It requires the xforms package, which is included as an rpm in /Binaries/Extras.

45 Share Information

Computers provide many methods of communication, though the most common for most people is e-mail. An Internet system that can be very useful for person-to-person communication is the Talk protocol. Talk is like an IRC chat room. When you know that a person is logged in to the network, you initiate a talk session by requesting a connection. After the connection is established, you "talk" by typing in messages that are communicated in real-time to the other person.

Several programs for using Talk are available for Linux. Gtalk and Ktalk (for KDE, as you've probably guessed) are both included on the CD at /Source/Business.

Ktalk is a graphical program that features

- ◆ An address book
- ◆ A command to test how fast the connection is
- ◆ Buffered output to avoid blocking other activity when you have a slow network connection
- ◆ Text manipulation, including word-wrap as you type, and copy/paste from other windows
- ◆ The ability to transfer a file to the person you are talking with by dragging an icon from a file manager (kfm) window

Ktalk can use the Ktalkd daemon to establish connections or the standard talkd daemon that Linux always includes. If you use Ktalkd, a message dialog box appears when you are receiving a message (that is, someone is trying to contact you). You can answer the message to establish a connection or ignore the dialog box.

Another "talking" utility is Speakfreely. This program enables you to hold a voice conversation over the Internet, just like the Internet Phone products that are now for sale around the world do. The quality of the voice and the speed that you can talk are determined by how much throughput your connection provides, but if your connection isn't fast enough for a regular conversation, several forms of data compression are available to help out. Encryption using DES, IDEA or PGP is also supported.

Speakfreely is also available for Windows, so all the people you talk with don't need to have Linux installed. To learn more about the program, visit the home page at http://www.fourmilab.ch/. Speakfreely is located on the CD at /Source/Business. To compile Speakfreely, you'll need to edit the Makefile, uncommenting the three flags set in the Linux section beginning on line 68 (after the explanatory notes).

If voice communication is not sufficient, several videoconferencing systems are available on Linux. Two are included on the CD: Confman and QSeeMe.

Confman is a huge package of about 10MB. It is located on the CD at /Source/Business/Confman is used to initiate and administer online conferences across the Internet using the "mbone" tools (vat, vic, nv, wb). Confman doesn't handle the multimedia data itself, but it helps a user plan, set up, and control a conference. More detailed information is available on the Confman home page at http://www.rvs.uni-hannover/confman.

Q-SeeMe is a videoconferencing client for Linux that uses the same protocols as the CU-SeeMe programs on Windows and Macintosh. Using Q-SeeMe, you can participate in a videoconference with users on these other systems. Q-SeeMe supports sending and receiving video using grayscale, JPEG, or H263. Audio conferencing is also supported.

More information about Q-SeeMe is available on the home page at http://www.pangea.org/~mavilar/qseeme/qseeme.html. The program is located on the CD at /Source/Business.

TeamWave Workplace is a groupware-type application designed to facilitate Internet communication for collaborating on projects, distance learning, or similar needs. Linux, Macintosh, Windows, and other Unix platforms are supported, so all members of a team can collaborate and share information using this product, regardless of their preferred platform.

TeamWave Workplace is located on the CD at /Binaries/Business. Note, however that the CD contains a 30-day demo copy for evaluation. You will need to contact the product's vendor at http://www.teamwave.com/ to learn more about obtaining a full copy if this product is one you are interested in. The cost is a minimal $99.00.

NOTE The conferencing software tools—SpeakFreely, Confman, Q-SeeMe, and TeamWave Workplace—require special hardware and/or configuration steps not detailed here. See the documentation included with each package for more information. We're providing these packages "as is" for users to try.

Both Gnome and KDE include nice utilities to manage personal contacts and information. These include the Gnome Personal Information Manager (PIM), and the utilities in KDE: kalendar and kab, which is the KDE address book. Beyond these, you can use the KOrganizer, part of the KOffice suite for KDE.

KOrganizer is a complete online day planner, with task lists, calendars, and many features similar to Microsoft Outlook. The initial screen of KOrganizer is shown in Figure 45.1. This program is part of the KDE distribution, located on the CD at /Binaries/KDE. If you're using KDE or have included the KDE submenu on Gnome in Red Hat 6, the Applications menu includes an Organizer item, which is actually KOrganizer.

FIGURE 45.1 KOrganizer **is a complete online day planner similar to Microsoft Outlook.**

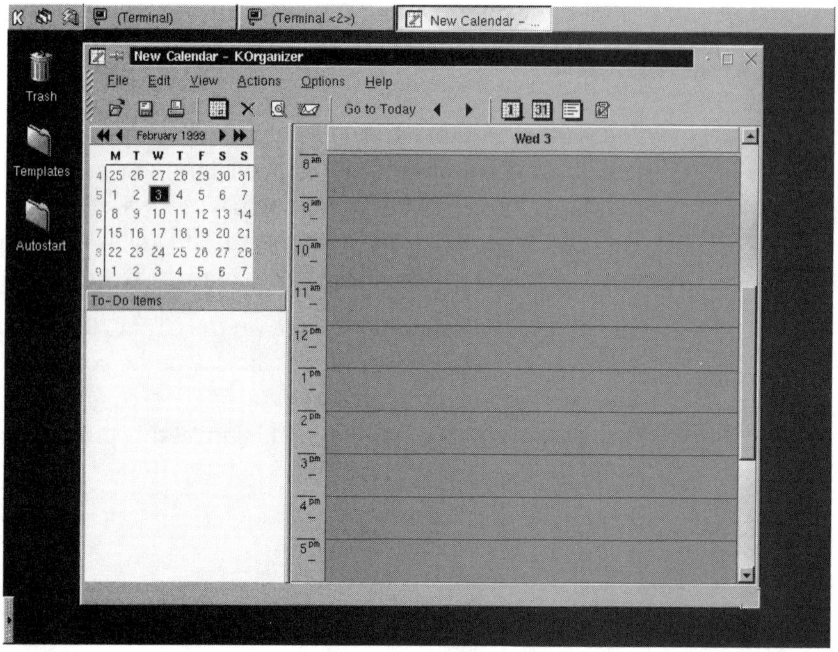

If you use many tools to communicate for business, you might also enjoy using IglooFTP. This program is similar to the FTP interface that many users are familiar with from Windows FTP programs. Unfortunately, Linux users often use Netscape Communicator or another browser to download files via FTP but must resort to the command line to upload files to another server or colleague.

IglooFTP provides a very nice interface in which you can connect to an FTP server, browse the file system of your local Linux system and the remote FTP site, then upload and download files to the directory you choose. IglooFTP is based on the GTK+ libraries, so it will work fine with Gnome platforms like Red Hat 6; KDE platforms will require the addition of GTK+ libraries. The IglooFTP package is located on the CD at /Binaries/ Business as an rpm-format binary. Figure 45.2 shows the main window of IglooFTP. Just use the rpm command to install the package, then execute the command IglooFTP.

FIGURE 45.2   IglooFTP **provides a very nice interface for downloading and uploading files to FTP servers.**

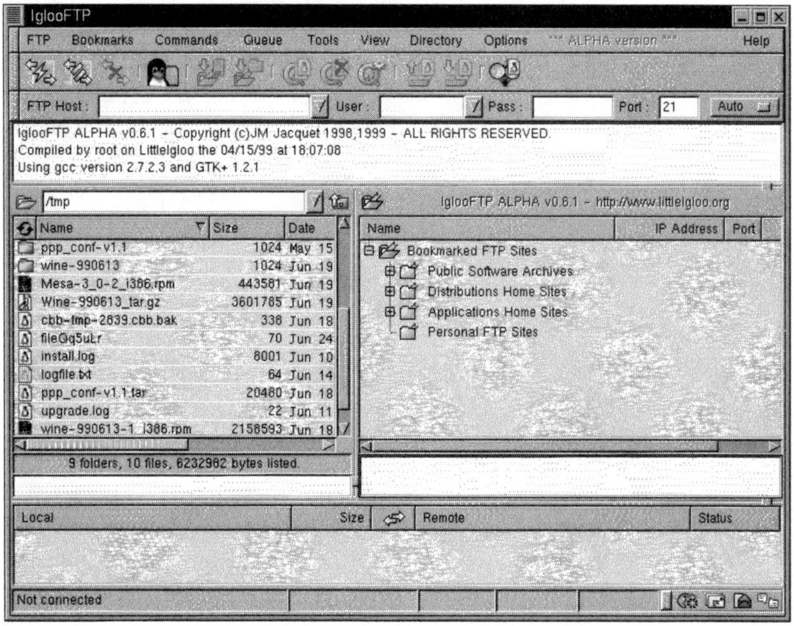

IglooFTP also includes many configuration options, including caching, browser launching to view files on an FTP site, viewer/file-type associations, and a fully configurable graphical appearance. The Preferences dialog box (see Figure 45.3) shows just a few of these options.

FIGURE 45.3   User Preferences for IglooFTP include the ability to cache documents, cross a firewall, and define viewer applications based on file types.

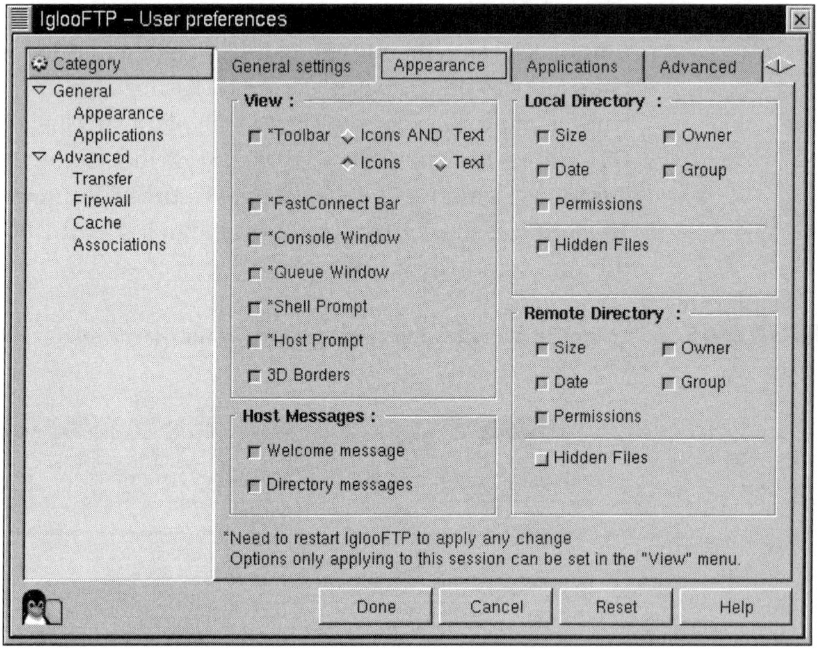

Disaster-Proof Your System

I don't want to be a pessimist, but the saying goes that there are two types of people: those who have had a hard disk failure and those who will have a hard disk failure. Now that your Linux system is loaded down with new toys and utilities, you should think about how to protect it from the inevitable disaster that will strike your PC.

This part describes some tools and procedures you can use to safeguard the valuable information on your Linux system, and it covers some basics about backing up your system and creating a rescue disk. But it also describes some of the more advanced disaster-proofing tools, such as how to set up software RAID (redundant hard disks) and connect an uninterruptible power supply to your Linux system.

If you're an experienced system administrator, you may note the folly of the term disaster-proof. Even so, the more preparations you make, the more trouble you can withstand and still come off the hero instead of the scapegoat.

46 Back Up Critical Files

Backing up a computer system is like buying insurance: no one wants to do it, but everyone eventually regrets it if they don't. Many full-featured backup utilities are included with Linux distributions or available from third-party software vendors.

The best backup utilities let you do things like

- ◆ Back up multiple remote systems from a single location
- ◆ Back up data to devices (such as CD writers or tape drives) located anywhere on your network
- ◆ Configure incremental backups (on only new or modified files) and full backups at specific time intervals
- ◆ Help you track the physical backup media in case you need to restore something
- ◆ Allow you to restore only certain files, based on multiple criteria
- ◆ Do all this in an intuitive (perhaps graphical) environment

Be certain to check the hardware compatibility list on your Linux vendor's Web site before purchasing a backup device such as a tape drive or writable CD drive. Not all devices are supported by Linux—for example, Universal Serial Bus (USB) devices and Winmodems can't be used with Linux. Once you get a backup device configured, some of the commercial backup tools you can use on Linux include

- ◆ ARKEIA, a centralized backup/restore/archiving solution for heterogeneous networks (see `http://www.knox-software.com/`)
- ◆ BRU Backup and Restore Utility (see `http://www.estinc.com`)
- ◆ Ctar, a powerful commercial backup program (see `http://www.unitrends.com`)
- ◆ Lone-Tar, a tape backup software package from Lone Star (see `http://www.cactus.com`)

A complete backup solution is often included with Linux products. An example is the BRU package that is included with Caldera OpenLinux and integrated with the default KDE Application menu (see Figure 46.1).

FIGURE 46.1 BRU is a commercial backup utility included with some versions of Linux.

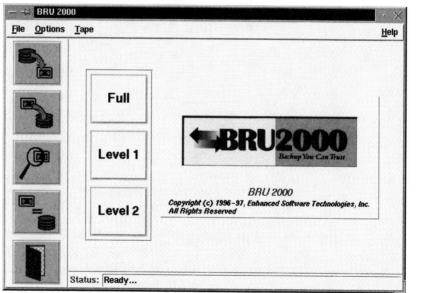

Use tar for Simple Backups

Linux has the inherent networking power to make many of these backup features easy to implement. In fact, once you become familiar with some basic Linux utilities, you can do a lot of quality system backup without resorting to additional third-party programs.

The Linux tar utility is a simple way to archive files to a separate device, such as a tape backup or floppy disk, or to another file (which should be located on a separate or remote hard disk).

You have probably been using tar throughout this book to unpack the archives stored on the CD. It's very easy to use tar to create your own archives.

For example, suppose you want to back up all the files in your /home directory. This would include the home directories for all users on your system. (You must be logged in as root to access these files to perform a backup.) Using the tar command, all of the files in /home are stored in a single compressed file called home_archive.tgz (TGZ is a standard extension for a compressed tar archive).

```
# tar cvfz home_archive.tgz /home
```

Each of the options in this example is described in the following table.

TAR OPTION	DESCRIPTION
c	Creates a new archive
v	Verbose mode
f	Indicates the name of the archive file to operate on
z	Compresses the tar archive using gzip

Notice that the options used with tar don't have to include the hyphen that precedes options used with most Linux commands.

Other options allow flexibility of where tar stores your archive file. For example, if you use the name of a device instead of a filename, you can store the archive directly to a floppy disk, tape drive, or writable CD-ROM drive:

```
# tar cvfz /dev/fd0 /home
```

```
# tar cvfz /dev/tape /home
# tar cvfz /dev/cdrom /home
```

If your /home directory is a little large to fit on a single floppy disk, use the M option to scan multiple volumes. The tar command will prompt you to insert another disk as each one is filled. (You might check the size of the /home directory with the du command to see if you have enough disks—and patience—for this operation.)

```
# tar cvfzM /dev/fd0 /home
```

When using tar to create an archive file, the last part of the command indicates what to include in the archive. For example, if you just want to combine three large files for more convenient storage and they've already been compressed into a tar archive, use this command (note the absence of the z option because the files have already been compressed in this example):

```
# tar cvf bigarchive.tar file1.gz file2.gz file3.gz
```

This design of tar leads to some convenient methods of backing up your data.

Suppose that you've backed up your large server hard disk. A lot of work has been done since then, but only a fraction of the files on the disk have changed. First, you can use the find command to see a list of all the files that have changed (based on the last modified date field for the file) in the previous seven days:

```
# find / -mtime -7 -type f -print
```

The list of files is printed on your screen. Because these files have been recently modified, they are the ones you want to back up. By combining the list from the find command with the tar command, you can create an archive that includes only the recently modified files. Two methods for doing this are shown here:

```
# tar cvfz update06-07-99.tgz `find / -mtime -7 -type f -print`
# find / -mtime -7 -type f -print >filelist; tar cvfz
  update0607-99.tgz `cat filelist`
```

Both of these commands make use of a feature of the Linux shell (command line). By placing a command between single back quotes, that command is executed, and the output of it is placed at that point in the command line.

The first command executes the find command. The file list that find produces is located in the last position of the tar command, so those files are archived. In the second command example, the find command is executed and the results are written to a file called `filelist`. A second command on the same line, separated by a semicolon, uses the single back quote trick to `cat` (dump) the contents of the `filelist` file at the correct location for tar to use the list of files.

Either method will work—use whichever you feel most comfortable with.

By using other options of the find command, you can back up files that a certain user has created or that have other characteristics. You can also use the file list generated by the find command as part of other Linux commands.

Back Up System Configuration Data

In the case of a system crash, you may want to access some of the more critical system configuration data before worrying about restoring users' home directories and other daily working files.

Most of the configuration data for a Linux system is stored in the `/etc` directory. Information in this directory can be critical when you're trying to rebuild your system because it includes things such as

- ◆ The `inittab` file, which is used by the core `init` startup process

- ◆ The startup scripts (in the `rc.d` subdirectory) that control what services to start at boot time

- ◆ The user database and password files

- ◆ Information about kernel modules used on the system (such as the `conf.modules` file on Red Hat 6 or the `modules` directory on some other distributions)

- ◆ The `lilo.conf` file, which may control how your system boots (and can show you how different partitions are used)

- ◆ The `sysconfig` and `network-scripts` subdirectories, which contain your networking configuration

- ◆ The X configuration file

- ◆ Configuration information for other key services such as Samba, HTTP, and FTP servers

If your Linux server is acting as a DNS server, Web server, or something similar, additional configuration files for those servers are stored in locations such as /var/named or /usr/httpd, but these additional files are not critical to getting your system up and running.

To back up your /etc directory, use this command:

```
# tar cvfz etc_backup.tgz /etc
```

Then store the etc_backup.tgz file on a separate system or floppy disk. Remember, however, that the /etc directory contains highly sensitive security information, such as encrypted passwords for all users. Be careful where you store the backup file.

You can use the procedure in the section below, "Restoring Files from a tar Archive," to extract a single file from the /etc archive if necessary or to restore the entire directory after reinstalling your Linux system.

Automate Backups

Earlier in this book, in Number 17, "Run Any Program Any Time," we discussed using the cron command for repetitive tasks. Backing up your system is the perfect example of why to use cron. Once you have determined the tar commands (and related find or other commands) that you need to successfully implement a backup policy, you can use cron to execute those commands while you're away from the office.

For example, if you create a text file with these lines in it and then hand it over to cron as described in Number 17, your entire system will be backed up every Sunday morning at 3 A.M. An incremental backup will also be done every night at 11:30. The list of files backed up is stored to an index file for your review the next morning.

```
* 3 * * 7 tar cvfz weekly`echo $DATE`.tgz / > /root/
  weekly_index.txt
30 11 * * * tar cvfz update`echo $DATE`.tgz `find / -mtime -7 -
  type f -print` > /root/nightly_index.txt
```

Restoring Files From a tar Archive

The critical part of having backed up your files is restoring them when the system has a crisis. The easy way to do this with tar is to unpack the entire archive in the current directory using this command:

```
# tar xvfz update03-05-99.tgz
```

If you have your archive stored on a device such as a tape drive, the command would be something like

```
# tar xvfz /dev/tape
```

To see a list of files in the archive without extracting them, use a t instead of an x:

```
# tar tvfz update03-05-99.tgz
```

With the list of files included in the tar archive, you can extract a single file that has become corrupted or lost. Use the extract command, x, with the full path name of the file you want to extract. For example, if the output of the t option shows a file named etc/inittab, you can use this command to extract only that file into the /etc directory:

```
# tar xvfz etc_backup.tgz etc/inittab
```

If you don't use the full path name, the file will not be located in the tar archive.

47 Boot Linux in Emergencies

One of the more serious problems you can have with Linux is not being able to boot your system. This can happen because of a hard disk crash, problems installing a new version of Linux or the LILO boot loader program, or even a minute corruption of key areas of your disk.

In these cases, you need to be able to boot your system into Linux so you can diagnose and correct the problem.

Most Linux distributions have a rescue disk image that you can copy from their CD or Web site. Using this disk, you can boot your system, access your Linux partition, and use a basic set of utilities to try to fix whatever problems have occurred.

As an example, the Red Hat 6 CD includes images for a boot disk and a rescue disk. You can't use rescue mode directly from the bootable Red Hat CD, but you can create a set of boot and rescue disks before problems occur, keep them in a safe place, and use them if a hardware problem or misconfiguration makes your system unusable.

To create these disks, follow these steps, using two blank formatted 3½ inch disks. You'll probably need to be logged in as root to use this procedure.

1. Mount your Red Hat 6 Linux CD number 1.

```
# mount /mnt/cdrom
```

2. Insert a blank, formatted disk in your floppy drive.

3. Change to the directory where images are stored on the Red Hat CD.

```
# cd /mnt/cdrom/images
```

4. Use the dd command to dump the boot disk image to the floppy (this command takes several minutes to reformat and write to the floppy disk):

```
# dd if=boot.img of=/dev/fd0 bs=72k
```

5. Remove the boot disk and label it appropriately.

6. Insert a second blank formatted disk.

7. Use the dd command again to dump the rescue disk image to the floppy:

```
# dd if=rescue.img of=/dev/fd0 bs=72k
```

8. Remove the rescue disk and label it.

If a problem occurs, boot your system from the boot disk and then use the rescue disk when prompted to enter rescue mode. Remember, the time to make these disks is before your system has a problem and you are unable to make them!

Other Linux distributions have similar features. Check the documentation for your Linux package to learn more.

48 Monitor System Logs for Trouble

Most of the important activity on your Linux system is logged to the system log. This file—/var/log/messages on most Linux systems—contains messages that nearly every important Linux program has written to the system. The system log includes information such as

- ◆ Each kernel module that is loaded
- ◆ Each attempt to log in as root
- ◆ Connections made via FTP or certain other protocols
- ◆ Failed login attempts
- ◆ Warnings about system resource limits
- ◆ Networking daemons starting and stopping

You can configure which types of events are logged to the messages file by reviewing and editing the /etc/syslog.conf file. This is rarely needed unless you're running a large Linux server or have specific security concerns, however.

Because the system log file can be a good way to see potential trouble brewing before it causes real problems, several programs have been developed to help you watch the system log file for warning signs. Some examples of these warning signs are

- ◆ Repeated failed log in attempts in the middle of the night by a user that is supposedly on vacation
- ◆ Network services being stopped and restarted when the system administrator is not aware of it
- ◆ Programs having trouble allocating sufficient memory to execute properly

Warning signs can pertain to both system maintenance—keeping your Linux system running smoothly and efficiently for all users—and to security issues.

The Log Scanner program is in the best Unix and Linux tradition: it can do wonderful things… if you can set up the text configuration file and know a little Perl programming.

The Log Scanner is a Perl script that works with the TCP wrappers package (a tool that checks whether network connections are allowed based on their service, location, etc.). Using Log Scanner, a system administrator can define anomalies to watch for in the system log file. A contact person is also defined so that when an anomaly is detected, an e-mail can be sent as notification.

A configuration file, `Rules.cfg`, is stored in the `/etc/lscan` directory. (As a starting point, you can copy the default `Rules.cfg` file from the `lscan` subdirectory where you have unpacked the `logscanner` archive.) The configuration file can be edited and extended to define what to look for in system log files. Though I've implied that the configuration format is cryptic, a quick look at some of the sample rules provided with Log Scanner demonstrate how useful it can be in watching for problems with your network and Linux system:

```
#o:badsu:"^month/^day ^time Bad su ... ^source tried to become
  ^user on ^host too many times."
#o:roottelnet:"^month/^day ^time Somebody from ^source tried to
  telnet to ^host as root."
#o:rootftp:"^month/^day ^time Somebody from ^source tried to ftp
  to ^host as root."
#o:badtelnets:"^month/^day ^time User from ^source had too many
  failed telnets into ^host (^user)."
#o:badftps:"^month/^day ^time User from ^source had too many
  failed ftps into ^host (^user)."
```

The Log Scanner is included in the `/Binaries/Business` directory on the CD.

A similar program to the Log Scanner is Log Watch. This program also lets you configure items to watch for in your log files, but Log Watch is a C program rather than a Perl script. Detailed configuration information is stored in the `/etc/log.d` directory. Sample configuration files, documentation, man pages, and so forth are all included with the Log Watch program.

Log Watch is on the CD at `/Binaries/Business`. It is in rpm format and can be installed using this command:

```
# rpm -Uvh /mnt/cdrom/Binaries/Business/logwatch-1_6_4-
  1_noarch.rpm
```

After installation, review the sample log file, `/etc/log.d/logwatch.conf`, as directed in the post-install message.

49 Add Redundant Disk Arrays to Linux

One of the best ways to protect against disk failures on critical systems is to use an array of redundant hard disks. The common term for this is RAID—Redundant Arrays of Inexpensive Disks. The inexpensive term is relative. Compared to mainframe-style hardware, anything you use for your PC is inexpensive. If a system is worth protecting with a RAID disk system, however, don't take needless risks by using low quality hard disks or cables when you set it up.

Linux can easily support hardware RAID devices that make an array of disk drives appear as a single device to the operating system. To Linux, these would be a single physical device, such as `/dev/sd0`, the first SCSI drive. Such hardware RAID systems often provide hot-swapping, allowing you to remove and replace a defective disk drive with a new one, never shutting the power off to the subsystem (or to your Linux system).

The problem with these dedicated RAID systems is that they can be prohibitively expensive. With the latest releases of Linux, software-based RAID is supported. By using Software-RAID, you can configure your RAID disks in just the way you want them, giving you a lot of flexibility and saving a lot of money. The catch is that you must learn more about your disks and the Linux system in order to make it all work (and especially to take care of any problems that arise).

This section describes in general terms how Software-RAID works on Linux. When you're ready to learn more, visit the RAID home Web page for the latest information: `http://linas.org/linux/raid.html`. Software-RAID support in Linux is difficult to use; the documentation states that it "is best attempted by experienced system administrators." I mention it here both because it's getting easier all the time and because it's a very powerful feature of Linux that few people seem to know about.

One of the first things that you need to know about RAID is the oft-misunderstood numbering of RAID devices. For example, you may hear that a device "supports RAID-5." RAID-1 and RAID-5 are the most used levels. All of them are explained here:

◆ RAID-0, or RAID-linear, is the grouping of multiple physical disk partitions into a single logical partition. This provides no fault tolerance, but it allows a single logical file system to grow beyond the bounds of a single physical disk. In some cases, striping (normally associated with RAID-0) is used to improve performance. Conceptually, striping splits blocks of data and writes them across two or more hard disks to increase the chance that both disk heads can read or write data simultaneously. Striping is used a lot in higher RAID levels.

◆ RAID-1 is mirroring. Two or more partitions of the same size have the same information copied to them. This may improve performance if the system is smart enough to read from both copies at the same time (deciding which disk head is closer to the desired sector), but its main purpose is to protect against disk failure. A commercial disk mirroring solution for Linux is also available from Twin-Com.

◆ RAID-4 is like RAID-0, but it adds (requires) a separate partition that is used to store parity information. This means that if you have, for example, five disk partitions, only four are storing data. The fifth is used by the RAID drivers to store a parity check of the other four partitions. This parity information degrades performances a bit, especially when writing to the disk, but it does create a system where one disk can fail and the data can still be reconstructed based on the parity partition.

◆ RAID-5 avoids the bottlenecks of RAID-4 while still providing fault tolerance based on parity information that is stored across all of the partitions in the disk array.

Selecting which RAID system to use and deciding how to configure your hard drives is part of the flexibility (and potential headache) of Software-RAID. You can even combine some levels. Linux, for instance, supports layering mirroring (RAID-1) over a multipartition logical device (RAID-0).

Software-RAID in Linux is implemented by selecting a set of kernel options (this requires recompiling your Linux kernel). These options are part of the "multiple devices driver support" and are shown in Figure 49.1 as part of the block devices configuration of the kernel (this figure shows the make menuconfig method of setting up the kernel).

FIGURE 49.1 Software-RAID can be set up in Linux by reconfiguring your kernel.

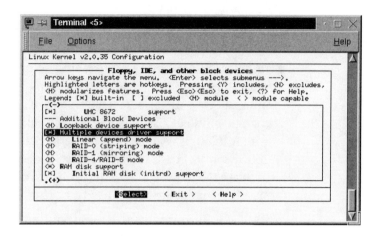

In addition to the required kernel support, a set of low-level (read "expert-level") administration tools can be used to configure and maintain file systems that are composed of Software-RAID devices. These tools are developing rapidly and should only be used by administrators who are very familiar with their RAID configuration. The RAID home page mentioned previously contains abundant documentation, benchmarks, tutorials, and other information.

50 Supply Uninterrupted Power to Linux

It's actually very easy to supply uninterrupted power to Linux. Simply plug your PC, monitor, and other peripherals into a diesel generator and keep filling it with gas until the main power comes back on. Battery-based backup systems are cleaner and quieter, but they don't last forever. In fact, most uninterruptible power supply (UPS) devices are designed to allow you a few minutes to save your files and gracefully shut your system down. This prevents file system corruption and gives you a chance to let any networked users know about the system going down.

Because a device that provides even a few minutes of battery-based power can cost several hundred dollars, most businesses don't choose to go far beyond this measure of power backup.

When you use a UPS on your Linux system, you can use the utilities described in this section to control your Linux system based on signals from your UPS device.

Modern UPS devices are connected both to your wall socket and the serial port of your computer. When the UPS detects that the power has been cut, a signal is sent to the serial port on your PC. By using a program that intercepts the signal and controls your Linux system, you can leave Linux unattended and still gracefully shut down the system in the event of a power failure. Three standard signals are sent to the serial port by a UPS (this list converts the signals to English):

◆ The power has failed, begin a graceful shutdown.

◆ The power has failed and I'm about out of battery life, shut down quickly.

◆ The power has been restored, there's no need to shut down.

To use a UPS on Linux, you need a program to receive and act on these serial port UPS signals and a configuration that instructs your PC how to behave. Before you buy a UPS, try to determine from the manufacturer whether or not it includes Linux support (or if they've used it on a Linux system). Generally speaking, if you can get the specifications for which pins on the serial cable are used to indicate a power failure, you can easily configure the Linux software to act on the UPS signals.

The init process is the program that starts all other programs when your Linux system is booted. A configuration file called /etc/inittab is used to control its actions. Part of that file looks like this:

```
pf::powerfail:/sbin/shutdown -h +5 "Power Failure; System
  Shutting Down"

# If battery is fading fast -- we hurry...
p1::powerfailnow:/sbin/shutdown -c 2> /dev/null
p2::powerfailnow:/sbin/shutdown -h now "Battery Low..."

# If power was restored before the shutdown kicked in,
  cancel it.
```

```
po:12345:powerokwait:/sbin/shutdown -c "Power Restored;
   Shutdown Cancelled"
```

Notice the signals in the control statements: powerfail, powerfailnow and powerokwait. For each one, a shutdown command is defined. The shutdown command halts the system either in five minutes (+5) or immediately. If the powerokwait signal is received, a new shutdown command is executed with the -c option to cancel the system shutdown.

You can edit these lines in /etc/inittab to change what happens when the UPS detects a power failure. You can even write a script that performs many different tasks and launch that script from the inittab file.

Several daemons are available that can manage the signals received by the UPS and issue the signals that the init program uses to start a system shutdown. Some of these daemons are

◆ powerd

◆ bpowerd

◆ upsd

The more commonly used daemons, powerd and bpowerd, are included on the CD at /Source/System Tools.

One of the most popular brands of UPS devices is APC. A comprehensive Web page with instructions for making an APC UPS device work under Linux is available at http://www.brisse.dk/site/apcupsd/. The APC device uses the apcupsd daemon, which is included on the CD at /Source/System Tools.

APC power devices can also use the apcmswitch utility (located at /Source/System Tools). This utility allows you to set individual usernames and passwords for each outlet on an APC MasterSwitch via a CGI interface.

Another source for commercial UPS support on Linux is the LanSafe III UPS Power Management package from Exide Electronics (see http://www.exide.com).

INDEX

Note to the Reader: Throughout this index **boldfaced** page numbers indicate primary discussions of a topic. *Italicized* page numbers indicate illustrations.

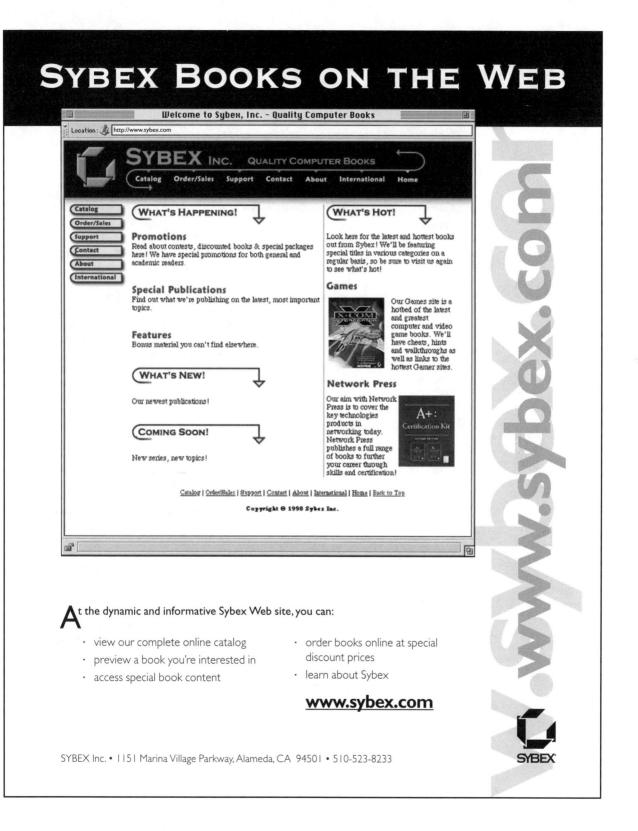

Finding More Linux Stuff

The following Internet resources are great places to look for updates and new programs for Linux.

Internet Site	Description
`http://www.linuxberg.com/`	**A huge site (mirrored worldwide) with categories and ratings for each Linux package. Intended for those desired, more stable programs.**
`http://www.freshmeat.net/`	**The place where all Linux-oriented developers announce new releases of their programs. Use the search function to find a specific package. Best for the latest release, which is not always the most stable (though you can usually find those as well).**
`ftp://sunsite.unc.edu/` **or** `http://metalab.unc.edu/`	**Probably the largest FTP site in the world, with many mirrors. Start with the** `/pub/Linux` **directory.**
`http://www.redhat.com/mirrors.html`	**A list of sites that mirror the Red Hat archives, which are too busy to be accessed directly. The core Red Hat files, updates, and contributed files are listed separately.**
`http://www.kde.org/`	**Use the Applications link on the KDE Web site to see tables of the latest KDE applications with links to the downloadable packages.**
`http://www.gnome.org/`	**Use the Software Map link to learn about Gnome software. The list is organized by category with icons to indicate Stable, Core product, Screenshot, etc.**

Internet Site	Description
http://www.linuxapps.com/	A catalog of Linux applications with descriptions, helpful icons, and a search function.
http://www.hongik.com/linux//linapps.html	The Linux Applications and Utilities Page has categories for applications. Not all that recent, but sometimes helpful in locating a needed package.
http://SAL.KachinaTech.com/index.shtml	Scientific Applications on Linux. A collection of esoteric stuff for mathematicians, chemists, and computer scientists. Sections for database, graphics, and programming tools are also included.
http://www.linuxhq.com/	Information on the latest Linux kernel updates as well as documentation and other resources.
http://www.slashdot.org/	This isn't a download site, but you should know about it if you're going to be a Linux fan. Read news items or use the search feature to locate specific package information.

What's on the CD

The CD-ROM contains most of the software packages that are described in the text of the book. (A few items described are commercial software and cannot be included here.) Highlights include

- The ApplixWare Office Suite
- Players for video clips, MP3 audio files, and audio CDs
- The best arcade and strategy games for Linux
- Virus scanners
- Personal finance tools
- Security add-ons
- Windows and NetWare integration tools
- Apache Web server add-on modules

You deserve some warning about these add-on packages: Some of them are easier to use than others. I've included a lot of tools that you can run right off the CD; others require that you work with the source code a little, especially if you're not running a standard Red Hat Linux distribution, which is what all the packages were tested on. If you're not a programmer, don't worry. I'm confident that you'll still find all sorts of useful tips and tools in this book. If some that you want to try are harder to use, consider that as incentive to learn more about the inner workings of Linux.

- All of the packages have been tested on a default Red Hat 6 Linux installation.
- The README file on the CD and the Introduction to the book provide additional guidelines on working with the source code files (if necessary for your Linux system).
- Some packages are only included as source code and must be compiled on your system before use. These packages are indicated in the text of the book.
- Some packages require additional preparation to your Linux system or additional hardware, as described in the text of the book.
- The rpm_list.txt file on the CD shows you what was installed on the test system.